Learning Anime Studio

Bring life to your imagination with the power of
Anime Studio

Chad Troftgruben

PUBLISHING

BIRMINGHAM - MUMBAI

Learning Anime Studio

First published: April 2014

Production Reference: 1260314

Published by Packt Publishing Ltd.
Livery Place
35 Livery Street
Birmingham B3 2PB, UK.

ISBN 978-1-84969-957-0

www.packtpub.com

Cover Image by Smith Micro Software

Credits

Author
Chad Troftgruben

Reviewers
Charles Brandt
Shawn Briscoe
Jim Mills
Timothy Sanders
Tom Thompson

Acquisition Editors
Pramila Balan
Nikhil Karkal

Content Development Editor
Priya Singh

Technical Editors
Dennis John
Pankaj Kadam
Adrian Raposo
Gaurav Thingalaya

Copy Editors
Janbal Dharmaraj
Sayanee Mukherjee
Karuna Narayanan
Alfida Paiva
Laxmi Subramanian

Project Coordinator
Kranti Berde

Proofreaders
Ameesha Green
Kelly Hutchinson
Dan McMahon

Indexer
Monica Ajmera Mehta

Production Coordinator
Arvindkumar Gupta

Cover Work
Arvindkumar Gupta

About the Author

Chad Troftgruben is a freelance media designer who has been working with Flash, Anime Studio, and other various software for a number of years. By applying methods from his cartoon animation and filmmaking background, Chad provides a simplistic yet creative approach to each lesson he teaches.

Beginning in 1996 with a program called Microsoft's 3D Movie Maker, Chad cut his teeth on the basics of animation, eventually graduating to Flash in 2002 and then Anime Studio in 2010. Live-action filmmaking was also a big part of Chad's life as he made short films with his friends throughout high school and college.

In 2007, Chad started providing free online video tutorials on Flash and other software. Since then, his tutorials have been viewed by millions of people, including entrepreneurs, teachers, students, and many others. In 2010, Chad was hired by LearnKey to present their Flash CS5 learning series, which was a six-hour course detailing the entire feature set of the software. Since then, he has been keeping busy with various animation and tutorial projects, such as creating Smith Micro's official Anime Studio 10 tutorial series and authoring for Virtual Training Company.

Acknowledgments

First, I would like to thank all the hardworking individuals at Packt Publishing for keeping me on track, raising the bar high in terms of quality, and allowing me the creative freedom in delivering my very first book to the masses.

I would also like to acknowledge Fahim Niaz and the hardworking team at Smith Micro for giving us reviewer copies of Anime Studio to keep the writing process going. Not to mention, their software is amazing!

One of the first books on animation I ever read (way back in the olden days) was *Flash 5 Cartooning, Mark Clarkson, Wiley*. I loved the style and approach of the book, and in some ways I hope my book will harken back to that easy-to-learn style Clarkson tapped into. Special thanks go out to Mark Clarkson for writing such a great book and helping me learn computer animation. Here's hoping I can do Anime Studio the same justice he did with teaching Flash animation!

Finally, I would like to thank my wife, Stephenie. Without her love and support, it's safe to say that this book wouldn't have been possible. I love you, Stephers.

About the Reviewers

Charles Brandt always loved animation, but he grew up on a rural farm far away from anyone who knew anything about it. Luckily, the Internet was invented, and with some determination and the help of some wonderful artists he met along the way, he has managed to figure it out. Since then, he has gone on to create animations on everything, from the existential crisis of a duck to the adventures of a team of crime-fighting Internet cyber cadets. Still very much in love with animation, he continues his work exploring the new frontiers of animating for handheld devices and creating tools to make animation quicker and simpler for everyone.

I would like to thank my animation mentor Brian Schrank, without whom I would have had no idea where to begin.

Shawn Briscoe pursued an art-related career from an early age, inspired by Japanese animation, also known as Anime. He majored in Graphic Design at Harding University in 1998, studied 3D Animation with Maya at New York Film Academy in the summer of 2003, and finally earned a Master of Fine Arts degree in Animation from Savannah College of Art and Design in 2007. Upon moving to the greater Los Angeles area, he found work as a freelance artist, working in graphic design, web design / development, motion graphics, animation, visual effects, interactive design, and teaching 3D animation with Maya. With his passion being animation, he pursues motion-related work and has worked primarily in motion graphics, visual effects, and animation for over seven years.

Jim Mills was born in Culver City, California. By the age of three, he was already displaying a preternatural understanding of drawing and art. But he found himself drawn to the beauty of cinema. Toiling away with his high school friends, what once seemed like an after-school hobby became a tangible dream. His hard work soon paid off with the release of *Switch Killer*, which was distributed by Lionsgate Entertainment. Soon after, his passion for drawing and films collided, which set Jim on the path of expanding into the realm of animation. With his recent partnership with renowned musical artist Ginuwine, Jim is currently working on a new animated series in hopes of bringing it to television. Along with freelancing and producing animation tutorials on the side, Jim is repeating history by carving a name for himself in a subsection of the industry he originally developed a passion for.

Timothy Sanders is a software designer and developer from Prince Edward Island, Canada. An Interactive Multimedia graduate, he was drawn into the world of computing by his love for story-telling through animation.

He has tried his hand at television, desktop programming, web design, animation, and video editing. Having recently completed a desktop/mobile software suite that controls his employer's staff schedules, invoices, and commissions, his attention is now turning toward artificial intelligence systems and returning to school for his Bachelor's degree in Computer Science. He also hopes to complete the game engine he started working on two years ago with C++ and DirectX.

I would like to thank my mom and dad; brother, Lee; sister-in-law, Joy; grandma, and best friend/partner Mary-Helen for their constant love and support through all my endeavors (no matter how big or small). Thanks to my friends, especially Andy K. (head of our Member Services division) and Dana (gaming companion) for helping me stay grounded... well, mostly grounded. And of course, thanks to my friend and employer, Catherine Arsenault of Atlantic Business Alliance for the lab and resources she trusts me to work and experiment with. Oh Piggly...!

Tom Thompson works in the field of e-commerce, marketing, and web design.

www.PacktPub.com

Support files, eBooks, discount offers and more

You might want to visit www.PacktPub.com for support files and downloads related to your book.

Did you know that Packt offers eBook versions of every book published, with PDF and ePub files available? You can upgrade to the eBook version at www.PacktPub.com and as a print book customer, you are entitled to a discount on the eBook copy. Get in touch with us at service@packtpub.com for more details.

At www.PacktPub.com, you can also read a collection of free technical articles, sign up for a range of free newsletters and receive exclusive discounts and offers on Packt books and eBooks.

http://PacktLib.PacktPub.com

Do you need instant solutions to your IT questions? PacktLib is Packt's online digital book library. Here, you can access, read and search across Packt's entire library of books.

Why Subscribe?

- Fully searchable across every book published by Packt
- Copy and paste, print and bookmark content
- On demand and accessible via web browser

Free Access for Packt account holders

If you have an account with Packt at www.PacktPub.com, you can use this to access PacktLib today and view nine entirely free books. Simply use your login credentials for immediate access.

Table of Contents

Preface

Have you ever watched a cartoon on television or the Internet and wondered, "How do they do that?". Perhaps you have a story you've written that you want to tell visually? Or maybe you just have some crazy ideas in your head and you want to spit it out onto a digital canvas and see what happens? Whatever the case, *Learning Anime Studio* will teach you the fundamentals of using Anime Studio Pro as well as animation in general.

Learning animation software requires hands-on training. While reading the step-by-step exercises will help, the real deal comes with the work files that accompany your book purchase. If you're not comfortable with drawing on a computer, don't worry; you can use the book's assets while going through the lessons!

When you are done with this book, you will have gone from a blank canvas to having an animated sequence on screen. Let this book be your guide while your imagination takes you to new heights!

What this book covers

Chapter 1, Stepping into the World of Animation, covers how to install Anime Studio along with configuring default settings for your documents. We will begin our journey with an overview of planning and scripting your cartoon.

Chapter 2, Drawing in Anime Studio, introduces us to Anime Studio's drawing tools. This chapter breaks each tool down, creating a guide you can refer to at any time in the course of the book.

Chapter 3, Exploring Layers and Timelines, teaches us which layer is right for certain situations with easy-to-understand exercises. The three timelines are also explored in this chapter.

Chapter 4, Enhancing Your Art with the Layer Settings Panel and Style Palette, demonstrates the main functions of each feature in the Layer Settings panel and Style palette that will help you add an extra "pop" to your work.

Chapter 5, Bringing a Cartoon Character to Life, introduces three different bone animation techniques so you know which options are available when it's time to animate. Smart Bones are also explored!

Chapter 6, Developing Your Cartoon's Scenery, covers how to draw a scene from scratch, preparing your character for his/her big premiere.

Chapter 7, Creating a Library of Actions and Assets, covers how to make organization easy with the Library and Actions panels.

Chapter 8, Animating Your Characters, covers different ways to animate the character. Along with multiple exercises for various character movements, you will learn how to create a short conversation between two characters. The new Bone Constraint functions are discussed as well.

Chapter 9, Exporting, Editing, and Publishing, discusses exporting your cartoon, using video editing software, and how to get you work in front of an audience.

What you need for this book

You will need the following:

- Anime Studio Pro 10 (while you can follow along with previous versions, some exercises were written for Version 10)
- iMovie or Windows Live Movie Maker for editing

Who this book is for

Learning Anime Studio is for newcomers to Anime Studio or animation in general. Hobbyists and newcomers with ambitions of being an animator will get the most out of this book. However, intermediate and long-time users of Anime Studio will be able to use various chapters as a reference to some of Anime Studio's tools and features. The book also serves as a guide for the new enhancements introduced in Anime Studio Pro 10.

Conventions

In this book, you will find a number of styles of text that distinguish between different kinds of information. Here are some examples of these styles, and an explanation of their meaning.

Code words in text, folder names, filenames, file extensions, pathnames, and user input are shown as follows: "Enter 25 into the stroke width field."

New terms and **important words** are shown in bold. Words that you see on the screen, in menus or dialog boxes for example, appear in the text like this: "Click on the **Apply** button in your **Layer Settings** panel."

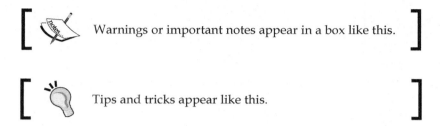

Warnings or important notes appear in a box like this.

Tips and tricks appear like this.

Reader feedback

Feedback from our readers is always welcome. Let us know what you think about this book—what you liked or may have disliked. Reader feedback is important for us to develop titles that you really get the most out of.

To send us general feedback, simply send an e-mail to feedback@packtpub.com, and mention the book title via the subject of your message.

If there is a topic that you have expertise in and you are interested in either writing or contributing to a book, see our author guide on www.packtpub.com/authors.

Customer support

Now that you are the proud owner of a Packt book, we have a number of things to help you to get the most from your purchase.

Downloading the example code

You can download the example code files for all Packt books you have purchased from your account at http://www.packtpub.com. If you purchased this book elsewhere, you can visit http://www.packtpub.com/support and register to have the files e-mailed directly to you.

Downloading the color images of this book

We also provide you a PDF file that has color images of the screenshots/diagrams used in this book. The color images will help you better understand the changes in the output. You can download this file from `https://www.packtpub.com/sites/default/files/downloads/9570OT_GraphicsBundle.pdf`.

Errata

Although we have taken every care to ensure the accuracy of our content, mistakes do happen. If you find a mistake in one of our books—maybe a mistake in the text or the code—we would be grateful if you would report this to us. By doing so, you can save other readers from frustration and help us improve subsequent versions of this book. If you find any errata, please report them by visiting `http://www.packtpub.com/submit-errata`, selecting your book, clicking on the **errata submission form** link, and entering the details of your errata. Once your errata are verified, your submission will be accepted and the errata will be uploaded on our website, or added to any list of existing errata, under the Errata section of that title. Any existing errata can be viewed by selecting your title from `http://www.packtpub.com/support`.

Piracy

Piracy of copyright material on the Internet is an ongoing problem across all media. At Packt, we take the protection of our copyright and licenses very seriously. If you come across any illegal copies of our works, in any form, on the Internet, please provide us with the location address or website name immediately so that we can pursue a remedy.

Please contact us at `copyright@packtpub.com` with a link to the suspected pirated material.

We appreciate your help in protecting our authors, and our ability to bring you valuable content.

Questions

You can contact us at `questions@packtpub.com` if you are having a problem with any aspect of the book, and we will do our best to address it.

1
Stepping into the World of Animation

While I'm sure you are excited to jump in and start animating a cartoon using Anime Studio, there are a few steps we need to take beforehand. Cartoon production, no matter how you approach it, is a very involved process and animating is but one piece of the puzzle.

In this first chapter, we will cover the following topics:

- Constructing your animation blueprint
- Installing Anime Studio
- Opening Anime Studio for the first time
- Editing preferences
- Setting up your first document

Constructing your animation blueprint

In this book, we will be creating a very simple animation that won't be using a script. However, once you have finished learning the basics of Anime Studio and it's time to move on to your own works, you will need to know the proper procedures in constructing a blueprint for your productions, especially when it comes to more complicated animations.

You may have an idea of what you want to do, and that's great. But it's important to form a more structured plan before getting started with production. This can be overwhelming, especially if you're not used to writing or expressing ideas on paper.

This chapter will help get you started and become comfortable with this process. You wouldn't build a house without a blueprint and the same applies to animation and film. Jotting down notes, mapping an outline, drafting a screenplay, and finally sketching a storyboard is the key to a well-planned and successful animation.

Coming up with ideas

When starting out, most animators usually have a basic idea of how they want to tackle their cartoon. This idea or premise is what drives the urge to animate in the first place. But what happens if you have no ideas? Maybe you have one idea but not enough content to base a substantial story off of it. Or maybe you want to create a series of episodes and you can't think of worthwhile concepts after a certain episode or point. This can be a real struggle for people starting off with animation.

Writing what you know is a good way to approach a story as it will allow you to create a rich environment for your cartoon to thrive. It will make your cartoon believable, allowing viewers to invest themselves into your narrative.

The following is a figure of Mr. Binek's Class, a cartoon that takes place in a school and is loosely based on real events and characters:

Let's face it; *write what you know* can be misleading. As an example, let's say you want to create a cartoon about a solider during World War II. Maybe you want this animation to take place from a certain perspective, or in a different country that you've never visited. It's safe to assume that most people reading this were not involved in World War II, which can make writing difficult. So how do you *write what you know* in this case? Simple; you make it your point to know! Research is the key. Learning as much as you can about a time, event, location, and so on will help build credibility towards the universe you want to conceptualize and mold. Even better, if possible, interview people who lived to experience these incidents. The same goes for traveling to the places you want to include in your story. Any information you gather will help shape the credibility and believability of your animated universe.

Identifying what is funny

Not all cartoons have to contain humor. However, most modern animations, especially on the Internet, are meant to invoke a laugh or two from their audiences. I'm sure you've stumbled across many cartoons you've found to be funny. There may also be videos that others love that you can't understand the humor behind. So, the big question is, what is funny? How can you be sure what you're writing is funny, and more importantly, it is going to stir up laughs from other individuals and gather positive feedback? The best advice I found on this subject comes from an older, but valued source, Mark Clarkson's **Flash 5 Cartooning**. If you think it's funny, it's funny. You cannot please everyone, but there's a good chance others will find humor in your creation. So stick with what makes you laugh and believe in your animation. If you do that, you'll at least make one person laugh.

Writing down your ideas

It's safe to assume that you have some ideas for your own works even before you picked up this book. Maybe you have a handful of ideas that you would love to see be applied to your future cartoon. This is great; the problem sometimes is that ideas can come so fast that we lose track of them; or maybe the idea had occurred to you months before, and you're having a hard time remembering the finer details. This can happen a lot and keeping track of great ideas is something that must be practiced. The advice you will hear a lot is to carry a notebook with you at all times. Understandably, this can be a bit of a pain, even with ample pocket room. However, we live in an age where cell phones and tablets can be used for note keeping. This may be more convenient, depending on your preferences and hardware.

One recommendation is a piece of software called **Evernote**, as it allows you to sync notes from your phone, tablet, and PC with ease. It will install on almost any OS, including iOS, Windows, Mac OS, Windows Phone, and Android. You can download the desktop version at `www.evernote.com`. You will find the mobile versions on whichever app delivery service your device uses. The following are a few tips to keep in mind if you decide to try out Evernote:

- Be sure to make an account (which is free) so that you can access your notes on multiple devices.

- Notebooks act like folders. If you find you are accumulating a lot of notes, be sure to create notebooks for organization.

- If you wish to share your notes between devices, all you have to do is hit the Sync button at the top to put your notes in the cloud, as shown in the following screenshot:

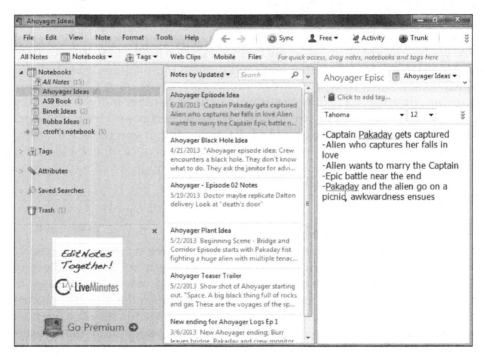

If Evernote doesn't do it for you, there are similar tools or services such as Google Docs or SkyDrive. However, if you prefer, go retro and wield the instruments our ancestors used: a piece of paper and pencil. Some people just prefer the traditional method of note taking. The bottom line is that even if an idea seems pointless or out of place, find a way to write it down. It may surprise you how relevant that seemingly insignificant idea can become as concepts evolve.

Piecing together the storm

The notes from your brainstorm sessions will more than likely end up as a pile of ideas without much cohesion or flow. This is normal because the note taking phase is meant to get standalone ideas formulated and written. You will want to organize these notes into an outline once your brain has spat the ideas out. How you outline will depend on your own comprehension skills. For instance, some people prefer bullet lists; others may want to get a mind-mapping software and organize everything that way. A software such as Scrivener allows you to create sections that can be easily rearranged, making it a prime choice for screenwriters and novelists. However, if you decide to do it, an outline is an important step in creating an animated cartoon.

The goal of the outline is to take your notes and organize them into a roughly structured narrative. Making the pieces fit is the key. Sticking to the main ideas is usually suggested when writing an outline, as other details such as character actions and dialog come later on during screenwriting. If a piece of a dialog that you must include comes to mind, include it. While your narrative flow may change over the course of the creative process, the outline will set up the building blocks to creating a cohesive blueprint for you to follow, as shown in the following screenshot:

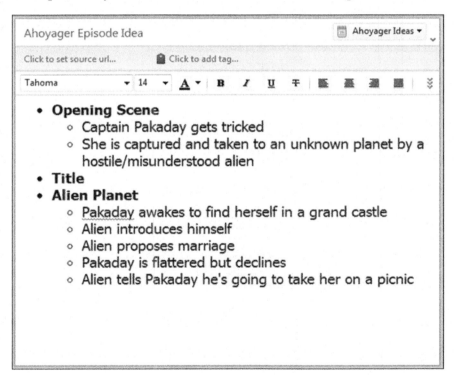

Writing your story

Screenwriting is where you'll want to write the story in full detail. This includes scene details, character actions, dialog, and so forth. Think of the process as if you watched your unfinished movie and are repeating every detail verbatim to a friend.

Screenwriting is special because of the following format that it uses:

- Your scene headings, in caps, describe the scene setting
- Characters are also capitalized
- Dialog is written underneath the characters in an almost center-justified format

The following is an example of a page from a screenplay; note how things are formatted:

```
EXT. SPACE - NIGHT

The Ahoyager is trying to hold its engines steady as a
massive black hole slowly sucks it in.

INT. AHOYAGER - BRIDGE - NIGHT

The bridge is covered with papers and books as crew members
read and run around in a panic.  PAKADAY is in the captain's
chair.

                    PAKADAY
          I need answers, people!

                    DALTON
          It kind of looks like a hole!

                    DOCTOR
          It kind of looks black!

                    BURR
          Well, maybe it's a black h...

                    PAKADAY
               (to Burr)
          Holder?  A black holder?  That
          doesn't even make sense.  Speak
          before you think!

                    CREWMAN JIM (V.O.)
          Captain!  The computer just
          analyzed the phenomenon.  It
          appears to be a black hole.

Pakaday's eyes widen as she gets up from her chair.  She
approaches one of the monitors with a diagram of the black
hole.  She pauses for a moment in an attempt to think.  She
turns her head back to the bridge crew.

                    PAKADAY
          Who here is an expert on big black
          things?

TITLE
```

When it's time to write your screenplay, you will want to download a piece of software that can put your words into the proper format. This not only makes the document more readable, but puts a professional spin on your creation, especially if you want to sell the draft to a production company.

My first recommendation would be Celtx (`http://www.celtx.com`). This free piece of software (with an optional premium version to access cloud-based and collaborative features) is streamlined, yet powerful enough, to draft up even your most ambitious screenplays. The software comes with a storyboarding template which allows you to order images, apply scene descriptions, text, and more.

You can download it for Windows, Mac OS, and Linux. On top of that, as of this writing, you can purchase a Celtx app for any of your iOS mobile devices, which allows you to write screenplays on the go.

If you want to use the same software that many of the professionals do, investing in Final Draft (`http://www.finaldraft.com`) may be up for consideration. The software contains many advanced features that may help with the creative process. Plus, as I said, it's widely regarded as a *pro's choice* type of software. Just be prepared to pay upwards of $200 for the fully-featured standard edition.

Whatever software you decide to use, the following are some basic rules to follow as you begin writing your first screenplay:

- A **scene heading** comes first. As previously stated, this is displayed in capital letters. **Int.** stands for an interior shot, while **Ext.** stands for exterior.
- Writing **actions** or descriptions is really no different from that of a novel. You want to be as descriptive as you can to paint a picture in the mind of the reader. Unless you are writing the script for yourself, you will want to avoid descriptions that would fall under the category of direction (camera movements, transitions, and so on). Also, it's proper to always write in the present tense.
- **Character headings** are always capitalized, just like scene headings.
- **Dialog** is always placed below character headings.
- When in doubt, use the special commands that your software provides. You shouldn't have to think much about the formatting with the aid of the software.

Constructing terrible first drafts

As you are discovering over the course of this chapter, your concepts, ideas, outline, and screenplay will continually be evolving up until you begin production. This can even continue after you start animating. Don't worry, this is normal. It may seem like most popular writers, whether they are novelists or screenwriters, are gifted with the hand of God. They can sit down and whip up several pages of a novel or screenplay in no time. The truth of the matter is, more often than not, a successful writer can sometimes draft a piece of literature up to three or more times. Your first draft is rarely your last.

When you first draft your screenplay, you shouldn't be concerned about more than just getting your ideas down as they come to you. Once this process is complete, you may want to step away from the script for a few days. If you have a friend or colleague who does similar work, such as writing, filmmaking, or cartooning, let them see the script. I can't tell you how many times I've struggled with a screenplay and a second pair of eyes discovers elements I had not considered. When becoming occupied in an activity or piece of work, especially a screenplay, it's almost as if you develop a tunnel vision. Flaws in character actions, dialog, and the narrative flow can go unnoticed.

The next figure shows an example of what a first draft may look like after notes have been implemented:

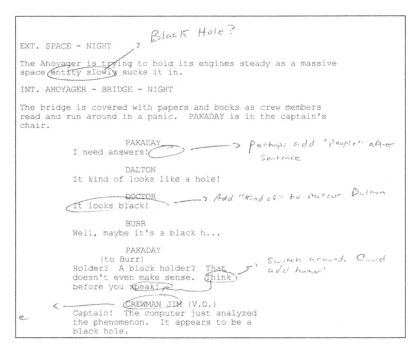

When it's time to do your second draft, the goal should be to critically analyze the flow of events and strengthen them if possible. Other elements you may want to consider are tightening your writing structure and correcting any grammar or spelling mistakes.

The second draft may be similar to or may completely contradict the first draft. Once you are finished, remember that a second pair of eyes doesn't hurt. By the time you take a swing at a third draft, things should be easier. It's possible you could have a total upheaval, and revamp the entire script once again.

If the concept was strong to begin with, a third draft usually requires small tweaks here or there. Comparing the first draft to the third usually resembles significant changes, most of which involve a tightening of narrative structure and character development. More tweaks may be required, but just keep this in mind that terrible first drafts tend to lead to terrific third drafts. Of course, not everyone's path will be the same. You could find yourself with more than three drafts by the time the process is done.

Illustrating a storyboard

After your screenplay is finalized, you may want to create a storyboard which will visually outline the scenes you will animate in your cartoon. Think of it as a comic book with multiple slides and written directions for the camera and character actions. This is helpful for when it's time to set up shots in your animation. It can be a visual guide as you or others dissect the written script. Storyboards don't have to be incredibly well designed. You will find artists who simply use stick figures to get a visual representation while others create more details for their drawings. South Park's storyboards sometimes look more detailed than the actual cartoon itself.

Storyboards can be sketched on paper or mapped in a computer software. In the end, it depends on how you intake information and approach material. Artists have been known to outline all of their scenes or slides on separate notecards and stick them on a wall. This allows them to view the entire sequence at once. Other people prefer the controlled structure a piece of software provides.

If you prefer using software to map out your storyboard, there are several options out there. Celtx, the same software that I recommended for screenwriting, has a storyboard template that allows for basic organization. You can dictate shot types and add descriptions, images, and sketches to create your storyboards in Celtx, as shown in the following screenshot:

Recording dialog

If you've written a script that contains words spoken by characters, your next step will be to record the dialog. It's best to record these lines early on, once you are satisfied with the script. While animating, you will find that it can be difficult to match mouth or body movements to the dialog without actually having any audio present.

First, you will need a microphone. There are several to choose from. Obviously, a $10 mic will be inferior to a $200 one. Shop around, check out reviews on Amazon, and see what you can find within your budget. If possible, avoid using headsets as some seem to leave a clicking sound whenever there is a slight movement with the head or jaw.

Some suggestions for microphones are: Blue Microphones Snowball USB Microphone, Blue Microphones Yeti USB Microphone, and MXL USB 009 24 BIT/96 KHZ USB Condenser Mic. These range from around $60 to $200 and are all great choices. If your budget doesn't allow for expensive equipment, a pop filter is a great, fairly inexpensive buy to get the most out of your audio quality, even with a consumer-based microphone.

Next, you will need to download an audio recorder. Anime Studio has a built-in recorder, but it's not very user-friendly as you can't trim or edit the clips to any real extent. You may find basic audio recording software on your computer. Again, this can be a pain to use, given the limited tools involved. If you're looking for a solid, free audio recorder, check out Audacity (`http://audacity.sourceforge.net/`), shown in the following screenshot. It's available for both Windows and Mac and has a robust set of tools to utilize. Best of all, it's easy to move or trim segments of a clip, if you need to fine-tune a line.

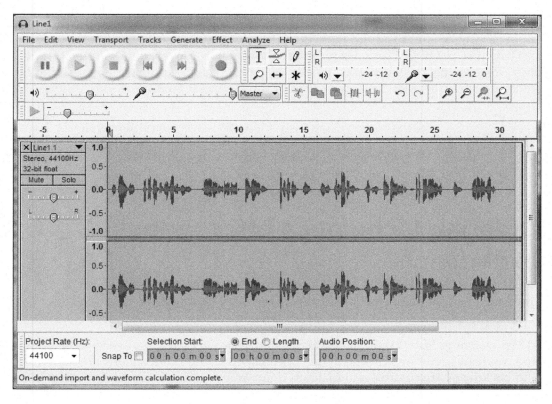

If you're ambitious, you can record yourself and star in your very own production. However, if you have a lot of characters, it may be difficult to create different voices for each one. There are effects you can apply through Audacity to change the pitch of your voice, but it may not be enough, especially if you're a male trying to imitate a female, or vice versa. For a large cast of characters, you may want to consider bringing in some friends or family to fill in the gaps. Additionally, you can always hire actors to do the lines for you. One idea is to network with others on places such as YouTube. Not only will you gain voice actors, but you will also make connections with other people who can later help promote your work. You may have luck finding people through a service such as Elance (`http://elance.com/`). Just note that it's probably in your best interest to know the individual personally, especially if you plan to give them direction or re-use them later for another cartoon.

The best way to approach this is to record one line at a time. Trim any dead space and use the noise removal effect in Audacity if you have a lot of static in the background. Save the line as a `.wav` or `.aiff` file. MP3s, while popular, tend to greatly compress the quality of the audio. If your voice actors are not in the same room as you, be sure to advise them of your guidelines so the lines you receive are as consistent as possible. This goes for microphone volume levels too. You don't want their voices to be quieter than yours or vice versa. While you can do some editing on your end to correct these issues, it's best to nail it right at the source.

For the cartoon in this book, the audio will be supplied for you in the project files that accompany this book. However, it's never too early to start thinking about what your characters will sound like for your own works.

Differing techniques offer various experiences

Looking at two-dimensional, non-Internet based cartoons, there is a world of difference that separates the big film spectacle of a Disney-created cartoon and a made-for-television Hanna-Barbera production episode.

When watching *Snow White and the Seven Dwarfs* or *The Lion King*, every scene, frame, and moment is vibrant and full of life. The characters are fluid, actions are varied, and backdrops are colorful and distinct. Companies such as Disney have artists that draw out every single frame, or cell, for these cartoons. To put this into perspective, the average film runs at 24 frames per second. That means for every second of footage you see on screen, 24 individual frames, or pictures, create that second.

In most traditional animation settings (and this number does vary), most animation sequences are shot in 2s, or in other words, one drawing is shown for every two frames. Take an average film that runs for two hours, convert that, and you end up with 7,200 seconds. Now take the seconds and multiply it by 12, the number of drawn images per second, and you get 86,400 drawings. This is again a rough example and doesn't take into account the different layers and composition of these frames. This should give you an idea of how involved frame-by-frame animation on a large scale can be. The luxury here is that large animation studios are well equipped, comprised of huge teams, and have millions of dollars at their disposal to meet tight timetables.

Now, looking at our other example, because television cartoon studios such as Hanna-Barbera were given little to work with financially (and had to adhere to tight schedules), new time and resource savings techniques were formed to offset production costs. The next time you stumble across an old Hanna-Barbera cartoon on television, stop and examine the animation on screen and compare it to one of your favorite Disney films. A majority of animation on screen, such as walking or running, is recycled. Background pieces will often repeat themselves when the camera follows a character. Watching *The Flintstones*, one has to wonder just how big Fred's house is as the scrolling background usually consists of 15 repeated windows and chairs.

Look at Fred Flintstone in the following screenshot when he speaks; typically, his mouth is the only movement taking place (and even those assets are recycled). This form of limited animation (or cut-out animation) is a method that has been adopted and used often through the decades as television animation has evolved. Compared to Disney cartoons, even conversations were full of life, with detailed and colorful movements in every shot.

Analyzing animation on the Internet

Given the history of how cartoon animation has evolved, it should come as no surprise that cartoonists on the Internet fall into two camps: frame-by-frame and cut-out. There is usually some debate as to which technique is superior, but like the example in the previous section, drawing comparisons is silly as they both have their merits. Additionally, many artists use both methods, blurring the line between the two extremes.

Breaking down frame-by-frame animation

There are many frame-by-frame animators making a name for themselves on the Internet. Artists such as YouTube user Harry Partridge have gained incredible popularity through animated works. You can tell that a lot of time went into crafting each frame to create a fluid and appealing sequence. Adobe Flash is a popular piece of software for its ability to create frame-by-frame motion. Toon Boom is another software that has gained popularity in recent years. Both programs use **onion skins,** or reference images, to allow artists to create their frame-by-frame animations with accuracy, as shown in the following screenshot. If done right, the results are pleasing. But, as we discussed in this chapter, frame-by-frame comes at the cost of time and resources.

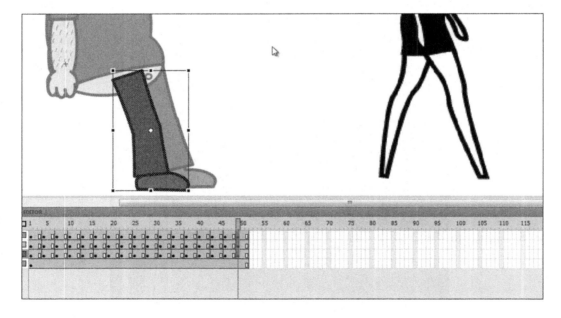

Exploring cut-out, tweening, and bone animation

Many animators carry on the tradition of Hanna-Barbera by using cut-out, tweening, and bone techniques to create their animations. Examples of this type of animation can be seen everywhere on the Internet. The benefit is that it saves time. Artists usually create a library of reusable assets and allow their animation programs to do the heavy lifting when it comes to calculating animated sequences. The term tweening comes from the two words *in between* and allows for the automatic animation between two points. Interpolation is another term that is used for this type of animation. Bone animation builds on this by allowing an artist to create a bone structure and letting the piece of software calculate movement by using keyframes.

In an interesting repeat of historical events, cut-out animation on the Internet was popularized due to a lack of resources. At the turn of the century, Internet cartoons were more simplistic in style due to the limitations of bandwidth and a computer's processing power. Cartoons were embedded onto web pages using the Flash `.swf` format and were streamed from there. If a cartoon contained immense detail, anybody with a slow connection or weak processor experienced lag, or worse, faced sound syncing issues. To help alleviate this, artists would make their web cartoons more simplistic to up the chances of viewership. This involved cut-out techniques, using limited reusable assets, and simplistic tweened animations. This has since changed with the invention of YouTube and better Internet connections. There are more opportunities to distribute work anywhere in the world without fear of bandwidth and processing limitations. Cut-out animation is now used more for workflow purposes rather than to avoid technical issues.

Introducing Anime Studio

Anime Studio was originally developed under the name of **Moho** in 1999 by Mike Clifton at LostMarble. In 2007, Smith Micro bought the rights and began marketing Moho as **Anime Studio**, and it has since then seen seven versions released under the new name. Anime Studio's claim to fame is it's easy-to-use bone system. The software makes cut-out animation easy to achieve and has other features from competing software, such as the ability to tween (or interpolate) between two points on the timeline. In other words, the software does most of the heavy lifting for the cartoonist. There are two versions the consumer has to choose from: Debut, that is designed keeping beginners and hobbyists in mind, and Pro, that is designed for professionals and serious animators. This book will be using the Pro version of the software, as shown in the following screenshot:

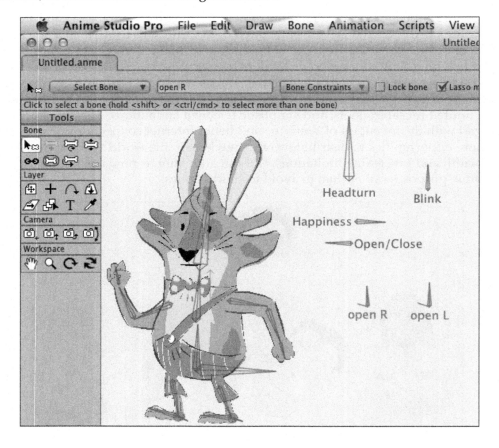

Because Anime Studio's focus is on cut-out animation, frame-by-frame isn't a primary focus. With a little tweaking (and a lot of patience), this animation type can be achieved. However, for this book we will be focusing primarily on the use of Anime Studio's bone system. It should also be pointed out that Anime Studio is not used just for the creation of anime-type cartoons. In fact, the majority of cartoons created with the software are similar to what you'd see on most American television channels. The software allows you to create any type of animation. There's nothing limiting you but your imagination.

Anime Studio Debut and Pro can be purchased from almost any software store and online at www.getanimestudio.incredibletutorials.com. A 30-day trial offer is also available for both versions.

Choosing between Anime Studio Debut and Pro

While Pro is the version we will be using to create our animation for this book, it's a good idea to go over the differences between the two versions that Smith Micro offers for its animation software. If you decide to go with Debut, just note that several of the lessons we will be going over in this book will not be able to be replicated on your end due to a lack of features. Both versions are shown in the following screenshot:

Debut, which is priced competitively at $49.99, contains most of the major animation features that the Pro version offers. The differences mostly lie in frame limits, the inability to export HD files, and limited layer types. The Pro version, which is priced at $299, gives you unlimited control over your animations. While the price is over double that of Debut, I believe the benefits you get outweigh that burden, allowing you to tap into the full potential of Anime Studio's architecture. The following is a more detailed breakdown of the major differences:

- Debut limits project files to 3000 frames; Pro gives you unlimited durations.
- Debut limits the resolution of your files to a maximum of 720 x 480; Pro can freely do HD resolutions.
- Debut lacks many of Pro's layer types, such as Switch, Patch, and Note.
- Pro gives you the ability to render out 3D objects.
- You cannot use the physics system in Debut.
- You cannot create particles with Debut.
- Onion skins are disabled in the Debut version.
- Camera controls are limited in Debut.
- Pro has introduced many useful features that cannot be found in Debut. These include Smart Bones, Patch Layers, GPU Acceleration, and Blend Morphs.

For a more comprehensive list on the differences between the two versions of Anime Studio, check out this handy chart provided by Smith Micro at http://anime.smithmicro.com/comparison.html.

If you decide to go with the Debut version, you can always upgrade to Pro at a special price through the official Anime Studio website. To do this easily, simply go to **Help | Upgrade to Professional Version**. Additionally, you can get great discounts through the official Anime Studio website if you are using an older version of the software and want to upgrade.

Installing Anime Studio

After making your purchase, you will need to install Anime Studio onto your computer, especially if you plan to follow the lessons in this book. Installation should be similar for both Windows and Mac versions. The following are the steps you will need to take:

1. If you purchased a boxed version of Anime Studio, insert the disk into your DVD drive. If you purchased the digital version online, locate the folder on your computer where you placed the download.

2. Double-click on the executable file to start the installation process (if you downloaded the file off the Internet, you may need to unzip it first).

3. If you get a security warning about running the executable, allow the process to continue.

4. You will have to click on **Next** once and accept the terms and conditions of the Anime Studio software. After you do that, click on **Next** again.

5. You will be asked to indicate which folder you want to put Anime Studio into. Usually, most people leave this as is. The next couple of screens will ask about the Start Menu (if on Windows) and desktop shortcuts. Once you've decided, click on **Next**.

6. The last screen will have you verify your selections. Once you're ready, click on **Install**. This may take a minute or two depending on the speed of your computer.

7. Once the installation is complete, you will be notified with a dialog box. Simply click on the **Close** or **Finish** button to end the installation process. The following screenshot is what you will see if the installation is successful:

Working with the 32-bit and 64-bit versions of Windows

If you're running a 64-bit version of Windows, Anime Studio will automatically install two separate versions of the software for you to use (64 and 32 bit). Mac users will only have one version of the software. If you can only install the 32-bit version, don't worry; you can still follow along and use this book.

The reason for this is because the Windows version of Anime Studio cannot import or export certain Apple-associated files (that is, QuickTime) when working in the 64-bit mode. This means that if you want to take advantage of the increased speed of the 64-bit version, you will need to switch over to the 32-bit version if you ever need to import or export any kind of Apple file (labeled as Anime Studio Pro 10 x86). This can be confusing at first, and some people prefer to stay with the 32-bit version just for ease of use. However, you will probably find the 64-bit version's speed enhancements to be well worth this minor inconvenience.

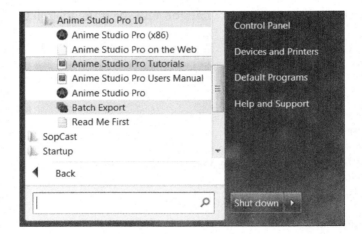

Opening Anime Studio for the first time

When you open Anime Studio for the first time, you will be greeted by a splash screen designed to help you get started with the software. Feel free to register your product if you wish to receive updates. You can download the bonus content package if you wish, and Content Paradise can be accessed at any time through the Help menu if you want to browse their items at some point.

However, we really have no use for the splash screen beyond this. This splash screen will launch each time you open the software, unless you click on the **Don't show this again** button on the bottom, as shown in the following screenshot:

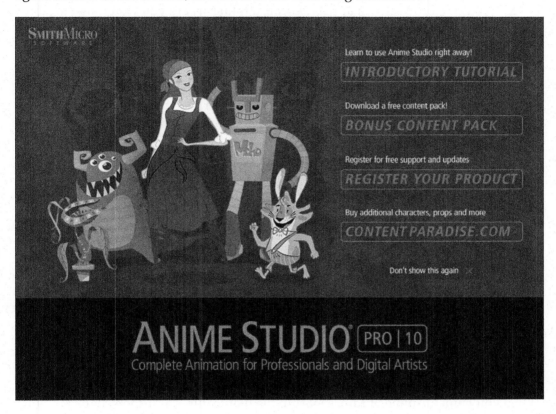

Creating your content folder

The next prompt you will have to deal with involves setting up a folder for your library. The library allows us to house reusable assets along with brushes, audio files, and so on. The library will be discussed more in a later chapter, but it may be best to set the folder up now so you don't have to deal with this message, as shown in the following screenshot, each time Anime Studio is launched:

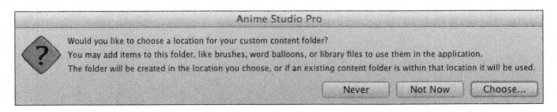

The following are the steps required to set up your content folder:

1. Select **Choose** from the prompt window.

2. Your file browser will appear. Locate a folder where you would like to store these assets. This is usually a folder that is easy to access and is in a safe spot so it doesn't accidently get deleted.

3. A progress bar will appear indicating the folder is being created.

4. If you go to your file browser and look at the folder you just selected, you will find subfolders indicating different library items, as shown in the following screenshot:

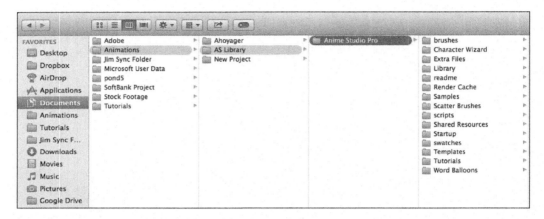

Playing with the startup file

When you launch Anime Studio, a startup file that features a cartoon character, will be the first thing you see by default. This quirky character is Anime Studio Pro 10's mascot and it gives you an opportunity to play with the tools or even use him in one of your own projects.

Let's create some movement for this character. If you page forward through the dots or keyframes on the timeline, you will see that some movement has already been placed. You can study this if you like or alter it in any way. The good thing about this is he's already rigged up and good to go. All we have to do is use the Manipulate Bones tool and the timeline, as shown in the following screenshot:

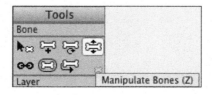

Perform the following steps to create movement:

1. Make sure you are on frame 0 on your timeline. That's the area on the bottom of your application with all the numbers and dots.

2. Select the Manipulate Bones tool from the left-hand side tool bar. It's the last one on the top row of the list in the **Bone** section and looks like a horizontal bone with two black arrows on the bottom and top.

3. Click and hold down on the character's front hand.

4. Move your cursor and notice how the character's hand follows. Also, note how the arm pieces bend and move in conjunction to the hand. This is the magic of bones at work.

5. Try moving another limb, such as a leg, to see how other parts of the character's body react.

This gives you an idea of how you can move the bones of a character. But what if you want to do some animation with these bones? Well, that's easy! If you look at the bottom of the program, you will notice a long area with numbers. This is referred to as the timeline, as shown in the following screenshot:

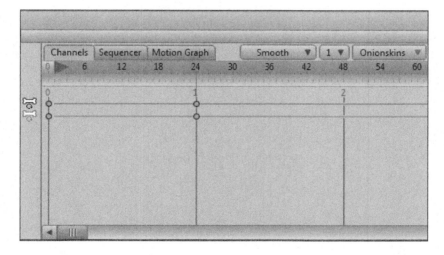

Let's have some fun and try to animate this character we have on screen by performing the following steps:

1. Hold down your mouse button and highlight all the keyframes on the timeline. You can also do this by holding *Ctrl* (*command* if you're on a Mac) and hitting the *A* key on your keyboard.

2. Hit the *Delete* key on your keyboard. This will ensure you have a clean slate when creating this test animation.

3. Try clicking on the number **24** and then moving the limbs of the character.

4. Click on frame 1 and then hit the play button located above the timeline. You should see these limbs now animate between frames 1 and 24. Congratulations! You just created your first animation!

Editing Anime Studio preferences

Before diving into creating our first document in Anime Studio, let's take a look at the program's preferences. This will allow us to adjust the colors of the user interface as well as set some of the more advanced options. Most options here will more than likely remain untouched. However, it's good to know what you can adjust should you decide to modify some preferences down the road.

Exploring the Options tab

In order to access the programs preferences, go to **Edit** at the top of the window and choose **Preferences**. A new window will appear, as shown in the following screenshot:

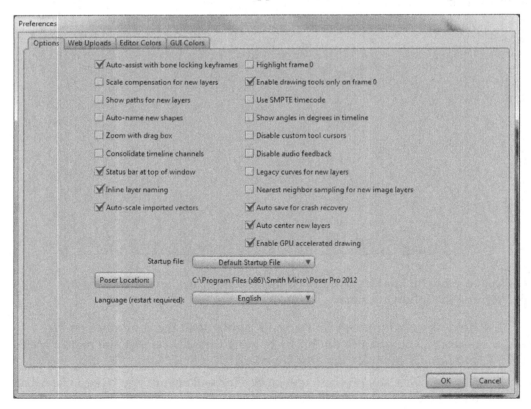

The following are some of the major preferences in the **Options** tab:

- **Consolidate timeline channels**: This is present by default in the Pro version of Anime Studio. This option, when checked, creates a less complicated timeline at the expense of flexibility. For this book, we will not be checking this option.

- **Enable drawing tools only on frame 0**: This disallows the user to use drawing tools past frame 0. When this is disabled, it can be useful for frame-by-frame animation. Since Anime Studio was not designed to work this way, it can cause conflicts and confusion in more complicated projects. For this book, the option will be left enabled (in other words, we will only be drawing on frame 0).

- **Startup file**: This drop-down menu allows you to select what file you'd like to see whenever you boot Anime Studio. By default, as we know by now, we get an anime style character rigged with bones as our current startup file. With this menu, you can choose a new file or opt out of having any file launch with the software.

 What about the other options? Don't worry; it's usually best to leave these set to their defaults when first starting out. Later on, if you decide you need to tweak some of these settings, you can always go back to this window through the **Edit** menu.

Using the Web Uploads tab

With the Web Uploads tab, you can export your videos straight to YouTube, without having to go through your web browser. This can be convenient if you want to upload your animations quickly and easily. For this book, we will be creating pieces of work that will need to be put through a video editor before being uploaded, so we will not be using this option. But you may find it to be of use should you decide to create simpler animations down the road. The **Web Uploads** tab is shown in the following screenshot:

Modifying properties with the Editor Colors and GUI Colors tabs

The last two tabs in the **Preferences** window allow you to change the colors in the Anime Studio interface. The **Editor Colors** tab deals more with the tools of Anime Studio. Here you can change the way the background color looks in your workspace as well as adjust the default line thickness when creating strokes with your objects, as shown in the following screenshot:

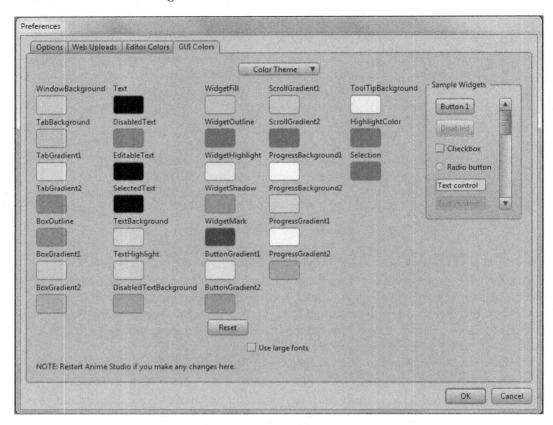

The **GUI Colors** tab allows you to adjust the color theme for the entire Anime Studio interface. There are built-in themes you can access from the **Color Theme** drop-down menu. Plus, you can adjust all of the colors individually to create your own look. This book will be taking screen caps using the default color scheme.

Setting up your first document

Now that you have configured your software settings, it's time to set up our first document that we will be working on in Anime Studio. Setting up your document parameters early on is important, especially when you consider how the frame rate and resolution can greatly alter the final outcome. Changing either of these settings when you have animation and assets on screen can greatly alter the performance of your animation. So be sure to set your parameters first!

Creating a document

You can create a document at any time by going to the **File** menu and choosing **New**. If you have a project file currently open, a tab will be created for the new document. The same applies if you are opening existing project files. You can jump back and forth between these documents by simply clicking on the corresponding tabs.

You can close a project file at anytime by clicking on **X** next to the document's tab. When closing a tab, you may be asked to save any changes before exiting. As a general rule, it's important to save often! Create a new document now so that we can adjust the settings.

Downloading the example code

You can download the example code files for all Packt books you have purchased from your account at http://www.packtpub.com. If you purchased this book elsewhere, you can visit http://www.packtpub.com/support and register to have the files e-mailed directly to you.

Adjusting Project Settings

With your new document now open, go to **File** and choose **Project Settings**. This will open up the settings panel for your current document, as shown in the following screenshot:

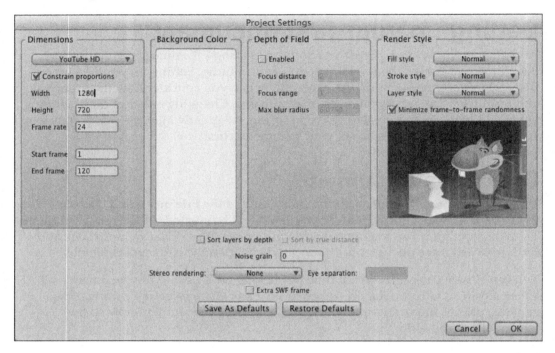

There are a few considerations to make when looking at this panel. These settings will change depending on your project's needs. In the case of this book, the following is what we will be doing:

- The **Dimensions** section dictates the size of our document or what we anticipate the resolution of the video to be at export. You can adjust the dimensions manually if you wish (by inputting numbers in the **Width** and **Height** fields). However, Anime Studio has some built-in presets that are useful when wanting to conform a project to an industry standard resolution. For the case of the cartoon we will be making, let's choose **YouTube HD** from the drop-down menu. This will give us a resolution of 1280 x 720. This is a good resolution for Internet distribution. You can go higher with this resolution if you wish, but this size should keep things manageable for most computers running Anime Studio.

- The **Frame rate** option, which is also adjusted when choosing a resolution template, dictates how many frames per second our animation will contain. It's very important to decide on your frame rate early because if you change it when animation is in place on your timeline, it can disrupt the flow, audio syncing, and more. The higher the frame rate, the smoother your cartoon is going to look. Of course, this also means you will need to animate more frames per second to compensate. A good rule of thumb is animations made for cinema run at 24 frames per second. Animations made for television run at 30 frames per second (usually converted from 24 or 12 frames per second). Nowadays, you may even find videos that push 60 frames per second. While in the end this will come down to personal preference, we will be using 24 frames per second for our project. This should already be set if you chose the **YouTube HD** preset from the drop-down menu.

- The **Start frame** and **End frame** fields allow you to control what part of your animation will be included when it's time to export. It's usually hard to determine this in the beginning as animated scenes can vary in length. These numbers can also be adjusted before you decide to export out a scene. For right now, leave the numbers as they are. These options are shown in the following screenshot:

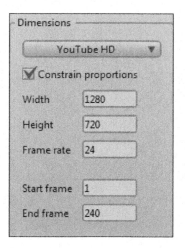

- The **Background Color** section adjusts the color of your background when you export out an animation. This will not adjust the color in the editor, so the changes are not apparent until you render out a frame or sequence. The background color can also be useful if you plan to export out separate elements of your animation and compile them in another program. This is referred to as **keying** or **matting**. We will be leaving the background color to the default setting for this book.

- The **Depth of Field** section allows us to simulate a camera lens and blur out certain objects, depending on their distance from our Anime Studio virtual camera. Sometimes, it's easier to create the depth of field effect manually, either through blurring layers in Anime Studio or through a video editor. For this book, we will be leaving this option off.

- Choosing options in the **Render Style** section can adjust the way your cartoon looks through various style filters. This can generate some interesting results if you're trying to spice up the look of your cartoon. Choosing a type of **Fill style** will alter all the fills of your objects while **Stroke style** will change the look of the lines. **Layer style** will apply the chosen effects to all your layers. We won't be using any of these styles for the cartoon in this book, but they may be useful for you in future projects.

- The **Save as Defaults** button, which is located at the bottom of the **Project Settings** panel will allow you to save the settings you just changed, so that for future documents you don't have to worry about adjusting the resolution and frame rate. Click on this button; that way you won't have to worry about adjusting these settings again as you move through this book. If you ever decide you want to have the default settings back, simply click on the **Restore Defaults** button, as shown in the following screenshot:

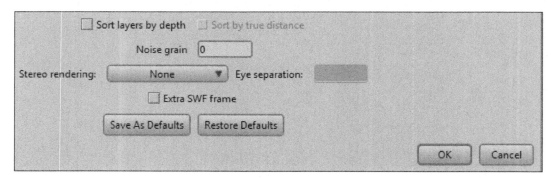

Summary

It may not seem like it now, but planning, outlining, and writing is incredibly important when creating a successful cartoon. This book will give you the tools you need to get going on your animation adventure with the creation of a simple animated scene. However, when it's time for you to start working on your own projects, you will want to take all of the suggestions for planning and writing in this chapter to heart. Finally, preparing your document and settings in advance will help with your workflow later on (and prevent some potential headaches).

In the next chapter, we will be going more hands-on with the software by working with all the draw and fill tools. We will also briefly discuss the differences between tablet and mouse drawing and the advantages vector drawings have over bitmap graphics.

2
Drawing in Anime Studio

Anime Studio offers a large selection of tools to help you craft the perfect character, environment, or prop. This can be a bit overwhelming if you are unfamiliar with Anime Studio's interface or drawing on a computer. This chapter will help ease you into the process.

In this chapter, we will cover the following topics:

- Mouse versus tablet drawing
- Vector and raster graphics
- The Draw and Fill tools

Mouse versus tablet drawing

If you're accustomed to drawing traditionally with a pen or pencil, you will discover quite quickly that drawing with a mouse requires a different skillset. The way a mouse moves, the difference in control, and the lack of intimacy can really take some time getting used to. While initially overwhelming, it is possible to map your mind towards mouse drawing.

A graphic tablet is like a digital drawing pad that allows you to sketch on screen using a utensil that resembles a pen or pencil. What's nice is that Anime Studio was built to work with certain graphic tablets, thus making Plug and Play easy.

In this book, we will be creating cartoon assets with a mouse. This is the most universal way as most users have this accessory for their computer. In addition, the book covers both freehand and point drawing styles. We will be using point drawing for the majority of this book.

Learning about Wacom tablets

Wacom is a very well-known brand of graphic tablets which work well with Anime Studio. This is because Smith Micro Software teamed up with Wacom while building Anime Studio to deliver seamless compatibility. What's great about Wacom tablets is that they correspond to the amount of pressure you apply to your lines. For instance, if you apply a lot of pressure at the start of a line and then end the line with light pressure, you will see a difference in width just as you would with a real pen or pencil. This option can be turned off in Anime Studio, but most artists welcome it. If you're interested in tablet drawing, Wacom has many different tablets varying in size and features. You can visit www.wacom.com for more details. The following is the image of a Wacom tablet:

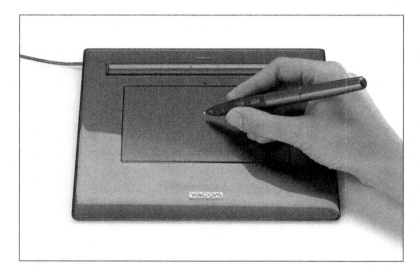

Understanding the basics of vector and raster graphics

Before we begin drawing in Anime Studio, it's important to understand the differences between vector and raster graphics. Anime Studio allows you to output both types of graphics, and each has its strengths and weaknesses.

Vector drawings are created whenever you use a drawing tool in Anime Studio. This is also the main format for Adobe Flash, Toon Boom, and Adobe Illustrator. Vector format is a popular choice and has been dominating the Internet cartoon scene for several years.

The following image is an example of a vector image. Notice how all the lines retain a sharp quality.

Vector graphics tend to have smaller file sizes compared to equivalent raster graphics. This not only makes streaming embedded **Shockwave Flash** (**SWF**) easier, but also keeps your project files lower in size, thus freeing up more space on your hard drive and cutting down on load times.

Raster or bitmap images are made up of pixels. Common file types include JPEG, BMP, PNG, and GIF. Basically, images you take with your camera, found on the Internet (at least the majority of them), or created in Adobe Photoshop are raster graphics. Raster graphics can be imported into Anime Studio and used for different functions. While they can contain great detail, raster graphics have many disadvantages when it comes to animation. As they are pixel-based, if you enlarge or zoom into a raster graphic past its original size, you will lose the image's quality. They also tend to bloat project file sizes up; this is due to the pixels needing more information to display the image.

Many artists do find raster images worthwhile; additionally, you have the ability to convert raster images into vector graphics if desired. This method is called tracing, and while it can be useful, it's definitely not 100 percent effective, especially when trying to make the image work with animation. The following image is an example of a raster graphic. Compare it to the previous vector image. Note how the raster graphic appears blurry or pixelated in comparison.

Now, you must be wondering which image type is the best. There is really no right or wrong answer to this question. It all comes down to personal preference and what you plan to do with your cartoon. We will explore a few uses of bitmap images in this book, but the primary focus will be on creating vector art through the drawing tools.

Exploring the Draw and Fill tools

As we start working with the drawing tools in this chapter, it would be best for you to have a new document loaded up so that we have room to play around. In order to do that, navigate to **File | New**. We will also use the example files provided with the book's code bundle.

Your document's dimensions and settings should be set from the previous chapter. New documents always open with a vector layer on the right-hand side **Layers Panel**, labeled **Layer 1**. This is perfect for us as all of the drawing tools require a vector layer to be used. We will be discussing the difference in layer types in *Chapter 3*, *Exploring Layers and Timelines*.

Some drawing tools have features that can be adjusted at the top of the Anime Studio window. We will refer to this area as the **top bar**.

The drawing tools are located on the left-hand side of your screen by default. The tools we will be looking at are divided into two panels: **Draw** and **Fill**. If you go in order while learning these tools, it may make sense, but we're simply too free-spirited for that. We will be going back and forth between these tools as some of them directly benefit the usage of others.

Drawing shapes and lines with the Add Point tool

The Add Point tool allows us to create lines and shapes using a series of points. All of Anime Studio's tools work with a point system, but this tool arguably gives you the most control in this regard. Points can then be moved or deleted depending on your needs. The following screenshot shows the location of the Add Point tool on the toolbar. As you can see, it looks like a curved line with a point at the end. You can also press the *A* key on your keyboard to select the tool.

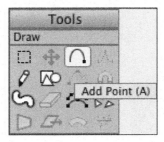

To get started, perform the following steps:

1. Go to the top of your toolbar and click on the Add Point tool. Next, you will find a few options just below your **File** menu at the top of the Anime Studio program window. This is your top bar area. Please make sure **Auto-Weld** and **Auto-Fill** are both selected (this will be indicated by a check mark next to the corresponding option).

Autowelding ensures that the two points we are joining will snap or weld together. Autofilling ensures that once two points are joined together to complete an enclosed object, the drawing will fill in with the colors from your **Style** palette. Try deselecting these options and redoing this exercise later on, to see what happens!

2. On the right-hand side of your screen is the **Style** palette. Right below the title, you will see two colors, each labeled with **Fill** and **Stroke**. Click on the **Fill** color swatch and select a color of your choice from the options given. With the **Color Picker** window, you have the ability to click on a color, adjust the color range, modify transparency, as well as adjust your colors numerically for precise control.

3. Once you have selected your color, click on the **OK** button.

4. Now, select the **Stroke** color swatch and repeat the preceding steps. Try to pick a different color than that of the fill. The following screenshot shows the **Style** palette and **Color Picker**:

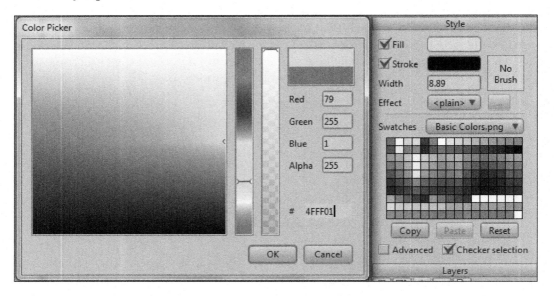

5. Move your cursor somewhere on the blank canvas. Click and hold down the left button of your mouse, drag in any direction, and release. You should now see two points connected with a link. Now, we are simply seeing an outline, or reference for this object. No physical line has been created yet.

6. Place your cursor on one of the two points. When correctly placed, your Add Point drawing tool will be highlighted in green.

7. Now, click and hold down the left button of the mouse and drag anywhere to add to your line. If you keep the left button of the mouse pressed and move the point around, you should notice that the placement of this point affects the line curvature from the other two points. If you don't like this effect, you can always select the **Sharp Corners** option on the top of your window to create perfectly straight lines from point to point. Release the left button of the mouse once you've found a spot for your point.

8. By repeating the preceding steps, you can continue to add interconnecting points to create an object; complex or simple, the choice is yours. If you desire, you can add points in between other established points by simply clicking on the line that interconnects them.

9. To complete your object, you must overlap one point over another. Click the left button of your mouse, hold it, and drag the mouse to your first point.

10. Once the area is highlighted in green, release the mouse button and notice how the object fills in with the colors you have selected from the **Style** palette. Have a look at the image in the following screenshot for an example:

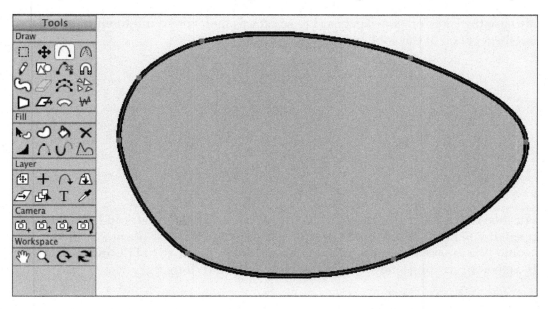

The Add Point tool offers a lot of control and is popular with mouse users. It may take some time to get used to, but if you prefer precision, practice will definitely pay off. This tool will be used quite a bit when we start drawing our assets. However, there are other tools that can get the job done, which we will be exploring momentarily.

Freestyle drawing with the Freehand tool

The **Freehand** tool allows us to draw in Anime Studio as if we were using a pen or pencil. This tool is a favorite amongst tablet users as it allows for absolute freedom of movement. It offers benefits for mouse users as well, especially if they plan to create a sense of stroke width variation. Just keep in mind, even though you can draw freely with this tool, you will still be creating points to make up your lines and objects, just like the Add Point tool. Just note that since Version 10, points will be hidden when using freehand drawing tools, to make the workspace less cluttered. In order to view and edit the points, you will need to select the Transform Points tool. The Freehand tool is the first tool in the second row (it looks like a pencil). You can also use the *F* key on your keyboard to select this tool. For your reference, you can see the location of this tool in the following screenshot:

For this exercise, you can keep the document you created for the Add Point tool open. If you need more room to draw, feel free to create a new document. If you would like to save the current document to work on later, go to **File** and click on **Save** before creating a new document. Now, let's start drawing!

The following steps will guide you on freestyle drawing with the Freehand tool:

1. Click on the Freehand tool. At the top, where you have your tool options, be sure that **Auto-Weld**, **Auto-Fill**, and **Auto-Stroke** are checked. Before trying this tool out, let's check out some of the other options we can adjust with the Freehand tool.

2. At the top, to the left-hand side of the **Auto-Fill** and **Auto-Stroke** settings, is a button labeled **Freehand Options**. Click on the button and a new panel will appear, as shown in the following screenshot:

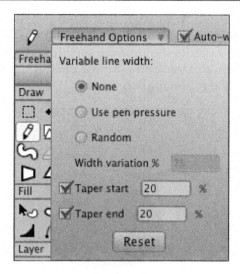

3. The **Variable line width** options allow you to change how the Freehand tool acts according to the pressure from your graphic tablet utensil. You can choose **None**, which will create a line with a consistent width; **Use pen pressure**, which detects how hard you are pressing on your tablet when drawing and adjusts the width accordingly (hard for thick, soft for light); or **Random**, which will randomize the line width as you place the points down. These options will work with a mouse, with the exception of the **Use pen pressure** setting.

4. In the same panel, you can also adjust the percentage of variation of line width. The higher the percentage, the more dramatic a shift you will have for your line widths. Finally, you can dictate if you want your freehand lines to taper at the start and end. This can be useful, especially if you're using a mouse and want to simulate the freehand pressure-sensitive look.

5. Once you have picked the appropriate options, let's start drawing! Place your cursor on the canvas, preferably outside of the other object you drew with the Add Point tool, hold down your left mouse button, and drag to create a line. You will notice that whichever settings you picked in the **Freehand Options** panel will be reflected in your line.

6. Since we have selected **Auto-Weld** and **Auto-Fill**, we can automatically create closed objects. Try drawing an oval with the Freehand tool. Your beginning and end points should snap together, creating an enclosed and filled-in object. You can view an example of a line and shape with the Freehand tool in the following screenshot:

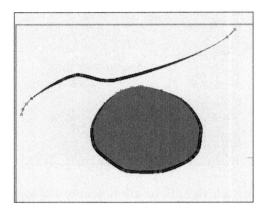

If you are drawing with a tablet or are familiar with traditional drawing methods, the Freehand tool may be a better choice over the Add Point tool. As we start to draw characters and props, the Add Point tool will be referred to a lot. However, don't be afraid to use the Freehand tool in its place if that's what you're more comfortable with. You can always combine these tools too. The more options you have, the better!

Creating perfect shapes with the Draw Shape tool

While we have the ability to draw whatever we want with the Add Point and Freehand tools, sometimes, being able to easily draw a specific shape can help save time. The Draw Shape tool allows us to draw different shapes, including rectangles, ovals, and stars. The tool looks like a rectangle, oval, and triangle overlapping one another, as shown in the following screenshot. You can also use the *S* key as a shortcut for this tool.

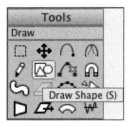

Like before, you can keep the same document open if you have room to draw, or you can create a new document. Let's start drawing shapes!

The following steps will guide you to create perfect shapes using the Draw Shape tool:

1. Go over to your toolbar and select the Draw Shape tool. At the top, you should have six shapes to choose from. Pick a shape that you would like to draw, select **Auto-Stroke** and **Auto-Fill** if you wish to automatically fill in your shape, and place the cursor on a blank part of the document.

2. Click and hold down the left mouse button, then drag to create the shape. Depending on where you drag, the appearance of the shape will alter. Releasing the button will create the shape, apply your stroke, and fill the settings if you have those corresponding options selected. Now, you will have a shape drawn like the image in the following screenshot:

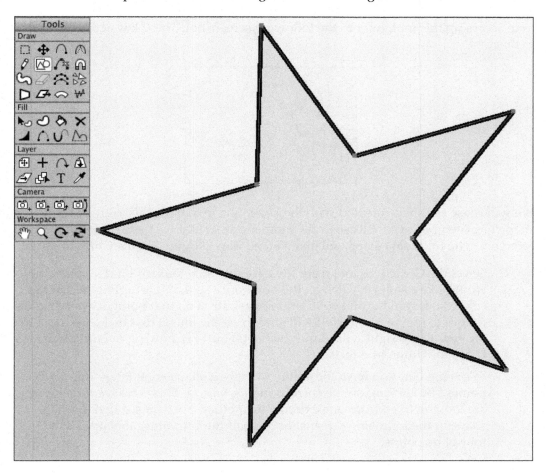

While we can draw shapes with the Add Point or Freehand tools, the Draw Shape tool can streamline the process. You can always use the Add Point tool to add points to your shapes to create more advanced objects.

Are you looking to create a perfectly proportionate shape? When using the Draw Shape tool, hold down the *Shift* key on your keyboard. This will lock the shape, so you can draw a perfect square, circle, triangle, or star.

Adjusting your bends with the Curvature tool

There will be times while drawing in Anime Studio when a line or curve isn't shaped quite right. While you can move the points of the line to create the desired shape, the Curvature tool allows us to straighten and bend lines with ease. To have an easier time accessing this tool, refer to the following screenshot. The C key acts as a shortcut to this tool.

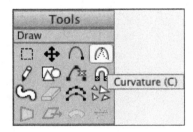

We will reuse the shape created with the Draw Shape tool for this exercise. If the shape has been removed, please draw another one so that we have something to reference. The following steps will give you an idea about using the Curvature tool:

1. Select the Curvature tool from the left-hand side toolbar. Find a point you would like to adjust. Click on the point once so that it is highlighted in red color. Now, hold down your left mouse button on that point. If your shape is rounded, moving to the left will straighten the line(s) that make up the shape. Moving to the right will round the line(s) out. Try moving in both directions to see the different effects.

2. In the top bar, you have the ability to make a shape completely rounded or pointed by clicking on the corresponding button. This can save time if you are looking to go from one extreme to another. You can see that the star shape in the following screenshot has had the Curvature tool applied to four of its points:

You can create interesting shapes using the Curvature tool. Additionally, it can help perfect a shape's design if you are having issues with moving points around. Be sure to keep it in mind when working on your own projects.

[Using the Select Points tool, you can easily alter the curvature of several points at once. All it requires is highlighting the desired points and then repeating the preceding steps.]

Altering points with the Transform Points tool

Up to this point, we have applied points to the canvas to create lines and shapes, but what if we want to alter points that have already been applied? The **Transform Points** tool allows us to select, move, scale, rotate, and delete one or more points. The tool looks like a crosshair and is the second one in your list of the **Draw** toolbox. The *T* key acts as the shortcut key for this tool.

 If you are a longtime user of Anime Studio, chances are you will recall that moving, scaling, and rotating points consisted of using three different tools. Version 10 has taken these functions and condensed them into one tool: Transform Points. The principles are the same, and you will discover quickly that it can help speed up your workflow, cutting down on time when it comes to selecting different tools.

The following screenshot shows the **Draw** tool panel with the **Transform Points** tool highlighted:

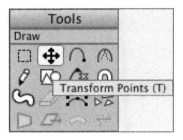

You can keep the shape, which we have been using, open for this exercise. If you don't have a shape on your screen, simply create one using the Draw Shape tool from the left-hand side toolbar.

The following steps will guide you to select, move, and delete points using the Transform Points tool:

1. Select the Transform Points tool from the top-left toolbar.

2. Try selecting a point from the shape on screen. To do this, simply click on the point. The point you have clicked on should turn red in color, which means it is currently selected.

3. Holding down the left mouse button on this point, try dragging it around on the canvas. As you alter the point's position, you will also alter the entire line or object that the point is part of. If you want to restrict movement of the point or object to the *x* or *y* axis, hold down *Shift* when moving your points.

4. If you were to click in the middle of an object (such as an oval) or in between points on a line, you will end up selecting all of the points making up that object. You can tell this by the fact that all the points are highlighted red. This can be useful if you want to edit a bunch of points at once. To deselect your points at any time, simply click off the shape or go to **Edit** and click on **Select None**.

5. When multiple points are selected, you may have noticed new options appear on your top bar. The most used of these are **Flip Horizontally** and **Flip Vertically**. If you need to quickly flip an object or points over from one direction to another, definitely give these buttons a try!

6. Select another point on your shape. Once that point is red, hit the *Delete* key on your keyboard. The point will disappear. Notice how Anime Studio compensates for this lost point by connecting the two nearest points together. This can alter the look of your shape, so be careful! This method is useful if you want to simplify an object or remove an unwanted point. You can see it really changes the look of our star, as shown in the following screenshot:

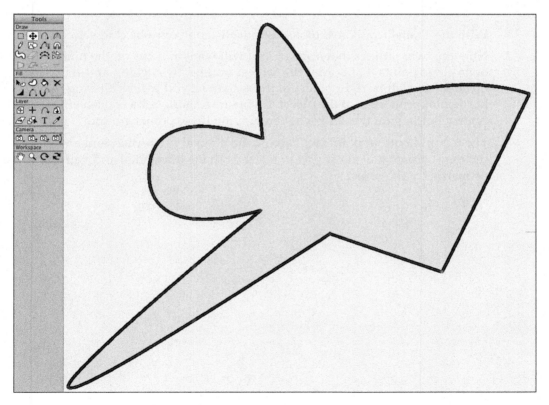

What we're using here is a simple shape, but as you start working with your own creations, you will discover all of what we'll be learning here is applicable.

 If at any point, you make a mistake when working on a project, simply go to **Edit** and click on **Undo** (*Ctrl* + *Z* on Windows and *command* + *Z* on Mac). You can undo several previous actions. Be careful though as there is a limit to how many backward steps you can take.

Sometimes, it's necessary to alter the size of a drawn object. When using the Transform Points tool, two red boxes will appear around the selected point or object. The second box contains nine points or handles that look like empty circles. You will use these to resize your shapes horizontally, vertically, and proportionally.

You can leave the current document open and use one of your existing objects as an example for this exercise. Making a new document and drawing a shape will suffice as well.

The following steps will guide you to scale points using the Transform Points tool:

1. With the Transform Points tool selected, click on your object to select it.

2. Note the two outlines that appear. You will want to focus on the nine open circle points that border the second outline. By clicking-and-dragging on either the left or right points of the rectangle, you will be altering the horizontal properties of the object. If you are looking for a squash effect, you can try holding on the *Alt* key when moving these points around.

3. The top and bottom points will adjust the vertical properties, and any of the four corners will allow you to resize both the horizontal and vertical properties of the object.

4. If you want precise control over the size values, you can enter numbers for both the horizontal (*x* axis) and vertical (*y* axis) properties on your top bar. As you can see in the following screenshot, things appear to be squished or distorted:

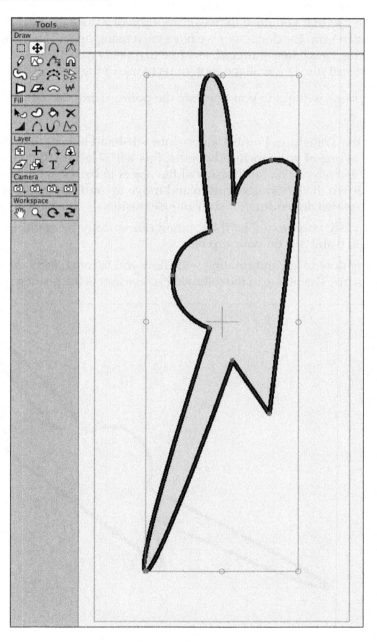

There will be times when you are working on a project where an object will be too small or big for what you want to achieve. Scaling points is invaluable in cases like this.

Now, let's talk about rotating points. Why would you want to do this in the first place? Rotating can be useful if you need to tweak a portion of a drawing or completely rotate an object. You can keep the document we have been using open. However, if you feel things are starting to become cluttered, feel free to quickly make a new document and create an object with the Draw Shape tool for us to use in this exercise.

The following steps will guide you to rotate the points using the Transform Points tool:

1. Select the Transform Points tool on your left-hand side toolbar. Select the center of one of your enclosed objects; this will select all the points in this object. Move your cursor outside of the object in between the two outlines. Hold down the left mouse button and move up and down. Notice how the object rotates depending on your mouse position.

2. If you wish, you can adjust the rotation numerically by entering a number between 0 and 360 on your top bar.

3. Holding down *Shift* and rotating will allow you to rotate in 45-degree increments. The image in the following screenshot is the result of point rotation:

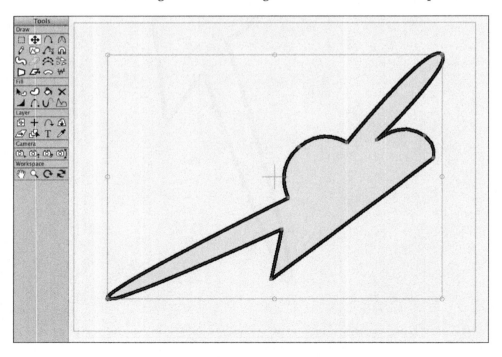

Sometimes, when drawing a character or prop, things may appear crooked or not line up with the other assets on screen. This tool will help you make those small corrections without having to redraw assets.

 Try using the Select Points tool and highlighting a small group of points on your object. Then, when rotating with the Transform Points tool, you can get some pretty interesting results. It can also help if you need to fine-tune some aspects of your object(s).

Selecting vector points with the Select Points tool

Sometimes, it's necessary to select more than one point. While you can select all points on an object with the Transform Points tool by clicking in between points, there are times where you may need to select specific points on an object. This is where the Select Points tool comes in handy. As you can see in the following screenshot, it's the first tool on your toolbar. The G key works as a shortcut too.

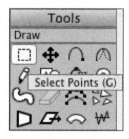

You can keep the document we have been using open for this. If you make a new document, just create another shape with the Draw Shape tool, so we have something to work with.

The following steps will help you to select vector points using the Select Points tool:

1. Select the Select Points tool from the left-hand side toolbar.
2. Find an object or line you have drawn, hold down your mouse button, and drag to encompass a certain group of points. Once you release your mouse button, you should see the selected points turn red.
3. From here, you can use the Transform Points tool (or another tool that alters points) to affect the selected group. In this case, the Transform Points tool allows us to move the entire object at once (since all points are selected). This can save a lot of time when it comes to altering an object on a larger scale.

4. Try selecting a small group of points on the object and then using the Transform Points tool. Notice how you can alter the object in a completely unique way.

5. If you're looking for a more detailed selection area, click on the box next to **Lasso Mode** on your top toolbar. This will allow you to select points freehand as opposed to using a rectangular area.

6. If you don't want to continually jump back and forth between the Select and Transform Points tools, you can also hold down the *Ctrl* key (*command* on Mac) while using the Transform Points tool to quickly do a selection. Give it a try! The star we started with is practically unrecognizable now as you can see in the image shown in the following screenshot:

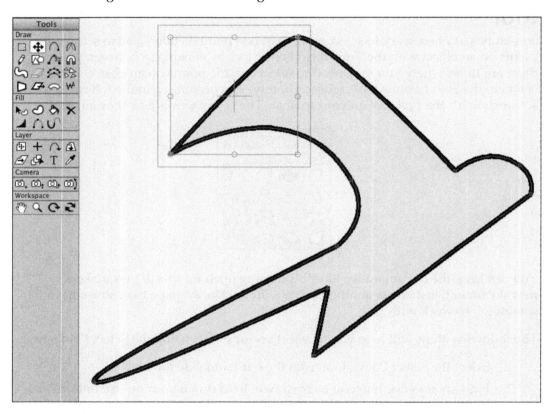

Being able to control which points you are altering is a huge benefit when it comes to creating and modifying drawn objects. This tool will also save you time with the ability to highlight several points at once.

 If you are looking to select all the points on a layer, try using the shortcut key, *Ctrl + A* (*command + A* if you're on a Mac). This can be easier than selecting all the points manually. Alternatively, you can go to **Edit** and click on **Select All**.

Filling in objects with the Paint Bucket tool

There will be times where you'll want to add fill or stroke properties to an object after you have drawn it. Alternatively, you may realize after setting an object's color on the **Style** palette, you need to make a change after drawing the object out. The Paint Bucket tool is used for these purposes. The only requirement for filling in an object is to make sure there are lines present to enclose the area. In the previous versions of Anime Studio, lines actually needed to be welded shut in order to use the Paint Bucket tool. This is no longer the case with Version 10. The icon for this tool looks like, you guessed it, a paint bucket! This is also the first tool we will be looking at that is located under the **Fill** section, as shown in the following screenshot. You can also use the *P* key as a shortcut to select the tool.

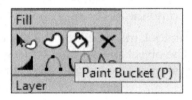

For a change of pace, let's open up an example file included within the code bundle of this book. You can save the current document if you wish to work on it further. To do that, go to **File**, click on **Save**, pick a location on your computer, name the file, and click on **Save**. The following steps will show you how to use the Paint Bucket tool:

1. Navigate to **File | Open**. Browse for the project file you downloaded with this book named `PaintBucketExample` in the `Chapter 02` folder. You should now see two un-filled shapes on screen.

2. Select the Paint Bucket tool from your left-hand side toolbar.

3. On the top bar, you should see three options: **Fill**, **Stroke**, and **Both**. With these options, you can choose to fill in the color, stroke, or both properties that are selected on your **Style** palette. If you like, you can choose your fill, stroke, and width properties from the **Style** palette before beginning this exercise.

4. To try this out, select the **Fill** option on the top bar and then take your cursor over to the first enclosed drawing on your canvas. Click inside the object and notice how the object fills in. However, we have no stroke surrounding the object as we are only using the **Fill** property.

5. Select the **Stroke** option from the top bar, go over to the second object in line, and click inside. Notice how your stroke properties from the **Style** palette have been transferred over. The inside of the object remains blank.

6. Select the **Both** option from the top bar and click on the first object again. As expected, both properties should transfer over to the shape.

7. The second shape in the lineup is broken or not complete. Select the Paint Bucket tool, then select the **Both** option from the top bar and try to fill in the object. The action cannot be carried out since the object is not enclosed. The same will apply when you try to use the **Fill** option to color in the object. However, if you select **Stroke** from the top bar and click on the outline of the object, the stroke properties will transfer over.

8. To complete the object, select the Add Point tool from your toolbar. Move your cursor on one of the points that is near the opening. Click-and-drag to snap your new point onto the next closest point to close off the object.

9. Select the Paint Bucket tool and try filling the object in again (make sure you select **Fill** or **Both**). The object should now fill in with no issues. The following screenshot should be similar to what you are seeing in the exercise file:

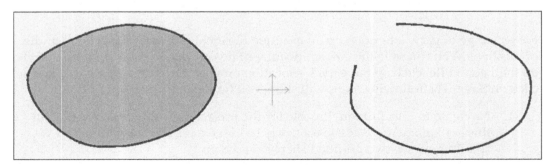

The Paint Bucket tool's uses are numerous, and it is the most used of the Fill tools. You'll be using it quite a bit as we progress through this book.

Altering shape properties with the Select Shape tool

The **Select Shape** tool is useful because it allows us to easily adjust the style properties of selected shapes. This can be useful if you want to quickly change a color, add a stroke, or remove a property. The tool is the first one located under the **Fill** section, as shown in the following screenshot. You can also use Q on your keyboard as the shortcut for this tool.

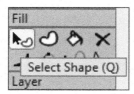

Keep the `PaintBucketExample.anme` file open. We can use the two example shapes for this exercise.

The following steps will guide you through altering shape properties using the Select Shape tool:

1. Select the Select Shape tool from the left-hand side toolbar. Click on the first shape that only has a fill applied to it. The shape's fill will become checkered, indicating it is selected.

2. On your **Style** palette, select the fill color and choose a different color from the color chooser. Once you click on **OK**, the color of the object will change to your newly selected color.

3. With the shape still selected, check the box next to **Stroke** on the **Style** palette. Now, notice how you can reapply the stroke line without having to use the Paint Bucket tool. You can do the same for the fill property as well. The following screenshot shows a selected object being changed with the **Style** palette:

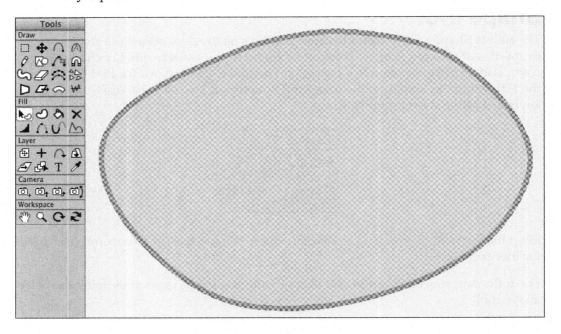

The Select Shape tool is great for those instances when you quickly want to change the properties of an object. You can use the Paint Bucket tool for similar situations, but using the Select Shape tool is arguably quicker in some cases.

By default, when you select a shape with the Select Shape tool, a checkered pattern will indicate your selection. If you'd like a simpler indicator, check off the **Checker** selection at the bottom of the **Style** palette. Now, a red outline will appear whenever a shape is selected as opposed to the checkered pattern.

Editing with the Magnet tool's influence area

Sometimes, it may be useful to select a group of points within the boundaries of a certain influence or magnet area. The Magnet tool allows us to do just that. We can even adjust the size of the magnet area to dictate what points will be affected. Think of it as another way to select multiple points at once. Finally, the closer a point is to the center of the magnet area, the more it will be affected. When looking at your toolbar, just look for the magnet icon. The *X* key will act as a shortcut. The following screenshot shows the Magnet tool in the **Draw** tool panel:

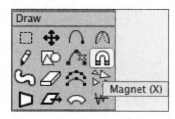

Feel free to keep the same `PaintBucketExample.anme` file open for this exercise. If you have altered the file heavily, feel free to reload it by going to **File | Open** and selecting the file again.

The following steps will guide you on how to use the Magnet tool:

1. Select the Magnet tool from the left-hand side toolbar.

2. When you move your cursor on the screen, you will notice there is a big red circle that appears. This is the influence area of your magnet.

3. To increase or decrease the size of the magnet area, you can enter a new value for the **Magnet Radius** field on the top bar. The default value is `.5`. Changing the value to `.25` will cut the size of the magnet area in half.

4. With the default radius size (`.5`), place your cursor between the two objects on screen. The radius area should contain points from both objects.

5. Click-and-drag your mouse around and notice how the points move between these two objects.

6. Place your cursor so that at least one point is near the center of the magnet area and at least one point is near the outside of the area. When you move your cursor, notice how the point(s) near the center move faster than the one(s) on the outside. Like a magnet, the pull is the strongest at the focal point. The red, oval selection area in the following screenshot is displaying the image after using the Magnet tool:

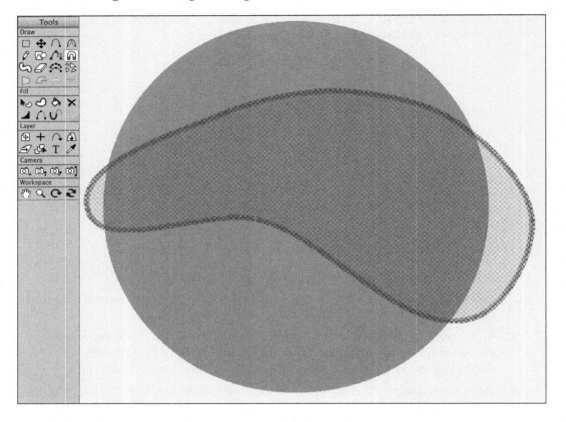

If you want to move a large number of points, the unique gravitational pull ability of this tool may suit you well. Give it a try and don't be afraid to mix and match different tools to fit various situations.

Filling in outlines with the Create Shape tool

The **Create Shape** tool is useful for creating or filling in shapes that have holes or gaps. It's also used for selecting outlined shapes and quickly filling them in. This is the second tool in the **Fill** section, as shown in the following screenshot, and looks like a blob of sorts. The *U* key acts as the default shortcut for this tool.

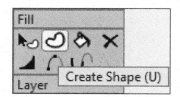

Let's open a new document for this demonstration by navigating to **File** | **New**. You can save the current file if you wish to come back to it later. The following steps will help you understand the use of the Create Shape tool:

1. Once you have a new document open, click on the Draw Shape tool, select an oval shape, and turn off **Auto-Fill** and **Auto-Stroke** on the top bar. Go to your canvas and draw out an oval.

2. Draw out another, smaller oval within the first.

3. Select the Select Points tool and highlight all the points that currently make up the shape. Alternatively, you can also use the Create Shape tool to select an object by clicking-and-dragging.

4. With the points still selected, click on the Create Shape tool on your left-hand side toolbar, which is next to your Select Shape tool. You should notice the shape turns a checkered red pattern, with the exception of the small oval inside the main shape.

5. Press the spacebar on your keyboard. The object, with the exception of the small oval, should fill in with the colors specified on your **Style** palette.

6. What if you want to fill in the small oval as well (or instead of) the large oval? That's easy! Select the points that make up the small oval.

7. The small oval should turn red and checkered.

8. Press the spacebar to apply the fill properties from your **Style** palette. The following screenshot show roughly what your workspace should look like before the fill is applied:

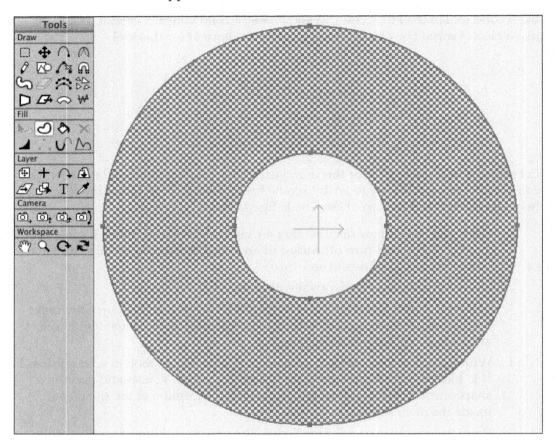

The Create Shape tool is one way to create shapes with holes in them. Most first-time users try to use the Paint Bucket tool to achieve this effect. It can be easily forgotten. You could highlight this section for future reference or make a note for yourself.

Hiding lines and shapes with the Hide Edge tool

The Hide Edge tool is useful because it allows us to hide a particular line or edge without breaking the overall construction of the object. This means that fills will not deactivate, which gives you more freedom when working with strokes. As shown in the following screenshot, the icon looks like a bent line with three points. The *H* key will activate this tool as well:

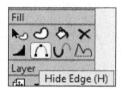

You can keep the same document open that you made for the *Filling in outlines with the Create Shape tool* section. We will use the Hide Edge tool on this object. You can make a new document and create a new shape too if you wish.

The following steps will help you understand the use of the Hide Edge tool:

1. Select the Hide Edge tool.

2. Go to the outside of the big oval and click in between one of the four points of the object. The stroke is now hidden.

3. Click again to bring the stroke back into view. You can toggle the visibility of all your lines using this tool. In the following screenshot, you can see we have hidden the line on the bottom-right of the oval:

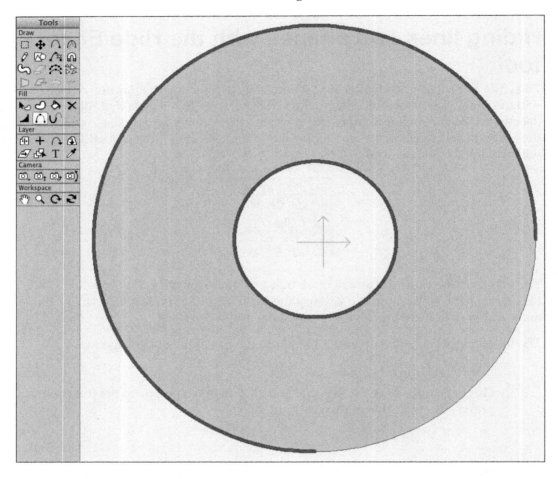

The Hide Edge tool can provide a lot of support when you are trying to stylize or hide lines from the audience. This will definitely come in handy later when drawing and connecting limbs together.

Revealing lines with the Stroke Exposure tool

Sometimes you may want to hide only part of a line between two points as opposed to the entire line. The **Stroke Exposure** tool gives you this control. You will find this next to the Hide Edge tool on your toolbar as shown in the following screenshot:

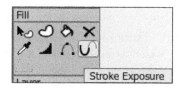

Keep the doughnut-looking object on screen. You can alternatively create a new document and object if you wish. Perform the following steps:

1. Click on the Stroke Exposure tool. Click and hold the top point of the oval.

2. Move your cursor to the left. Notice how the line disappears as you move further left.

3. You can stop at any time to create the exact stroke exposure you are looking for when working on any project. You should see something like the following screenshot:

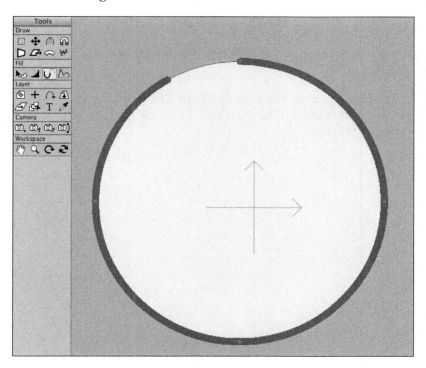

Stroke exposure is similar to the Hide Edge tool. However, if you're looking for more control, selecting this tool may be the way to go.

Removing lines and shapes with the Delete Edge tool

The **Delete Edge** tool allows us to quickly and effectively delete points from an object. Unlike the Hide Edge or Stroke Exposure tools, this will permanently do away with whatever line the point is attached to, creating a gap in the object. This will break the object's fill, but may be necessary when editing a drawing or undoing a misplaced point. This tool looks like a curved line with an X-like symbol on it. You can use the *D* key as a shortcut if you wish. The following screenshot shows the Delete Edge tool:

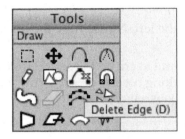

You can keep the doughnut-looking object on screen or create a new shape for the following exercise.

Click on the Delete Edge tool. Move your cursor to a point on one of the objects and click. The line for that point will be removed, breaking the fill of the object, as shown in the following screenshot:

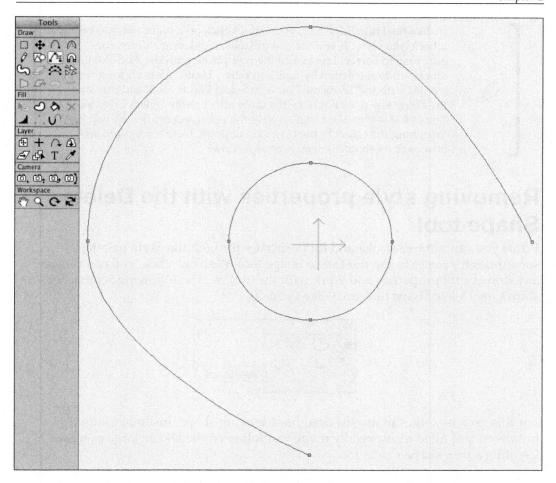

You will probably be doing just as much deleting as drawing when working in Anime Studio. It's all a part of the process of perfecting and creating assets. Be sure to keep the Delete Edge tool handy in cases like this.

Unlike the Hide Edge tool, you cannot click on a point twice to bring it back into view. If you make a mistake in deleting a point, the only way to correct it is to add the point back with the Add Point tool or undo the action by going to **Edit | Undo**. Also, clicking on a point with the Translate Points or Select Points tools and pressing the *Delete* key does not have the same effect as the Delete Edge tool. The *Delete* key method will remove the point, yet bridge the gap by morphing the object to the next closest point. Give it a try and see how each method changes your workflow!

Removing style properties with the Delete Shape tool

While you can remove stroke and fill properties through the **Style** palette, sometimes it's easier to use the Delete Shape tool. With one click, you can remove any draw or fill properties and work with the outline. The following screenshot shows the Delete Shape tool, an X-like symbol:

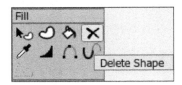

For this exercise, you can use the doughnut-looking shape. Just make sure it's unbroken and filled in, especially if you just followed the Delete Edge exercise. Creating a new shape works too.

The following steps will guide you to remove style properties using the Delete Shape tool:

1. With your oval still in place, click on the Delete Shape tool from the **Fill** section of your toolbar.

2. Click on the oval with this tool. Notice how the drawing properties (the stroke and fill) are removed yet the outline remains in place.

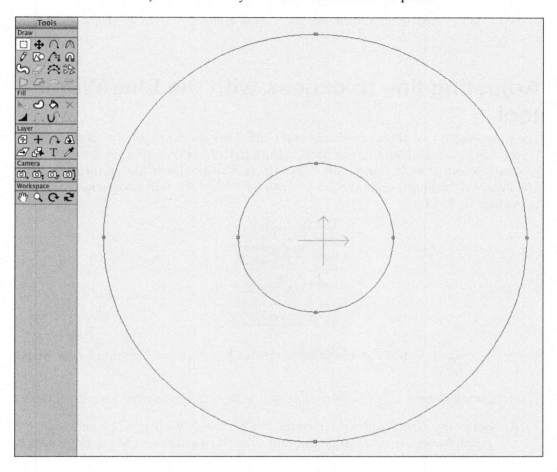

The Delete Shape tool can work great if you don't want to deal with breaking a shape to remove its fill properties. The best part is you can retain the shape's outline to fill or alter later on.

Once you delete a shape, you cannot retrieve the drawing properties unless you go to **Edit | Undo** or use the Paint Bucket tool to color the outline back in. So be sure you want the shape gone before you use this tool!

Adjusting line thickness with the Line Width tool

The **Line Width** tool allows us to adjust the line's thickness at specified points. If you don't own a tablet, this is a good feature to have as you can simulate the pressure-sensitive look, along with other effects. The tool looks like an incline. The *W* key is the shortcut for the Line Width tool. View the following screenshot to confirm its location:

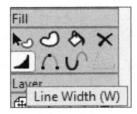

You may continue to use the doughnut shape for this exercise. Creating a new shape is also an option.

The following steps will teach you to adjust line thickness using the Line Width tool:

1. Select the Line Width tool from the left-hand side toolbar. Click and hold a point that contains a visible line and drag the mouse from left to right. Notice how the line's thickness changes depending on where you move the mouse.

2. If you select multiple points with the Select Points tool, you can adjust more than one line at once.

3. With a point selected, you can adjust the width numerically with the field on the top toolbar.

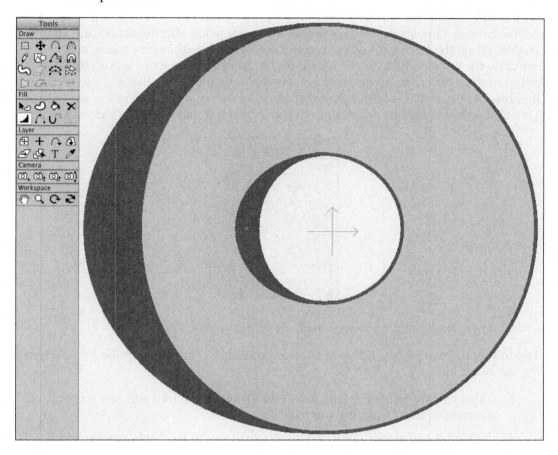

The Line Width tool is great for creating different stroke types without the use of a mouse. It also works in a pinch for when you don't want to adjust the stroke width through the **Style** palette. Play with this tool and see what type of effects you can come up with!

Creating pseudo 3D effects with the Perspective Points tool

Anime Studio allows you to work within 3D space when altering layers and camera angles. While the Perspective Points tool doesn't work within true space, it does simulate the effect, which can be useful if you don't want to work within the 3D environment, yet create an effect of perspective. The tool looks like a white rectangle that has one edge that is larger than the other, as shown in the following screenshot. This tool will also give us an idea of what effects it will have on selected vectors.

Create a new document for this exercise by going to **File | New**.

The following steps will guide you to create pseudo 3D effects with the Perspective Points tool:

1. With your blank document, select the Draw Shape tool and select the rectangle preset from the top bar.

2. Pick a fill and stroke color of your choosing from the **Style** palette and then draw a rectangle on your canvas.

3. Using the Select Points tool, draw a selection area around the rectangle to highlight all of the points.

4. Select the Perspective Points tool and place your cursor on the rectangle you just drew.

5. Click and drag the mouse to adjust the rectangle. As you go from left to right, you will notice how it looks like part of the rectangle is moving closer to the screen. If you move the cursor from top to bottom, the same effect will occur, but this time vertically. To visualize what this means, look at the image in the following screenshot. Notice how the right-hand side of the rectangle appears to be coming closer to us, creating the illusion of perspective.

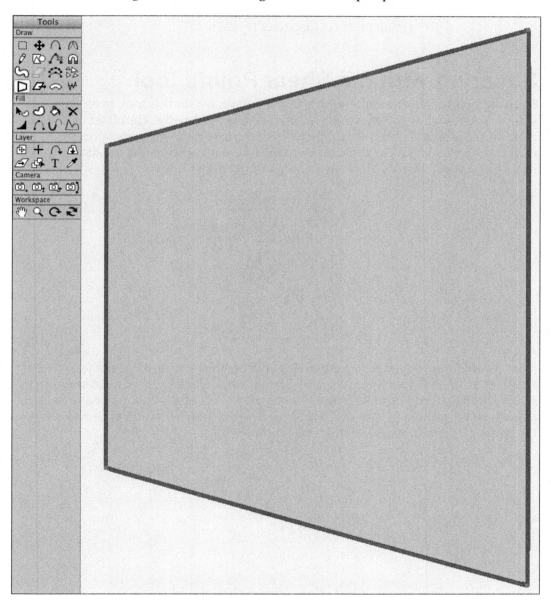

Like most of Anime Studio's tools, you could manually adjust the points of the object to achieve the same effect. However, the Perspective Points tool can make certain tasks easier, especially when it comes to creating the illusion of perspective.

> The Rotate XY Layer tool allows us to achieve a similar effect, but has the benefits of working within the true 3D space. We will learn more about this tool as we start to explore layers in *Chapter 3, Exploring Layers and Timelines.*

Shearing with the Shear Points tool

Shearing points creates similar effects to the Perspective Points tool. In essence, it allows you to alter and move the selected points diagonally. The effect may look simple with a rectangular shape but it can create more interesting results with advanced shapes. As you can see in the following screenshot, the tool looks like a parallelogram with an arrow pointing to the right:

Let's use the same rectangle we created for the *Creating pseudo 3D effects with the Perspective Points tool* section. To restore the rectangle back to its original state, go to **Edit | Undo** (or *Ctrl + Z* on Windows, *command + Z* on Mac). You may have to do this a few times if you made a lot of alterations. If you're having a difficult time restoring the rectangle, you can create a new one if you wish.

The following steps will help you understand the use of the Shear Points tool:

1. Select all four points of the rectangle using the Select Points tool and highlighting the rectangle with your selection area.

2. Select the Shear Points tool.

3. Move your cursor to the center of the rectangle.

4. Holding down your mouse button, move from left to right. Notice how the top portion of the rectangle moves away from the bottom portion. It's almost as if the rectangle is trying to tear itself apart. Notice the shearing effect in the following screenshot:

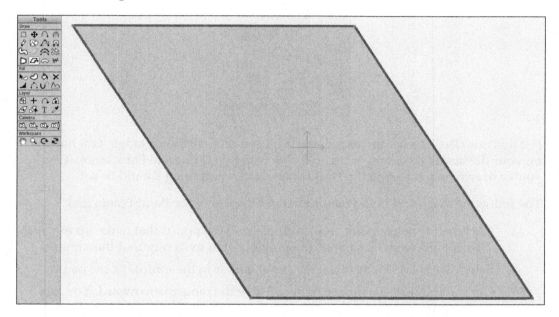

5. Moving your mouse up or down creates a similar effect, except with the vertical properties.

Shearing an object can have similar benefits to adjusting the rotation. An object may not be sitting right; shearing can give an object that extra push it needs. Plus, it can be used to create more experimental effects.

Making flexible-looking lines with the Bend Points tool

Bending points allow you to distort objects in interesting ways. It's almost as if you are creating the effect of snapping the selected object in half. The Bend Points tool isn't hard to miss as it looks like a rectangle that is bending downwards, as shown in the following screenshot:

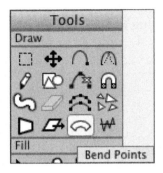

For this exercise, let's use an oval shape. You can remove the rectangle you have on your document or simply set it aside (by using the Translate Points tool). Once you've drawn an oval using the Draw Shape tool, everything should be set.

The following steps will help you understand the use of the Bend Points tool:

1. Click on the Select Points tool and select all the points that make up the oval. This should seem familiar as the previous two tools required the same step.

2. Select the Bend Points tool. Place your cursor in the middle of the oval.

3. Click and hold your mouse button. Move the mouse downward. You will notice a similar effect as to what the icon of the tool is expressing. Try moving the mouse up and to the left and right. It will appear as you are bending an eraser or a piece of rubber. The following screenshot will give you an idea of the effect:

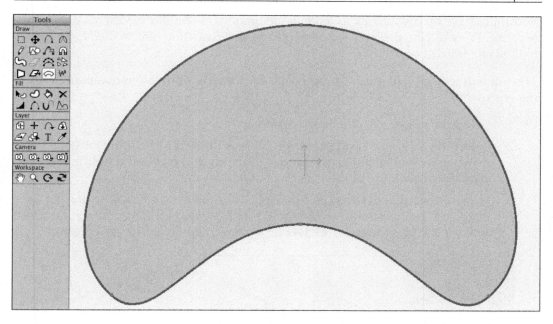

More often than not, bending points will be used more in an experimental setting. The best way to see this tool in action is to use it during your own projects and see what kind of benefits it can bring.

Creating random line movements with the Noise tool

The **Noise** tool allows you to alter the points by moving them in random directions. This could be useful if you're looking to create a unique or distorted look for an object. The tool itself looks like a line graph sharply dipping up and down, as shown in the following screenshot. It's the last item in the **Draw** section on the toolbar. You can also use the *N* key to select the **Noise** tool.

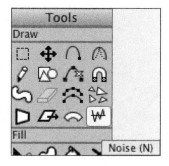

Be sure to have an object such as a rectangle or an oval on your screen for this exercise. We will be using this shape to try out the distortion effects the Noise tool has to offer.

The following steps will guide you through creating random line movements using the Noise tool:

1. Select the object with the Select Points tool.

2. Select the Noise tool and place your cursor in the middle of the object. Hold down your mouse button and move to the right. You should notice some movement with the points.

3. Release the mouse button and then click and hold it again. Now drag to the right. The points should move again but this time in different directions. You will see the image similar to the one shown in the following screenshot:

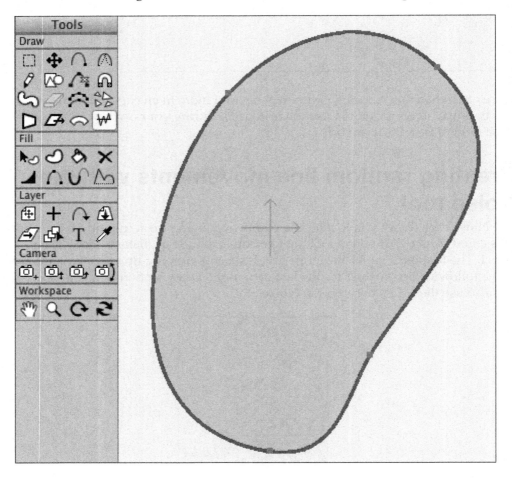

The Noise tool may not have an obvious practical use, but it can be helpful if you are looking to create a unique shape.

 The Noise tool will move your points in random directions each time you release and click the mouse button.

Transferring line formations with the Curve Profile tool

There may be times when you want to create a wavy or jagged line for one of the objects on your canvas. This could be done by creating a series of points and altering them accordingly. Or you could take advantage of the Curve Profile tool, which allows you to reference outlines and apply them to any shape. The tool icon has a point, followed by a rounded line, as shown in the following screenshot:

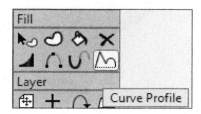

We will be using another example file for this exercise. Don't worry, you will find it in the code files that came with this book.

The following steps will help you understand the use of the Curve Profile tool:

1. Open up the example file CurveProfile.anme in the Chapter 02 folder. You can save any changes to your current document if you wish to come back and play around with it later.

2. You will see a red-colored oval, plus three outlines to its left. Click on the Select Points tool and highlight the oval so that all of its points are highlighted in red.

3. Click on the Curve Profile tool. Click on the first outline on the left-hand side (the wobbly looking one). You should observe that the outline has been applied to the stroke of the oval.

4. With the oval still selected, click on the second outline on the left-hand side (the jagged one). Your oval should appear to have a series of spikes.

5. With the jagged line effect still in place, direct your attention to the top of the screen. You should see a field entitled **Repeat count**. Delete the value 16 and enter 2 into the field. Upon pressing *Enter*, you should see a dramatically different shape on your screen. Perhaps this could be used as a flower or some other prop?

6. Feel free to click on the third outline to see what that looks like applied to your shape. If you decide you no longer want a curve profile applied to the selected shape, simply click on the canvas to revert back to a normal line. The results will be similar to the ones shown in the following screenshot:

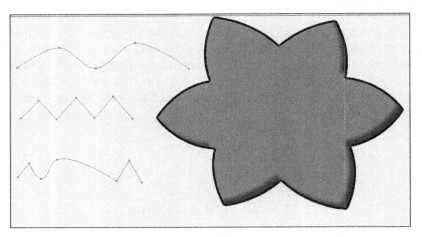

While they may not be immediately obvious, the Curve Profile tool has many uses. You could apply a wave outline to a bush, a cloud, the surface of water, and so on. It can save a lot of time compared to entering points manually.

Creating varied copies with the Scatter Brush tool

If at some point when working in Anime Studio, you have a need to create a bunch of objects that share similar traits, the Scatter Brush tool may be your best bet. It is possible to copy and paste an object multiple times and then slightly alter each of the copies. However, the Scatter Brush tool is much more user friendly and can save you a lot of time. The tool looks like four triangles, so it shouldn't be hard to miss. The following screenshot shows the Scatter Brush tool:

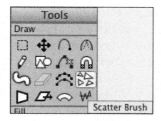

For this exercise, please open the example file `ScatterBrushExample.anme` from the `Chapter 02` folder, which has been included in the code bundle of this book. We will first start with using some of the built-in brush types for this tool.

The following steps will help you understand the use of the Scatter Brush tool:

1. Select the Scatter Brush tool from the left-hand side toolbar. In the top bar is a list labeled **Scatter Brush Options**. Click on it to reveal settings for this tool.

2. The **Angle jitter** feature will place each brush stroke at a slightly different angle in accordance to the value you put in. The angle will not exceed the specified number. The **Spacing** feature dictates how much space will be put between the brush strokes as you use the tool. The **Fill color jitter** and **Stroke color jitter** features allow for some color variance. Like the other values, the higher the value, the bigger the difference will be with your strokes.

3. **Flip X** and **Flip Y**, the last two options on the bottom of the options panel, will allow your brushes to randomly flip horizontally or vertically when using the brush. If you are looking for greater variation, you may want to select these options.

4. On the top bar, you also have the ability to adjust the minimum and maximum width of the brush strokes (**Min width** and **Max width**). This can allow you to control the size and variation (if any). For this example, we will set the maximum width to 60 and the minimum width to 40. The **Scatter Brush Options** list in the top bar is shown in the following screenshot:

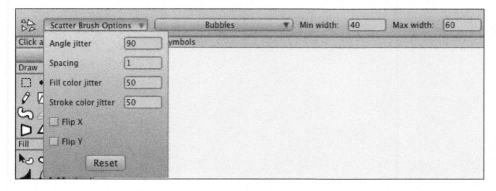

5. With your objects set, place your cursor on the screen. Hold down the left mouse button and move your cursor around the canvas. Bubbles should appear on the screen. This is because **Bubbles** is the default brush for the Scatter Brush tool. Here is where your previously specified scatter options will matter. You will see color, spacing, and angle differences with each brush stroke, based on the values you inputted earlier.

6. Click on the list labeled **Bubbles** in the top bar. You will find a list of built-in brushes. Select **Leaves** and try using the brush again. You should now see a series of leaves being drawn as you drag your mouse.

7. While using built-in brushes is great, the real power of the Scatter Brush tool lies in the ability to use custom-made objects as brushes. Use the Select Points tool and highlight the tree image that is in the document.

8. Go to **Edit | Copy**. You can also use *Ctrl + C* on Windows or *command + C* on Mac as a shortcut.

9. Go back to the brush selection button and choose **Clipboard** from the drop-down menu. This will now allow you to paint whatever you have copied (in this case, the tree image). The **Bubbles** list in the top bar is shown in the following screenshot:

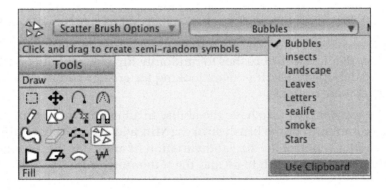

10. Hold down your left mouse button and start moving the cursor. You should see variation in the tree image just like you did with the built-in brushes. The following screenshot shows the variations in the tree image:

The Scatter Brush tool is terrific if you need to create a group of assets that share similar traits. With the options panel, you can choose just how different each of these assets look from one another. A great time saver!

Creating freehand shapes with the Blob Brush tool

Version 10 has introduced three brand-new drawing tools to Anime Studio's ever expanding toolset. The first tool we will be looking at is **Blob Brush**. This tool is neat because you can now create freehand shapes that automatically fill once you are finished drawing. It could definitely have its uses when working on more complicated projects. The following screenshot shows the of Blob Brush tool:

To get started, let's create a new document. The following steps will help you understand the use of the Blob Brush tool:

1. Select the Blob Brush tool. It is the squiggly-looking tool located below the Freehand tool. You can also use the *J* key as a shortcut.

2. With the Blob Brush tool, you can adjust the thickness of your drawn shape. You will find this setting on the top bar. The lower the value, the smaller your drawing area will be.

3. Place your cursor on the canvas, hold down your mouse button, and do a quick scribble. When you release your mouse button, notice how what you have drawn has had the fill and stroke properties you have on your **Style** palette applied to it.

4. If you continue to draw, and intersect with the original shape you made, the Blob Brush tool will live up to its name and push everything together, creating one shape.

5. If you want to remove portions of your new freehand drawing, hold down the *Ctrl* key (*command* on Mac) and start drawing. Anything you click will get erased. The cool thing here is that the shape will continue to blob together and maintain a cohesive form. This method is also useful when you want to punch holes into different objects and don't want to go through the method we outlined earlier when using the Create Shape tool. The following screenshot shows the Blob Brush tool in action:

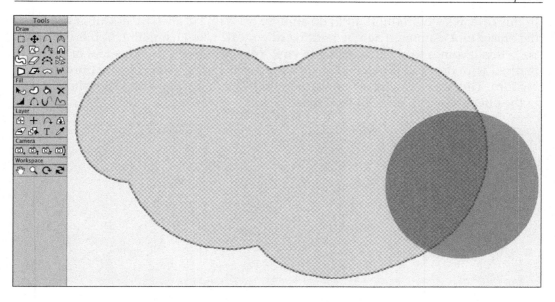

The Blob Brush tool opens up many possibilities for streamlining the process of shape creation. Be sure to consider it when working on your future projects!

Creating gaps with the Eraser tool

Eraser is one tool that has been requested for quite some time by Anime Studio users. So rejoice, the Eraser tool is here! It's to the right-had side of the Blob Brush tool and can be quickly selected by pressing *E* on the keyboard. The following screenshot shows the Eraser tool:

In this case, it's a bit redundant to do another exercise because we essentially used the eraser tool a moment ago by holding down *Ctrl* when using the Blob Brush tool. So, when it comes to erasing, it's up to you! You can either select this tool or use the method with the Blob Brush tool we just practiced earlier (step 5 in the previous section). The basic principles remain the same. The following screenshot shows some of the effects you can do with the Eraser tool:

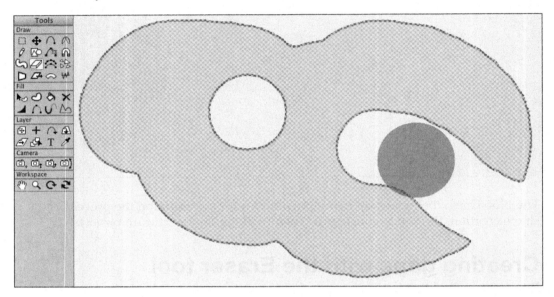

Polishing with the PointReduction tool

Sometimes when creating an object, especially with the new Blob Brush tool, a large number of points can make up an object. This can make things difficult to work with and sometimes you only need a small number of points to get a job done. This is where the new PointReduction tool comes in. The following screenshot shows the PointReduction tool:

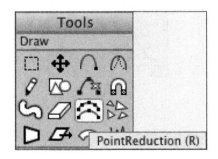

If you still have a shape that we used in the previous exercise on your canvas, we can use that for this example. If not, make a new document and apply a shape using the Blob Brush tool. Don't be afraid to make it a complex shape.

1. Select the PointReduction tool. It is to the right-hand side of the Eraser tool. *R* is the shortcut key.

2. On the top bar, you will find the **brush radius** option. The bigger this is, the bigger your influence area will be when applying this tool. We can leave the default value .25 for now.

3. The **Tolerance Angle** feature dictates how many points will be removed during this process. While the tool tries to maintain the original shape, if this number is set really high, it will remove so many points that it can alter the shape of the object. The best way to figure out what works best for you is to play around with different tolerance settings until you find the sweet spot. Different shapes will require different tolerances.

4. To apply this tool, simply hold down your mouse button and paint over the points you want to reduce. When you release, you will see the results as shown in the following screenshot. Pretty nifty, right?

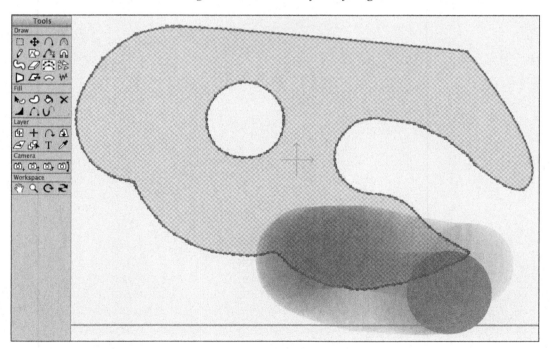

In the past, when one had too many points, the only solution was to go in, delete points, and manually reshape the object. The new PointReduction tool makes this process much more bearable.

Summary

There are a lot of tools in Anime Studio and learning all of them can be an overwhelming process. The key is to pick up certain tools that will be used most (such as the Add Point, Freehand, and Paint Bucket tools) and slowly learn the others as they become needed in your projects. Following along with this book will help too, especially when we start drawing more complicated objects and characters. Finally, keep practicing! Like anything, the more you practice, the easier things will get.

In the next chapter, we will take a look at the Layer tools as well as the different layer types and the beginning stages of mapping out our animations.

3
Exploring Layers and Timelines

Now that we have an understanding of how the drawing tools work, it's time to take a look at the different features that will allow us to bring our characters and scenes to life. As our projects progress, it will become clear that layers play a huge role in organization and enable different features for us to use. Our success will also rely on how well we are able to utilize the different timeline types and camera tools.

In this chapter, we will cover the following topics:

- Simplifying layers
- Layer tools
- Layer types
- Mapping out animation
- Changing your view of the action

Simplifying layers

Have you ever made a sandwich? You probably have. At the very least, you've seen or eaten one (and if you haven't, you should stop reading this book and explore life a bit more because, seriously, everyone should know what a sandwich is). Typically, a sandwich is made up of different ingredients. As an example, you have a slice of bread on top, lettuce and tomato underneath, a piece of cheese, then some meat, and finally another piece of bread. Looking at this sandwich overhead, the top slice of bread hides the rest of the ingredients, unless the lettuce, tomato, meat, or cheese tends to poke out from the sides. There's usually a certain order to the ingredients, but they can be removed or rearranged to change the makeup of the sandwich. When you examine one piece of the sandwich by itself, it's not very remarkable.

Combined with the other ingredients, it creates something more complex and unique. This, in a nutshell, is how layers work in Anime Studio. If this analogy made you hungry, go make a sandwich. This book isn't going anywhere.

Each layer in Anime Studio is its own entity or ingredient that makes up the entire animation. You can make as many layers as you wish; it just depends on how you want to organize your project file. For instance, it's usually standard practice to create separate layers for most elements of a character: head, eyes, nose, mouth, and so on. There are other artists who will only make one layer for all the items on the face, as an example. You may want to place multiple assets on a layer should you plan to use actions, which is a bit more complex and something we won't be touching on much in this book. As we start creating more complex assets, you will slowly discover which workflow best suits you.

Layers can be arranged by clicking and dragging in the **Layers** panel on the right-hand side. When one layer overlaps another, the objects in that top layer will appear over the bottom layer on the canvas. This can be adjusted so that layers are based on the depth of your canvas, but we won't be exploring that option in this book as the layer hierarchy method is the default and most commonly used. When you select a layer in the **Layers** panel, you can only edit that layer, which prevents you from accidentally altering anything else in the project file.

The **Layers** panel, along with housing our layers, allows us to create, delete, and duplicate layers. This will become very important as we start to create layers for the cartoon we will be making. Duplicating a layer has the advantage of retaining all of the properties of another layer. This could then allow you to use the copied layer as a reference and make adjustments with a foundation in place. The **Layers** panel can be seen in the following screenshot:

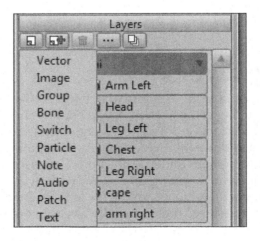

Layers have options that can be accessed by double-clicking on the desired layer in the **Layers** panel (or by clicking on the icon with three dots). From there, in the **Layers Settings** panel, you can do many different things including renaming and choosing a label color. Layer options can change depending on which layer type you have selected. We will be exploring this panel between now and *Chapter 4, Enhancing Your Art with the Layer Settings Panel and Style Palette.*

Controlling layers with different tools

Before diving into the different layer types, it's important to understand how to control layers using our layer tools in the toolbar on the left-hand side. You don't have as many options as you would with the drawing tools, but they're just as important. You will also discover that some of these tools act similar to the drawing tools but ultimately provide different effects. The layer tools will have options located on the top toolbar that you can interact with to affect how different tools work. These will be noted as we move through the exercises.

With Anime Studio open, go to **File | Open** and load the file entitled `LayerTools.anme`. This will be included with the companion files for this book. You should see a bowling ball, as shown in the following screenshot:

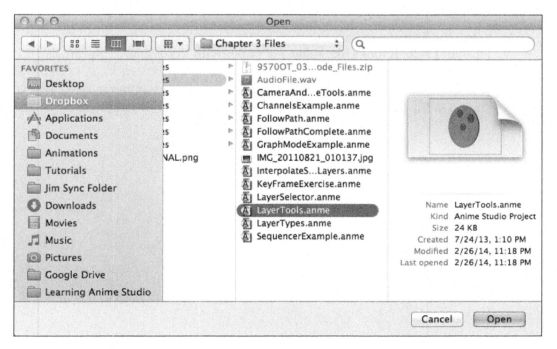

The layer tools (located underneath the **Fill** section on the toolbar) affect whatever layer we currently have selected on the **Layers** panel on the right-hand side. In the case of this project file, we have one layer to worry about. Everything on the bowling ball will be changed as we use the layer tools. Let's take a closer look!

The Transform Layer tool

The Transform Layer tool is probably the most popular layer tool as it performs three separate functions: move, rotate, and resize. If you are a previous user of Anime Studio Version 8 or lower, you may recall that these functions were designated to three separate tools. Things have been condensed since Version 9. The Transform Layer tool can be seen in the following screenshot:

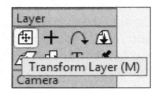

So, how do we use these three separate features? Let's find out by performing the following steps:

1. Select the Transform Layer tool under the **Layer** tools on the toolbar on the left-hand side. It looks like a sheet of paper with a crosshair. You can also use the M key to select it.

2. A red box should form around the layer (the bowling ball) on the screen as shown in the following screenshot:

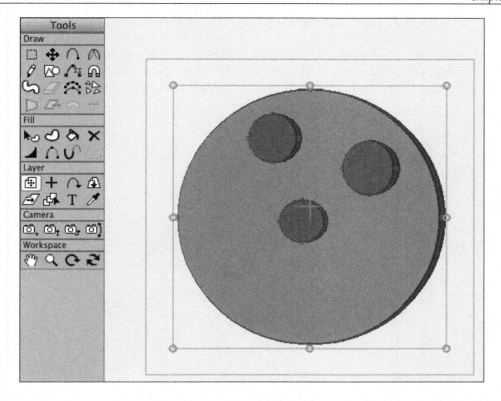

3. Placing your cursor on the outside or inside of the box will allow you to move the layer around. Simply hold down your left mouse button and drag to do so.

4. Placing you cursor in between the two red outlines allows you to rotate the layer.

5. Placing your cursor on one of the nine points surrounding the inside box will resize the layer. Like the Transform Points tool, the left and right points resize the *x* (horizontal) properties of the object, the top and bottom points control the *y* (vertical) variables, and the four corner points allow you to alter the size proportionately, as shown in the following screenshot:

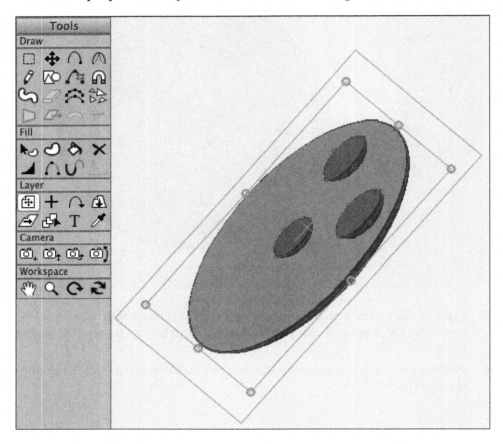

6. If you're more of a numbers person, you can enter your positioning (via the *x*, *y*, and *z* fields), size, and rotation values on the top toolbar.

7. What does the *z* position do? It allows us to move the object closer or further away from the camera (or viewer). This can be useful when creating a sense of depth for your animation. We will touch on this as we start designing your scene in *Chapter 6, Developing Your Cartoon's Scenery*.

If you have **Scale Compensation** enabled in the Anime Studio **Properties** panel, as you enlarge a layer, the lines will thicken to compensate for the size difference. When you enlarge objects with the Transform Points tool, this will not happen. Keep this in mind if you are particular on how your lines look when editing layers and objects.

You will be using the Transform Layer tool quite a bit as we progress and you start building your own assets for your projects once you are done with this book. It can be very handy, especially since it has three functions. If you're a user of an earlier version of Anime Studio, be sure to remember that scale, rotation, and movement have all been condensed into this tool!

The Set Origin tool

The origin point of a layer dictates the anchor in which your layer will be resized or rotated. By default, the origin point is positioned in the center of the layer. However, let's say you want the layer to pivot from the top-right side of the window when using the rotation function on the Transform Layer tool. Or perhaps you want the layer to expand from the bottom-left when resizing as opposed to the center. Placing your origin with this tool will allow you to control these elements. Use the following screenshot to help you locate it:

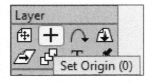

For this exercise, please keep the LayerTools.anme project file open. Perform the following steps to use the **Set Origin** tool:

1. Click on the Set Origin tool. It looks like a plus sign or crosshair. You can also use the *0* key to access the tool.

2. You should notice a crosshair in the middle of the layer. This is your anchor or origin point.

3. Select the Transform Layer tool and place your cursor in one of the corners of the red outline box. Rotate the layer. Notice how the rotation is dictated by the origin point in the center.

4. Select the Set Origin tool again and click on the top of the layer. The origin point has now changed its position as shown in the following screenshot:

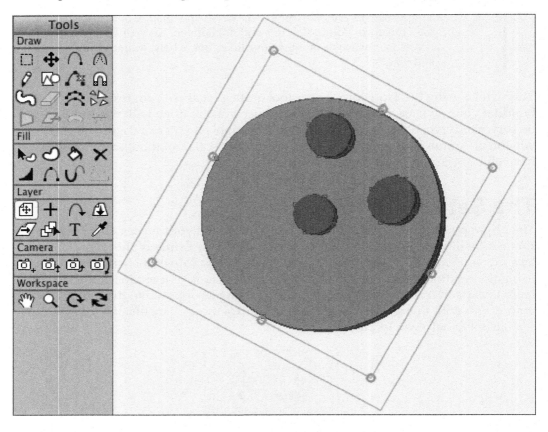

5. Select the Transform Layer tool for the second time and use the rotate function to notice how the origin point at the top changes the way the layer rotates.

6. Try scaling the layer down with the Transform Layer tool. The layer should shrink towards the top of the window, where the origin point sits.

7. Move the origin point around in different positions and use the Transform Layer tool to see different results.

Setting your origin point can really help, especially if rotation or resizing is involved. This can be used to create many different effects. As an example, maybe you want to create a swinging object and need to lock the origin point so that it moves correctly. If you can't get a layer to resize or rotate properly, keep this tool in mind.

The Follow Path tool

The **Follow Path** tool allows you to create a line or path in one layer and have your target layer follow it. As we haven't touched on animation yet, we will try to keep things simple. So don't worry!

The Follow Path tool is shown in the following screenshot:

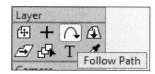

To begin, please open up the Anime Studio project file entitled `FollowPath.anme` and perform the following steps:

1. Click on the layer labeled **Line** on the **Layers** panel. Note that a wavy outline exists on this layer.
2. Click on the **Ball** layer.
3. Select the Follow Path tool from the toolbar on the left-hand side. It looks like an arched arrow pointing downwards.
4. The line from the second layer will become visible on your **Ball** layer.
5. Click on the left-hand side of the line. Try to get as close to the left edge as you can. This will indicate the ball's starting position.

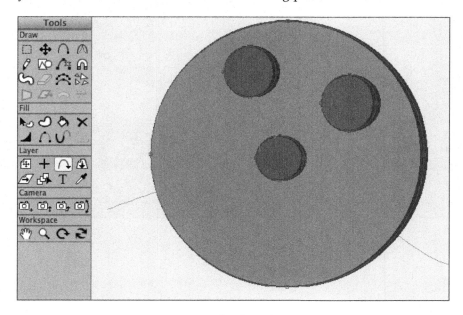

6. Go down to the bottom of your window. Be sure that the **Channels** tab is selected.

7. Click on **48**. We are moving forward on the timeline to create an animated movement for this layer.

8. Click on the right-hand side of the line with your Follow Path tool. You should now see two dots on the timeline. These dots indicate that the animation is taking place on your timeline.

9. Click on **0** on your timeline to go back to the beginning. You can also use the shortcut *Shift* + left arrow on your keyboard to return to **frame 0**.

10. Hit the **Play** button located on the bottom of your canvas to play the animation.

11. Your layer should follow the path of the outline. The following screenshot is also an example of what you should be seeing:

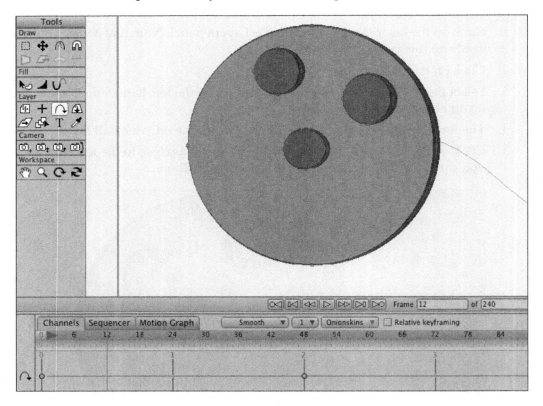

The Follow Path tool is great if you are looking for a layer to move in a very specific pattern. Just make sure to keep your outline path and moveable object on separate layers. Otherwise, the follow path technique will not work.

 An outline is always invisible to the audience. It's also not visible to the user in Anime Studio unless they select the layer the outline is on. An outline will only become visible to the audience once the stroke or fill properties are applied.

The Rotate Layer XY tool

The **Rotate Layer XY** tool works similar to the Perspective Points drawing tool in that we can adjust the 3D rotation of a layer. The exception here is that when working with the layer, we are modifying its properties in true 3D space. The point of the object that appears to be closer to the camera in reality is closer. When using the **Camera** tools, such as panning, you will be able to see different sides of the object, depending on where you move the camera. This is unlike the Perspective Points tool where the effect is simply mimicked. The following screenshot shows where you can find it on your toolbar:

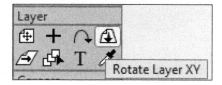

For this exercise, please reopen the file labeled LayerTools.anme.

1. Select the Rotate Layer XY tool. It looks like a piece of paper with an arrow pointing down on it.

2. With your cursor placed on the layer, hold down the left mouse button and drag to the left. You will notice that the perspective of the layer seems to change, similar to that of the Perspective Points tool.

3. Select the Transform Layer tool.

4. Place your cursor back on the document and start moving around the screen. It doesn't matter in what direction. The following screenshot demonstrates this:

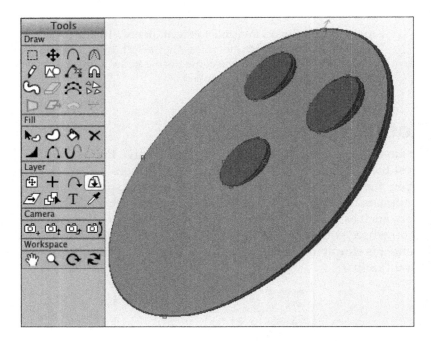

5. It will appear as if you are getting a different view of the object as you move it in different directions.

This tool is terrific when you want to create an object that reacts to Anime Studio's 3D space. This can be especially useful when coupled with the **Camera** tools, which we will be exploring in this chapter in a little bit.

The Shear Layer tool

Shearing a layer works similar to shearing points, except that you don't get a distorted effect, especially if you have a lot of points on the layer. This can be great if you're looking to tweak the layer without having to mess with the points.

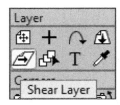

Please open up the `LayerTools.anme` work file. Make sure it's in its original state, meaning no Rotate Layer XY tool applied. The steps to be performed to use the **Shear Layer** tool are as follows:

1. Select the Shear Layer tool.

2. Place your cursor on the document.

3. Hold down your left mouse button and drag in any direction. You should notice a change in the layer's appearance similar to the following screenshot:

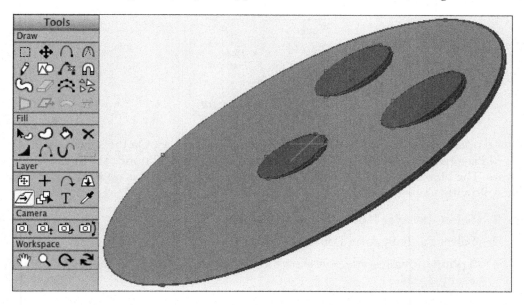

4. As a test, undo this action (**Edit | Undo**).

5. Choose the Select Points tool.

6. Highlight all the points that make up the bowling ball.

7. Choose the Shear Points tool.

8. Put your cursor on the document, hold down your left mouse button, and move the cursor around. Notice the difference in how the points distort versus the result after using the Shear Layer tool.

Depending on your needs, the Shear Layer and Points tools can provide different shearing effects. It never hurts to have choices!

The Layer Selector tool

In Anime Studio, you are only able to interact with objects that belong to the layer you have currently selected. This means, for instance, if you want to alter a vector on another layer, you first need to select that layer it belongs to. This is great for an organization but can be frustrating if you have several layers to page through in order to locate where you placed an object. The **Layer Selector** tool gives you an alternative method to select your layers. The Layer Selector tool is shown in the following screenshot:

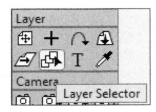

Please open up the work file entitled LayerSelector.anme. On the screen, you should see two bowling balls. On the **Layers** panel, you will notice we have two layers. The blue ball is on the **Ball 1** layer, while the green ball is on **Ball 2**. Perform the following steps to use the Layer Selector tool:

1. Select the layer **Ball 1** on the Layers Panel.

2. Select the Transform Points tool from your toolbar.

3. Trying moving some points on the blue bowling ball. You should be able to easily do this.

4. Now, try moving some points on the green bowling ball. Notice how you cannot interact with this vector graphic. This is due to the green bowling ball being on **Ball 2**, which is currently not selected, as shown in the following screenshot:

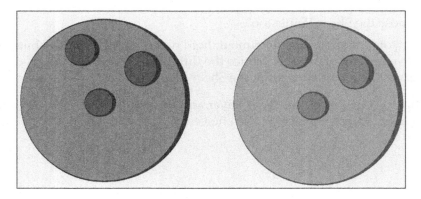

5. Select the Layer Selector tool, which looks like three small rectangles with a black cursor placed on the top, and click on the green bowling ball. Notice how you can now see the outlines of the vector shape of the green bowling ball; **Ball 2** is now selected on your **Layers** panel.

6. If you take the Transform Points tool and try to modify the green bowling ball, you will now be able to do so.

With the Layer Selector tool, you now have two ways of selecting layers: through the Layers Panel tool or directly in your document. Which method you use will come down to your workflow and how many layers you have to sift through.

This tool was previously known as the Vector Shape Selector in Version 8 of Anime Studio Pro. The tool was only able to select vector layers. Since then, the tool has been updated to work with all layer types.

The Eyedropper tool

The **Eyedropper** tool allows us to pick colors and properties from existing layers or objects and transfer them to a new location. This is beneficial for copying colors or replicating certain objects on your canvas. The Eyedropper tool is shown in the following screenshot:

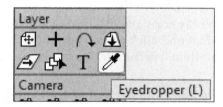

Please keep the `LayerSelector.anme` project file open for this lesson. The steps to use the Eyedropper tool are as follows:

1. Select the Eyedropper tool from the **Layer** section of the toolbar. You can press *L* as a shortcut if you wish.

2. Click on the blue bowling ball. Notice that whichever part you clicked on (the smaller circle or the main piece), the colors and stroke properties have transferred over to your **Style** palette, as shown in the following screenshot:

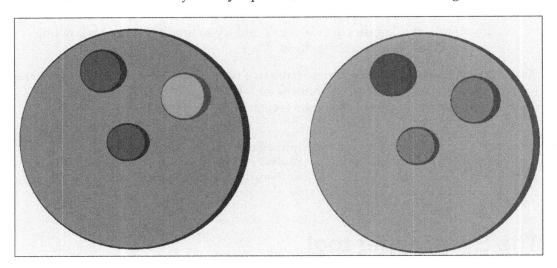

3. Take your cursor to the other bowling ball (make sure the **Ball 2** layer is selected on the **Layers** panel in order to do this) and hold the *Alt* key while clicking on one of the smaller ovals. This will transfer the color from your **Style** palette and fill in the object.

4. If you're looking to only copy the fill color of a layer, hold down the *Ctrl* key (*command* on Mac) and click to transfer only the fill to your Style palette. From there, you can then use the *Alt* key to transfer your fill color wherever you wish.

5. You can also use the **Paint Bucket** tool to apply the copied properties if you wish.

6. Now, using the gradient on the right-hand side of the window, hold down the *Shift* key and drag your mouse up and down on the gradient. Notice how whichever color you are selecting will show up in the Eyedropper circle icon. When you release, this new fill color is applied to the **Style** palette, as shown in the following screenshot:

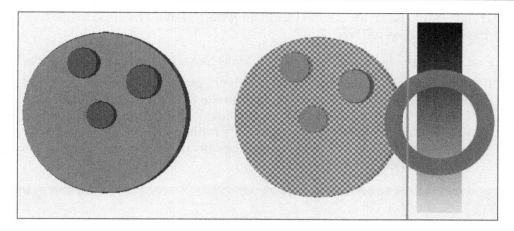

7. If you click on an object with the Select Shape tool and then use the Eyedropper tool on another object, the properties will instantly be transferred over to the selected object. This works while holding down the *Shift* key on another color too!

> The Eyedropper tool was positioned in the **Draw** panel of the toolbar prior to Version 9.5. Beyond this location change and the enhancements to transferring colors with shortcut keys, the tool works just like it always has.

The Eyedropper tool makes transferring colors easy. It beats trying to match the colors manually, especially if you have a lot of objects that share the same properties. And keep the shortcut keys in mind too, as it streamlines the process of filling in colors.

The Insert Text tool

There are two ways to insert text in Anime Studio. The first is to use the **Insert Text** tool and the second is by creating a layer. Since Version 9, Anime Studio has allowed you to create text layers, which lets you alter the font, size, and color later on. The Insert Text tool is shown in the following screenshot:

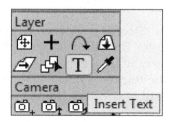

To get started, please create a new document (**File | New**). The steps to use the Insert Text tool are as follows:

1. Click on the Insert Text tool, which looks like a **T**, from the **Layer** toolbar.

2. A new panel will appear with a wealth of options. Our first focus should be on the text itself, which you can enter in the first section titled **Enter text:**. Let's type `Have a Great Day!` in this box. When typing out the last two words, place them on the second line by hitting *Enter* before typing. You will see what your text looks like on the canvas as changes are made. This is shown in the following screenshot:

3. Now, let's select a font for our text. Your choices will depend on what type of fonts you currently have installed on your computer. You can get more fonts through various software installs (such as Adobe's design programs) and websites dedicated to type design. For now, let's choose **Arial Bold**. If you don't like this font, choose the one you like.

4. Let's look at the **Fill** and **Stroke** properties. These work similar to the options found on the Style palette. The **Fill** property will change the color of the text while the **Stroke** property will give the text an outline. Enabling a stroke also allows you to choose the thickness of the line. Let's enable both options and choose a black stroke with a width of **2** and a blue fill color.

5. You can choose the justification of your text (left, right, and center). If we select **Left**, you can see that the top line of the text hugs the left-hand side of the preview box. Selecting **Right** will give us the opposite effect and center justifying will bring the lines of text to be centered over one another. Let's choose **Center** from the list for this exercise.

6. **Create one shape** and **Create text layer** allows us to convert the text either into a vector graphic or a text layer. With a text layer, you can re-enter this panel at a later time and make further adjustments to your text. Just know that once you choose the text layer option, you cannot convert the text into a vector shape. The advantage of a vector shape is that you can modify points and change colors just like any other vector graphic. It will all come down to preference when working on your own projects. For this exercise, we will keep the **Create text layer** option checked as shown in the following screenshot:

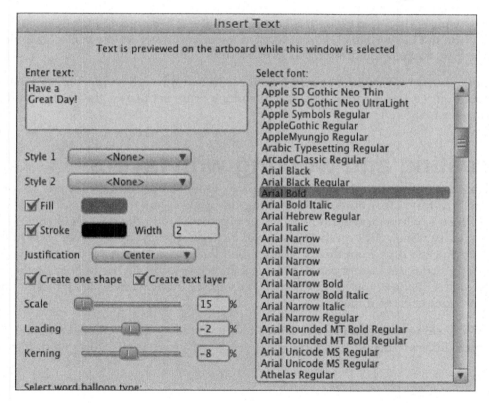

7. The **Scale** dial allows you to adjust the size of the text. While you can alter the size after the fact using the Transform Layer tool (or Transform Points tool if the text is vector-based), it's sometimes easier to adjust the size in this panel. Let's put the scale at 100%.

8. **Leading** adjusts the amount of space between your lines of text. If you only have one line, this option won't have much use. Setting this property at about -26% seems to give us a good amount of space between lines.

9. **Kerning** adjusts the horizontal spacing between characters. The lower the value, the less space there will be. Leaving this at 0% should give us the right effect.

10. The bottom of the panel is where you can choose to add a text bubble to your words. To see how this works, select **Standard_01_Top_Bottom** from the drop-down menu. A series of options will appear below this selection. You can also adjust the fill, stroke, and size settings to the right.

11. Once you have finished adjusting your settings, click on the **OK** button.

12. The text will appear on your document. You are free to move and modify the text with your **Layer** tools. If you need to modify the text, simply double-click on the **Text** layer that has been created for this text on the **Layers** panel. If you decided to convert this text to a vector graphic, you can use the drawing tools to modify.

Sometimes, it may be easier to add title or credit text through a video editor when editing your cartoon's video files. But in a pinch or for set pieces, the Anime Studio Text tool works well.

Creating and working with layers

Besides separating elements out in your project file, Anime Studio's layers can serve a host of different functions. Picking the appropriate layers for certain jobs is the key, which is why you will find each layer type detailed in the next sections. To add a layer at any time, click on the **New Layer** button on your **Layers** panel and choose the appropriate type from the list. Remember, you can only edit a layer if you've selected it from the **Layers** panel. Using the **Layer Selector** on the toolbar on the left-hand side will allow you to select any layer you see on the canvas; keep that in mind if that's your preferred method.

To follow along and gain a better understanding of layer types, please open the Anime Studio project file entitled LayerTypes.anme from your book's work files.

The Vector layers

Vectors are the most common type of layer found in Anime Studio. These layers serve a simple purpose, drawing. If you want to use the drawing tools in Anime Studio, make sure you are on a vector layer before attempting it. Otherwise, you will find that the drawing tools will be disabled. Until this point, all of our exercises have been done using vector layers (with the exception of the Insert Text tool). The steps to use the **Vector** layer are as follows:

1. In your example file, locate and click on the layer entitled **Vector** layer on the **Layers** panel on the right-hand side. This layer on the canvas is the first one on the left-hand side and contains a drawn line.

2. You will notice that your drawing tools will become available to you as shown in the following screenshot:

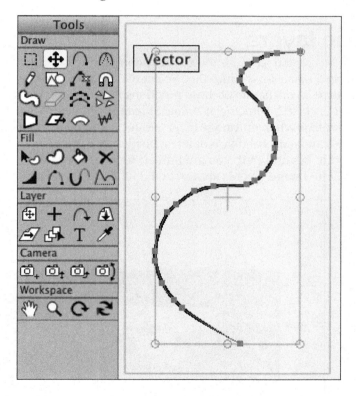

3. Click on the second layer in the **Layers** panel entitled **Image** layer. Notice how you can no longer draw with any of the drawing tools while in this layer.

Did you know you can convert 2D vectors into 3D objects? Yes, it's true! Some people even refer to Anime Studio as a 2.5D software due to its ability to work with 2D assets in 3D space. Double-click on any vector layer in your **Layers** panel and choose the **3D Options** tab in the **Layer Settings** panel. From here, you can select different render types and customize your new 3D object. Once you accept the changes, you will have a 3D vector layer appearing in your **Layers** panel (which holds the newly created 3D object). Just note that Anime Studio wasn't built for 3D animation. While it's an option, it's not the recommended method of animation for this software.

You will quickly discover that vectors are the most commonly used layer in Anime Studio. Unless you plan to use bitmap images for the bulk of your work, you will be selecting this layer type often.

The Image layers

Image layers can be created through the **Layers** panel like any other layer type or through importing a raster image into the project file. You have limited options when working with **Image** layers (some of these functions were detailed in our discussion on raster graphics in *Chapter 2, Drawing in Anime Studio*). The Image Mask tool, which is located on your toolbar when an **Image** layer is selected, allows you to clear pixels out of the image. This can be useful if you delete a portion of the image and want to place something behind it. Beyond that, you are limited to the layer tools detailed in the previous section. The **Image** layer is shown in the following screenshot:

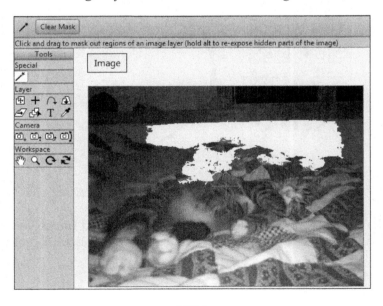

When importing an image, Anime Studio will link the image's location on your hard drive. This means if the image is moved, it will no longer appear or function properly in your document. When opening a document with a broken image, you will be asked to relocate the file. You can go through this process or manually reset the location by double-clicking on your image layer and then going to the **Image** tab and clicking on the **Source Image** button in your **Layer Settings** panel. You have another option for creating a *toon effect*, which can make the picture look painted when rendered.

 In addition to linking your image's location, if you decide to alter the image with another program, that change will be reflected in Anime Studio. The same goes for any external file.

Raster images are not included in Anime Studio's strong suit. But the option is there if you need it. Mixing animation with the images usually doesn't result in smooth results. You sometimes get a stutter effect during pans, zoom-ins, and so on. Images usually work best when stationary.

The Group layers

Group layers are essentially folders that contain any type of sublayer. This means you can group all layer types together in one group layer (even more group layers to create nested layers). It's like creating a folder on your computer and putting different types of files and documents into it. This can be useful if you are building complex objects. Also, all sublayers are controlled by the **Group** layer. As an example, if you use the Transform Layer tool to resize the **Group** layer, all the sublayers will be resized as well. The following screenshot shows the **Group** layer:

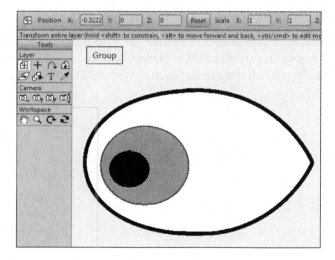

Let's take a look at the **Group** layer in our opened example file.

1. Click on the **Group Layer** on the **Layers** panel.

2. To see the three vector layers contained within the group, click on the arrow next to the layer.

3. With the **Group** layer still selected, take the Transform Layer tool and move, rotate, or resize the eye onscreen. Notice how all sublayers in the group layer are altered:

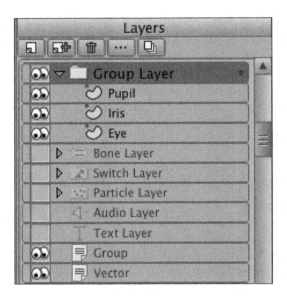

4. If you want to alter just one of the sublayers, you will need to click on one and then make your changes.

You will call on this layer type a lot when you get into more complex prop making. Some artists also choose to put all of their elements for a scene into a **Group** layer so that they can easily edit all the elements at once without affecting any of the nested animation.

The Bone layers

Next to the **Vector** layer, the **Bone** layer is probably the most used in Anime Studio. This is the layer that makes *cut-out* or bone animation possible. A series of bones are drawn on the layer itself, which controls all sublayers underneath. In a way, it acts like a **Group** layer in that it controls whatever layers are in the folder. Let's take a look at the **Bone** layer.

1. Select the **Bone Layer** from the **Layers** panel. You should notice three bones appear over the arm. They will look like blue and red (if selected) triangular shaped figures. These were drawn ahead of time for this exercise. We will learn how to draw bones and use the bone tools in depth in *Chapter 5, Bringing a Cartoon Character to Life*.

2. If you click on the arrow next to the **Bone Layer** on the panel, you will see the three sublayers that currently make up the layer.

3. Select the Manipulate Bones tool (it looks like a horizontal bone with arrows pointing up and down from it) from your toolbar on the left-hand side.

4. Left-click and hold on the hand bone. Now drag your mouse back and forth, as shown in the following screenshot. Notice how the bones work in a hierarchy and cause the sublayers to move. This is a very basic example and we'll be getting into more detail when the time comes to construct and animate characters.

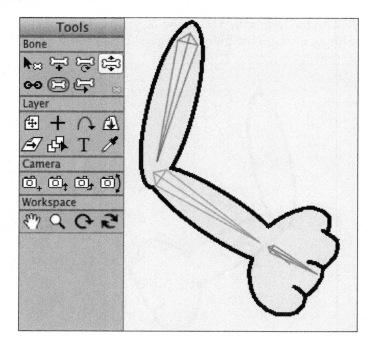

Anime Studio was built to use bones, so it makes sense that you will be accessing this layer type often. Mastering how to rig a character can be a rigorous process. What's important now is you understand the function and the use of the **Bone** layer.

> Did you know you can organize your layers by coloring them on the **Layers** panel? It's easy! Simply click on the area to the left of the show and hide option (the eyeballs). Here, you can choose from a variety of colors. This is great in order to identify layers at a glance.

The Patch layers

The **Patch** layer works in conjunction with the **Bone** layer and is best used to patch lines or seams between two objects. A good example of this would be if you have an arm or leg made up of two or more layers (just like the arm bone example we previously played with), a patch could be applied between the two layers to hide any ripping, gaps, or glitches that may occur in the animation process. The steps to be performed on the **Patch** layer are as follows:

1. While still on the **Bone** layer, make sure you have the sublayers exposed by clicking on the arrow next to the **Bone** layer.

2. You should see a layer entitled **Arm Bottom-Patch**. This layer is currently acting as a patch between the top and bottom portions of the arm.

3. If you click on the hide icon next to the layer, you will see what the patch is hiding. Simply click on the hide icon again to reapply the patch.

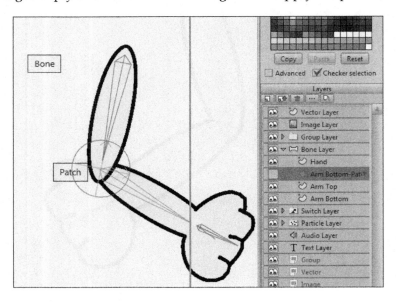

4. When you make a patch, you are asked to assign a target. In this case, we are targeting the **Arm Bottom** layer. The patch remains above the **Arm Top** layer to seal off the intersection.

5. A patch can be moved and resized with the Transform Layer tool.

Like the bones, we will be looking at how to apply patches in a more practical setting after we master the basics of Anime Studio.

The Switch layers

Like the **Group** and the **Bone** layer, the **Switch** layer is set up to house different sublayers. The difference is that the **Switch** layers will only display one sublayer at a time. This is useful if you want to create a talking mouth, blinking eye, and so on. Think of it as creating a flipbook for a certain portion of your animation by performing the following steps:

1. Click on the **Switch Layer** in the **Layers** panel.

2. You will notice on the canvas we currently have a closed mouth displayed in the **Switch** layer.

3. Right-click on the **Switch Layer** in your **Layers** panel and choose **Mouth Open** from the list. Now notice how the mouth on the canvas appears to be open. This is how you switch back and forth between sublayers in a **Switch** layer.

4. If you'd like to see which sublayers are in the switch, simply click the arrow next to the **Switch** layer, just as you would with a **Group** or **Bone** layer.

5. When animating, you would advance forward on the timeline; right-click on your **Switch** layer and choose the desired sublayer. This will swap the layers out as your animation plays out.

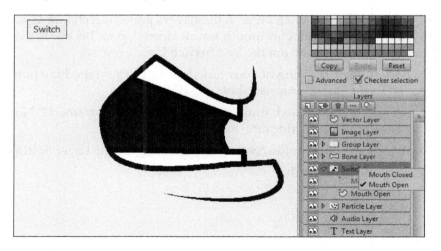

Switch layers are just one of the many ways to create animation in Anime Studio. Once you have your sublayers set up, you can move quickly when it comes to changing poses on the timeline.

 With Anime Studio 9.5, you can quickly switch between sublayers by holding in *Alt + Ctrl* (*command* for Mac) on your keyboard and right-clicking on the **Switch** layer on the canvas. A drop-down menu will appear that will allow you to change the sublayer that is currently visible.

One turn off with this layer is that it can make things look choppy. If that's a concern you have but still want to integrate **Switch** layers into your workflow, you can try using the interpolate points method. If your **Switch** layers contain the same points with the vector shapes, the object will appear to animate between the two objects with this option checked.

To see how this works, let's open up the work file `InterpolateSwitchLayers.anme` from your book's work files. Just keep the `LayerTypes.anme` work file open in its current tab, so we can return to it after this exercise.

You should see one **Switch** layer in the document. In the **Switch** layer, we have two vector layers: one indicating a closed mouth and the other an open mouth. Let's have Anime Studio create the opening animation for us by performing the following steps:

1. Click on **1** on your bottom timeline. This will ensure we are on frame 1 to start our animation.

2. Right-click on the **Switch** layer in the **Layers** panel and choose **Closed** from the drop-down menu. The mouth is now closed.

3. Page forward or click on **frame 12** on the timeline.

4. Right-click on the **Switch** layer in the **Layers** panel and choose **Open** from the drop-down menu. Our mouth is now open. Up to this point, everything should seem familiar from the first **Switch** layer exercise.

5. Go back to the beginning of your timeline and click on the **Play** button located in the previous screenshot.

6. The mouth will be closed. Jump to its open position at frame 12. Nothing new here. Now, let's add some magic!

7. Double-click on the **Mouth Switch** layer to bring up the **Layer Settings** panel.

8. Click on the **Switch** tab.

9. Check the **Interpolate sub-layers** option as shown in the following screenshot:

10. Close the panel.

11. Hit the **Play** button again.

12. You should now see an animation take place with the mouth going from closed to open. You did this using only two layers and a setting change. No manual animation necessary!

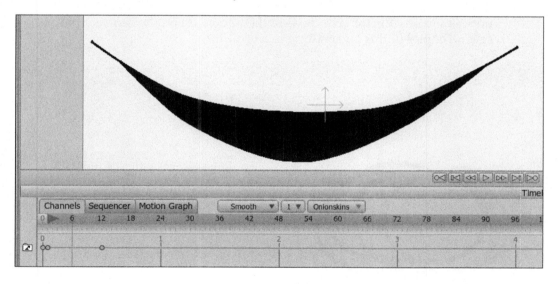

The **Switch** layers have many functions and how you use them will depend on your animation style and workflow. We will be using the **Switch** layers for our mouths as we dive into animating our cartoon, so you will see how they can work practically in an animation.

When you want to interpolate your **Switch** layers, they must contain the same points. If you are having issues with this, the best way to ensure everything will work is to create your layer with the desired points and then duplicate the layer in the **Layers** panel. Rename the layer and reposition your points. If you add a point to one layer later on, be sure to add it to the others as well. Think about your most complicated poses. Once those are drawn, creating other poses should be easier.

The Particle layers

Particle layers allow us to create multiple instances of an object by tweaking a few settings in the **Layer Settings** panel. These particles are usually generated and animated through the **Layer Settings** panel on the **Particles** tab. All you need to get started is create some sublayers for the particle effect to generate off. The steps that can be carried out in the **Particle** layers are as follows:

1. Click on the arrow next to the **Particle Layer** in the **Layers** panel. You will notice only one **Vector** layer rests in the folder; yet on the canvas, we have several copies of this layer sitting in a group.

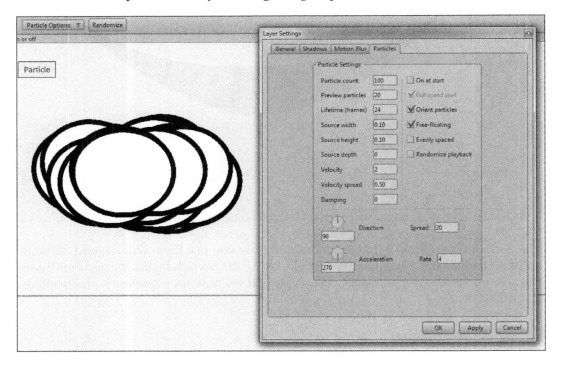

2. The **Particle** layer generates these copies using the settings we have in the **Layer Settings** panel. To access those options, double-click on the **Particle** layer in the **Layers** panel.

3. Select the **Particles** tab. From here, you have the ability to alter many different settings, including how many particles you want to generate, the velocity, direction, and so on. This can be useful for creating smoke, an explosion, rain, and more.

4. It can sometimes be tough finding the right series of settings to create the effect you're looking for. This may require some trial and error. Once you have adjusted your settings, click on **OK**.

5. Some settings may not render until you preview the frame. To do this, go to **File** | **Preview** (*Ctrl + R* on Windows, *command + R* on Mac). While this will only allow you to see the current frame, it will give you an idea of what the particle will look like. To fully view a particle effect, you will have to render out the project as a video.

6. A new addition in Anime Studio Pro 10 allows you to use a vector graphic as the source for the particle effect. To do this, create a **Vector** layer and draw any shape you want. It can be as complex or simple as you like. Multiple shapes will also work.

7. Now place this **Vector** layer at the very bottom of your **Particle** sublayers.

8. In your **Particle Layer Settings**, make sure **Use base layer as source** is selected.

If you are interested in seeing some premade particle effects made with Anime Studio, go to **Scripts** | **Particle Effects** and choose one from the list. You'll find that you can make some pretty robust effects with particles.

The Audio layers

The **Audio** layers, like the **Image** layers, are generated when you import an object into Anime Studio. In this case, audio files such as .wav, .mp3, or .aiff will create an **Audio** layer and house the file properties within.

You won't be able to see the audio file on the canvas. But if you click on the **Audio** layer, you will see an audio file icon show up, indicating that this is indeed an **Audio** layer. On the timeline, you will see a sound file present; this can help when trying to sync sounds to certain movements. If you scrub through the timeline or hit the play button underneath the canvas, you can hear the audio file play out. The following screenshot displays what an audio file looks like on the timeline:

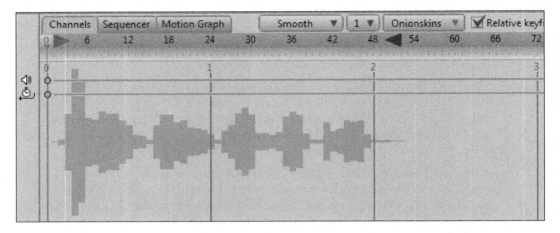

We will discover that sometimes it's best to add your audio files, especially music, when editing your cartoon in a video editor. Adding audio files while animating is essential when it comes to syncing sounds, especially voices.

The Text layers

As discussed in the previous section, the **Text** layers allow you to edit your text properties at any time. To do this, simply double-click on the **Text** layer in your **Layers** panel and choose the **Text** tab. If you decide to create text as a layer through the **Layers** panel, you will be presented with the same options and settings as the Insert Text tool.

The Note layers

Notes are not used in the actual animation. They are meant to display information on the canvas for the animator to read. This can be useful if you have multiple animators working on a project or if you don't want to forget something. You can see notes currently on the canvas labeling different layers. You can change the information on a note by double-clicking on its layer and entering the appropriate information in the **Note** tab. You can also alter the layer like any other with the Transform Layer tool.

Mapping out animation

While the layers provide the ingredients that make up our animation, the timelines set up and map out all the motion we will witness in the movie. The timelines are broken down into frames and seconds, allowing us to gauge when events or keyframes occur in the animation. Depending on your needs, there are three different timelines in Anime Studio Pro: Channels, Sequencer, and Motion Graph. We have worked a little bit with the Channels timeline in some of our exercises. This section will expand on that further, so we are clear on how to use all the timelines moving forward.

Understanding keyframes

The easiest way to remember the function of a keyframe is that it is a change that occurs on the timeline. Your timeline is made up of individual frames, which is indicated by the numbers you see at the top of the panel. When a keyframe or change is inserted, you will see a circle appear on the selected frame. If you create two keyframes that are 10 frames apart, any movement that occurs between the two points will interpolate, or in other words, automatically move and fill in the movement, saving you time. You witnessed this when we interpolated the **Switch** layer in the previous section.

To demonstrate this, open up `KeyFrameExercise.anme`, located in the files that accompany this book. Perform the following steps on the oval:

1. Place your timeline scrubber so that it's on frame 24. You can do this by simply clicking on **24**.

2. Select the Transform Layer tool, left-click and hold on the oval and drag to the left or the right.

3. When you release the mouse button, you will notice that two dots or keyframes have been placed between frames 0 and 24 on the timeline, as shown in the following screenshot:

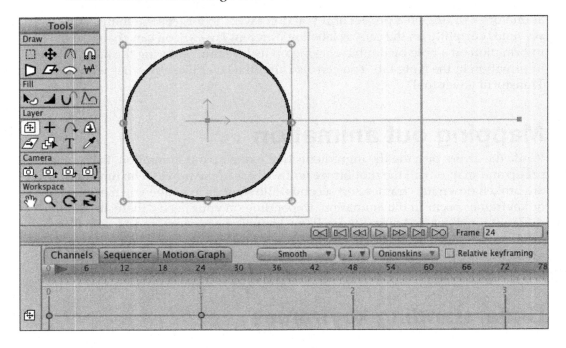

4. Click-and-hold on the red scrubber that is above frame 24 and drag back to the beginning of the timeline. This method is called scrubbing and you can see that between the two keyframes that Anime Studio created automatic movement on for the oval.

You can use keyframes to interpolate different functions such as size, distance, vector point movement, and more. These functions will become clearer as we move forward. Each layer has its own set of keyframes, which can only be viewed on the layer that is selected in the **Layers** panel.

Just like objects and layers, keyframes can be copied, pasted, and deleted in Anime Studio. This can be useful if you want to repeat an action or if you want to get rid of unwanted movements. If you're familiar with Anime Studio 8 or an earlier version, these methods have changed slightly in the newer versions. The steps to copy, paste, and delete keyframes are as follows:

1. To copy a keyframe, simply click on the desired frame (or highlight multiple frames by clicking-and-dragging a box around them).

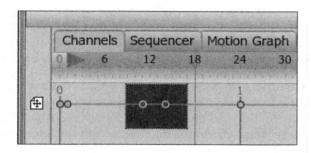

2. Go to **Edit** | **Copy** or use the convenient shortcut command *Ctrl + C* on Windows and *command + C* on Mac.

3. To paste that keyframe, find the spot on the timeline you want to place it and go to **File** | **Paste** (*Ctrl + V* or *command + V*).

4. Deleting keyframes work in a similar manner by highlighting and hitting the *Delete* key on your keyboard.

Just now you altered objects on your canvas using the previously discussed methods. The difference to keep in mind is that if an object and keyframe are both highlighted, the keyframe will take precedence over the object. So if you want to copy, paste, or delete an object, make sure no keyframes are selected.

 Just like layers, you can color code keyframes. To do this, simply right-click on a keyframe, choose label, and pick your color.

Also, once you highlight a keyframe on one layer, it stays selected even when moving to another layer. This can make things easier when working with multiple layers with various durations.

The Channels timeline

This is what you would consider your main timeline as most of the movements and effects that you create will be done on this tab. To access this timeline, simply click on the **Channels** tab that appears above your timeline panel. What's most useful about the **Channels** tab is that it shows you which channels or functions are currently being animated or executed. This means you can easily distinguish which keyframes control object movement, rotation, camera movement, and so on.

To get a better idea of how channels work, let's load up the example file ChannelsExample.anme located in your book's work files. What we have here is a simple rectangle that has some movement attached to it (you can do much more complex stuff in Anime Studio but it's easier to start with the basics).

If you look on the **Channels** timeline, you will see that we have four different channels. The first one looks like four dots, followed by three icons representing different layer transformations, as shown in the next screenshot. If you ever need a reminder of what these channels represent, just move your mouse over the icon and the tooltip will appear indicating its function.

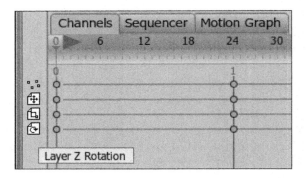

Now, let's have some fun by performing the following steps:

1. The first channel icon shows us the keyframes for the points of the vector graphic. If you take the Transform Points tool and click on the rectangle, another channel will appear. This one looks like a group of red dots.

2. The black dots at the top represent all the points on the vector, while the red dots at the bottom indicate the selected frames (if any) you are altering.

3. Let's move our timeline scrubber to frame 12. With the Transform Points tool still selected, grab one of the points on your rectangle and reposition it. Now, notice how a new keyframe has been created for the **Points** channels on your timeline.

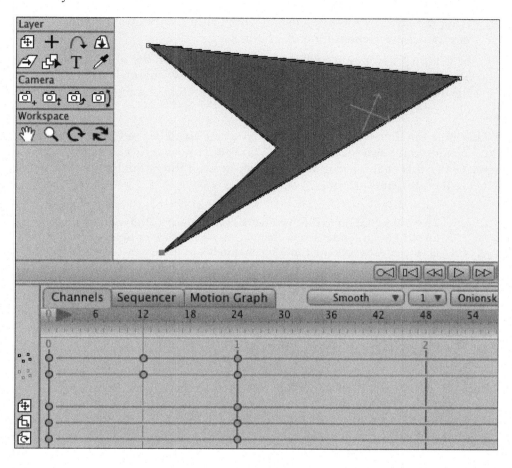

4. If you scrub through, you can see the keyframes interpolate this new keyframe and seamlessly transition the movement from one point to the other. You can move more of the points if you wish or even relocate the timeline scrubber and add more keyframes.

5. For practice, try copying, pasting, or deleting some keyframes. Practicing these functions will enhance your workflow, which is important when working on complex animations.

6. The previous steps also apply for the other channels. Select the Transform Layer tool.

7. Place your scrubber anywhere between the original two keyframes on your timeline.

8. Alter the layer by moving, resizing, or rotating and notice how new keyframes are created for each channel.

9. Select the XY Rotation tool, find a place you like on the timeline, and alter the layer. You should now see that two new channels have been created for the *x* and *y* properties of the rotation. Creating channels is as easy as altering them.

The **Channels** timeline is so powerful that you can do all of your animation in this tab and never open **Sequencer** or **Motion Graph**. However, it's best not to limit yourself. After this chapter, you will discover how all three timeline types can help you create the ultimate cartoon.

There is an option in the **Preferences** panel (**Edit | Preferences**) that allows you to condense the channels to keep a cleaner timeline (which is labeled **Consolidate timeline channels**). In some ways, this makes working with the timeline harder as you have less control over the channels. We made sure this setting was checked off in *Chapter 1, Stepping into the World of Animation*, but you can change it if you feel the need.

The Sequencer timeline

If you've ever worked with video editing software, you are probably familiar with moving clips around on a timeline to sequence them in a certain order. The Anime Studio Sequencer works similar to this. Let's say you've mapped out some animations for a character. However, after extensive work, you realized the animation happens too soon in the cartoon. Maybe you need the animation to sync up to a certain sound. This is where the **Sequencer** timeline comes in handy. No need to redo the animation.

Please open the file `SequencerExample.anme`, which came with the book's work files. What we have here is an explosion, followed by a sound effect. Ideally, we would like the sound to go off when the explosion does.

1. Let's click on the **Sequencer** tab and see what we can do.

2. With the sequencer now displayed, we should see two items: the explosion and sound effect. Here, we can click-and-drag these items around to rearrange where they begin in the animation, as shown in the following screenshot:

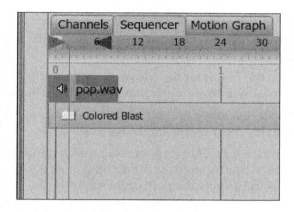

3. Give it a try! Line up the explosion and sound effect so that they occur at the same time.

4. In this case, we could move the sound effect to frame 1 with the explosion animation or move the explosion up to where the sound effect is. Either that or we could relocate both files to meet somewhere else on the timeline. Whatever the case, the sequencer allows you to easily move these assets around.

Just know that if you move an asset forward, it will still appear in the previous frames, just that it will not be animated until the timeline hits the point where you moved the sequence. To hide an object temporarily or permanently, you will need to access the object's visibility controls in the **Layer Settings** panel.

 Frame 0 is our work area in Anime Studio. This is where we have access to all the drawing tools as well as the ability to add bones and set up rigs. With Version 10, if you move a sequence to the left, frame 0 can still be accessed. This is an updated feature from previous versions.

The Motion Graph timeline

The **Motion Graph** timeline allows us to view the intensity of movement for an object and its layer through a graphical interface. With this, we can alter the lines or paths on the graph to create more complex animations.

Please open up `GraphModeExample.anme`. What we have here is a simple path of a ball that has several keyframes sprinkled throughout. The steps to be carried out on the **Motion Graph** timeline are as follows:

1. Click on the **Motion Graph** tab.

2. You will see the **Move Layer** channel on the left of the timeline; double-click on it.

3. You are now in the graph for the **Move** properties of the layer. You will see three different colored line graphs that you can alter at the keyframes.

4. For this example, the green and blue lines are stuck together, so click on the blue line keyframe of frame 36 and move it up.

5. You'll see that the green line (Z property) is located underneath, plus the path on the canvas has been altered. Try doing this with a few more keyframes to see how the position alters the path of the layer.

6. Right-click on a keyframe and choose **Bezier**. You should now see handles appear around this keyframe.

7. Move the handles around to alter the path even further. This can be useful for creating more complex animations.

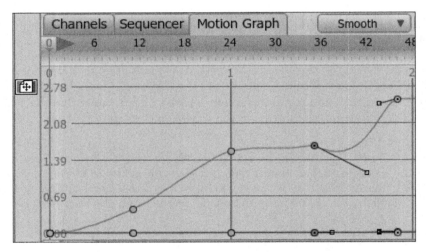

The **Motion Graph** timeline is great for those fine tweaks you cannot achieve with the standard Layer tools. Be sure to use it if you're looking to add extra detail to your animated works.

Changing your view of the action

One of the coolest things about Anime Studio is the ability to control the camera, effectively altering how every asset appears on screen at once. You can move, zoom, pan, and rotate a scene to simulate many different effects. The tools are very easy to use and act just like any other tool in regards to how keyframing and the timelines work.

On top of that, the **Workspace** tools allow us to alter the view of the document without affecting the animation in any way. You will be using these a lot when you need to get a different angle of the action when molding your creations.

Camera tools

Let's open up the work file for this section, CameraAndWorkSpaceTools.anme, to see these tools in action.

1. While on frame 0, select the Track Camera tool from the bottom of your toolbar on the left-hand side (under the **Camera** heading). This looks like a camera with a plus sign next to it and the shortcut key is 4.

2. Click and hold down your mouse button in the center of the document and move around. Notice how we can move the scene anywhere we want. This is great if we want to do a tracking shot of someone walking down the street or if we want to slowly reveal something that was originally off-screen.

3. Now take the **Zoom Camera** tool, the next tool in the camera list (it has an up arrow on the icon), and perform the same steps as you did with the Track Camera tool. You can also press 5 on your keyboard to select this tool.

4. You should notice how you can zoom in and out. This, of course, has noticeable benefits with being able to create close-up shots for your characters or to zoom out for wide-angle shots.

5. The last two tools on the list, rotate and pan (6 and 7 on your keyboard), allow us to rotate the view of the camera as well as do a 3D panning effect.

6. Animating a camera works just like anything else in Anime Studio. Select the Track Camera tool again, advance to frame 1, and click once on the document to set a keyframe.

7. You'll notice that the Track Camera icon appears in the **Channels** tab.

8. Go to frame 20 and drag the document to the left using the Track Camera tool.

9. Go back to your first keyframe and hit the **Play** button. Notice how movement has been interpolated between the two keyframes. The same premise applies for every camera tool on the list.

Like many of the tools, you can adjust the values of the camera numerically on the top toolbar. This can be useful for precise movements.

The **Camera** tools can make moving several layers at once easier. Plus, it brings a cinematic quality to your work. Be sure to keep these tools in mind.

Workspace tools

Keep the same document open for this section as we explore the **Workspace** tools by performing the following steps:

1. Click on the hand icon underneath the **Workspace** label on your toolbar. It will be labeled as **Pan.**

2. Put the cursor in the center of the document and click-and-drag around. What we are doing here is adjusting the view for you, not the movie itself.

 This is useful if something is off-screen and you need to move the workspace to see it. Or perhaps, you'd like to center an asset on your screen for easier access when working.

3. Additionally, if you have a right mouse button, you can hold it down and move around to generate the same effect. If you only have one mouse button, you can use the spacebar. This is a useful shortcut and can save time.

4. The **Zoom** tool, which is next to the Pan tool (and looks like a magnifying glass), allows you to zoom in and out of your workspace.

5. Just hold down the left mouse button and move from left to right. Left will zoom out, while right will zoom in.

6. You can do the same thing if you have a wheel on your mouse by scrolling it up and down (scrolling up will zoom out, scrolling down will zoom in).

7. The Rotate tool, which is the third tool in the **Workspace** section, allows you to rotate the canvas like a piece of paper.

8. This may make certain things easier to draw (if you need an upside-down perspective, for instance).

9. The **Orbit** tool, which is the fourth and last one on the list, gives you a 3D view of the canvas.

10. When you first click the canvas with this tool, you will be introduced to a completely different perspective of the workspace.

11. You can hold down your left mouse button to move the workspace around in this view. This is great if you need to see how all the elements are working within your document's 3D space.

12. The purple arrow on your workspace represents your camera. As you can see in the following screenshot, it truly does inhabit 3D space! If you track the camera with the Z properties, you can choose how close or far away it sits from the action.

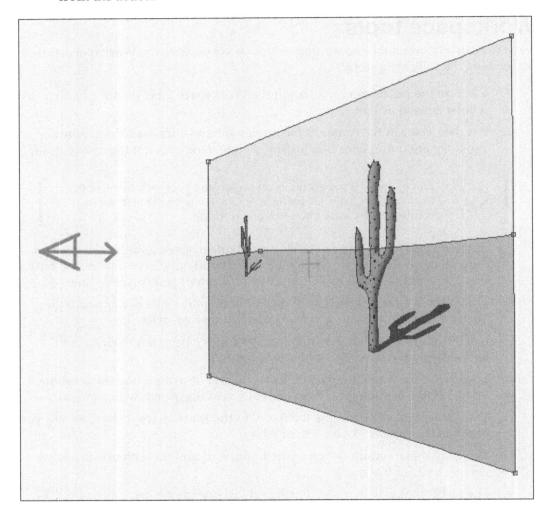

13. When you're done, click on **Reset** to bring the view back to the default point.

While the **Workspace** tools don't affect the action your audience will be seeing, they are just as important. You need to be comfortable with your workspace to achieve the best results. The easiest way for you to do this would be to take advantage of the mouse shortcuts. That way everything will become second nature when working with the other tools.

> Near the bottom of your Anime Studio window are four square icons. One looks whole, the second is split into two, while the third and fourth ones are split into threes and fours. Clicking on these will give you multiple views of your canvas. You could use the Orbit tool in one while keeping the canvas stationary in the other. This is great if you want to get multiple views of the action while building your scenes.

Summary

There are many elements when it comes to mapping out and perfecting animation. Becoming accustomed to the different **Layer** tools and layer types will be vital in your success. While the **Channels** timeline controls all the movement in our projects, don't forget to take advantage of the **Sequencer** and **Motion Graph** timeline. Finally, the **Camera** and **Workspace** tools will help you change the view of action for the audience and yourself. All of these basic concepts will come into place as we prepare to start creating our cartoon.

In the next chapter, we will be focusing on some of the settings that you can find in the **Layer Settings** panel. We will also be taking an in-depth look at the **Style** palette and different brush types, which will help when we start animating our cartoon.

4

Enhancing Your Art with the Layer Settings Panel and Style Palette

Learning what is in the Layer Settings panel and Style palette will help when it comes to creating different effects for your drawings and animations. We touched briefly on both of these areas in the previous three chapters. Now we will be taking a closer look at what these panels can do.

In this chapter, we will cover the following topics:

- Exploring the Layer Settings panel
- Designing with the Style palette
- Animating layer effects
- Applying shadows and shades to the layer

Exploring the Layer Settings panel

You can access the **Layers Settings** panel for any layer by simply double-clicking on a layer's name in the **Layers** panel. You will discover that different layer types contain additional tabs. We will be focusing on the standard settings you will find for all types. As we start creating our animation in the coming chapters, we may reference some of these tabs to achieve certain results.

The following screenshot shows the **Layer Settings** panel. There's a lot going on here, but don't worry, we'll break down the main parts!

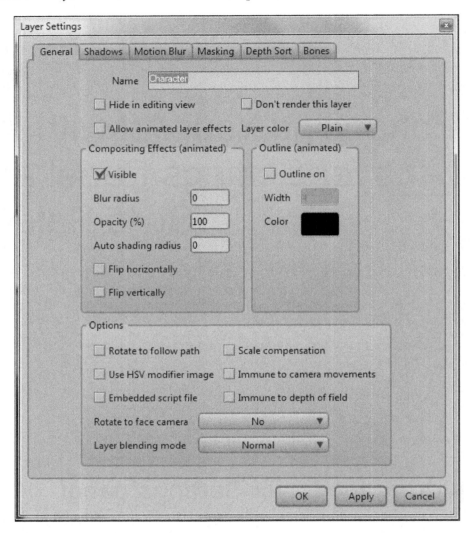

For this exercise, please open the LayerSettings.anme file. This file is available in the code bundle provided with this book. Double-click on the **Character** bone layer in the **Layers** panel to open up the **Layer Settings** panel. We will focus on the key items in the **General** tab first.

Whenever you make a change in the **Layer Settings** panel, it's important to either click on **OK** or **Apply**. This will ensure that the change you made is applied to the layer. The difference between the two buttons is that **OK** will close the panel after applying the change while **Apply** keeps the panel open. We will be using the **Apply** button more, so we don't have to keep reopening the panel as we view the changes. In some cases, it may be required to use the **OK** button. A note of this will be made if needed.

The Name field

When you create a layer, you have the option to immediately enter a name for it. This is great for organization, especially when a lot of layers come into play. Sometimes though, it may be necessary to change the name of a layer later on. You can do so with the **Name** field. Simply enter the new name of your layer in the field to change the name.

You can also quickly change the name of the layer by clicking on the down arrow next to the layer name on the **Layers** panel. This will bring up some other quick options you can adjust.

The Layer color menu

Along with naming your layers for organization, you can also color code them with the **Layer color** drop-down menu. The layer (in this case, the **Character** bone layer) will then be colored quickly, by selecting the color when working on your document. The color will be applied once you click on **OK** or **Apply** on the **Layer Settings** panel. You can also use the shortcut we mentioned in the previous chapter, which involves clicking to the left of the **hide** or **show** buttons. You can see the **Layer color** drop-down menu in the following screenshot:

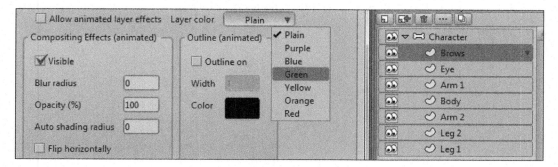

The Visible checkbox

Using the **Visible** checkbox, you can dictate whether the layer is visible in the animation itself, and not just the workspace. This can be useful if you want to hide something from view permanently or for a certain amount of time. The following steps will help you understand the use of the **Visible** checkbox:

1. Click on the **Visible** checkbox to uncheck it.

2. Click on **Apply** at the bottom of the panel.

3. Notice how the character layer disappears from view.

4. Click on the **Visible** checkbox again (so that it's checked), and then click on **Apply**. This will bring the **Character** layer back into view.

This function is used a lot when you have objects waiting on the sidelines to be brought into action as a scene is taking place. It can help with clutter (and reduce resource needs) and keep those assets visible only when needed.

The Blur radius field

The **Blur radius** field allows us to set how blurry a layer looks. This can be useful in instances where you want to create a depth of field effect, or if you need to stylize the layer so that it appears out of focus. The following steps will help you understand the use of the **Blur radius** field:

1. Enter the number 20 and click on **Apply** at the bottom of the panel. The higher this number, the more blurry your layer will appear. The maximum value you can enter is 256.

2. The blur effect will not appear unless we render the document. To do this, go to **File** | **Preview** (*Ctrl + R* on Windows and *command + R* on Mac).

3. You should see the character appearing out of focus in the preview window, as shown in the following screenshot:

4. Close the preview window.

5. Change the **Blur radius** value back to 0 and click on **Apply**.

We briefly discussed about the **Depth of Field** setting in the **Project Settings** panel back in *Chapter 1, Stepping into the World of Animation*. While that method allows you to automatically blur objects based on camera distance and position, sometimes it's best to manually blur layers.

The Opacity field

Opacity allows you to set the transparency of the layer you are editing. Perhaps you're looking to create a ghost or a piece of glass. The **Opacity** setting can help you achieve a more convincing effect. The following steps will help you understand the use of the **Opacity** field:

1. Opacity intensity can be adjusted between 0 and 100. The value 0 will make your layer completely invisible while 100 will make it opaque. Let's enter in 50 for this exercise to set the value in between.

2. Click on the **Apply** button at the bottom of the panel.

3. Like the blur radius effect, we will not see a change until we preview the current frame. Use the **Preview** shortcut command (or go to **File | Preview**) to see the result. If you look at the image shown in the following screenshot, we can see through the character. Perhaps he has crossed over to the other side.

4. Once you've viewed the preview, close the window and return to **Layer Settings**.

5. Change the **Opacity** value back to 100 and click on the **Apply** button.

Changing the opacity of a layer can really add some visual flare to your project. Be sure to keep it in mind when tackling different tasks.

The Auto shading radius field

While you will find most of the robust shading options in the **Shadows** tab (which we'll be learning about shortly), the **Auto shading radius** option allows you to create a shading effect that goes around your strokes. The following steps will help you understand the use of the **Auto shading radius** field:

1. Enter 50 in the **Auto shading radius** field, as shown in the following screenshot:

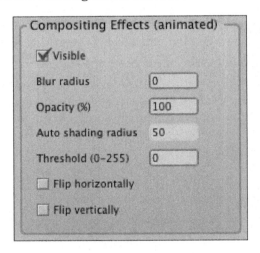

2. Click on **OK** and preview the current frame. This is another layer effect that needs to be rendered before you see it.

3. You will notice that the autoshading radius feature creates a softer look for the layer. This is due to the shading effect on the stroke lines. The higher the number, the more blurred the shading will be. You can see the shaded effect surrounding the strokes in the following screenshot:

4. You can turn the **Auto shading radius** field's value back to 0 once you are finished viewing the result.

This effect is great if you're looking to do something a little more with your lines. Keep in mind, the lower the number, the more defined the shading area will be.

The outline settings

The outline settings allow you to create an outline that encompasses the selected layer. This is yet another tool for you to use when it comes to stylizing layers. The following steps will help you understand the use of the outline settings:

1. Check the **outline (animated)** box on the right-hand side of your panel.
2. You can enter a value for the thickness of the outline; enter 8 against the field.
3. You can also change the color. Click on the color selector box and choose a dark blue color.

4. Preview the frame by going to **File | Preview**. Notice how we now have a blue line surrounding the layer, as shown in the following screenshot:

This effect is great if you are looking to create a cut-out look for your animation. It can also be useful, to an extent, if you didn't add stroke lines to your layer and are looking to achieve a similar result quickly.

The Layer blending mode menu

At the bottom of your **Layer Settings** panel is a drop-down menu named **Layer blending mode**. You are given a list of different blends you can use for the currently selected layer. These can achieve a variety of effects and rely on at least one more layer in order to work.

Make sure you have the group layer **Forest 1** visible, which is listed under your **Character** layer on the **Layers** panel. Remember, to make a layer visible, click on the eyes icon beside the layer name on the **Layers** panel. The following steps will help you understand the use of the **Layer blending mode** menu:

1. With the **Layer Settings** panel still open (and the **Character** layer selected), click on the **Layer blending mode** drop-down menu and select **Screen** from the list.

2. Click on **OK**.

3. Preview your frame to see the results. This is yet another effect to create a ghostly visual, or perhaps, a way to overlay a color or gradient over a backdrop to enhance the scenery. The choice is yours! You may have the same effect applied to your character, as shown in the following screenshot:

Layer blending modes are widely used in photo and video editing applications. They can also create some neat effects when animating. Each blending mode will have a different effect. You will notice, in this case, that **Screen** tends to remove all blacks from the layer and creates a transparent effect for the green. These modes also depend on the colors you are using and which layers are involved at the time.

Do you want to apply a transparency or blur to multiple layers but don't want to click through each one?

You don't have to! With Anime Studio Pro 10, you can now go to the **Layer Settings** panel of a specific layer, highlight multiple layers on the **Layers** panel, and then edit the current layer's settings. Any shared parameters will be applied to all layers. Give it a try!

Animating layer effects

The visibility, blur radius, opacity, and auto-shading radius settings can all be animated, if you choose. This can be useful if you want to make something appear to fade in or out via the **Opacity** setting, or perhaps, you want to create the effect of a layer coming into focus—that is going from blurry to sharp—with the blurred radius. You can also choose to make something invisible, and then have it reappear anytime you want using the visibility setting. All it requires is checking a box and placing your keyframes on the timeline. The following steps will help you understand how to animate layer effects:

1. At the top of the **Layer Settings** panel is an option named **Allow animated layer effects**. Make sure it's checked.

2. Advance to frame 24 on your timeline.

3. Adjust the **Blur radius** to 40.

4. Click on **Apply**. Notice how there is now a **Blur radius** channel on your **Channels** timeline along with two keyframes. This is shown in the following screenshot:

5.   The effects can only be witnessed by exporting out an animation. You could also page through a few select frames between the keyframes and do a preview to see the transition. This can be done for any of the effects mentioned earlier.

Other general options for layers

You will also find a list of other settings in the **General** tab of the **Layer Settings** panel. Some descriptions on a few of these options are as follows:

- **Scale compensation**: This option will keep your lines from getting thicker as you enlarge or zoom in on vector layers.

- **Immune to camera movements**: This option will keep the selected layer from being affected by your camera tools.

- **Immune to depth of field**: This option will disable that layer from being blurred if you have the depth of field option checked in the **Project Settings** panel.

- **Rotate to face camera**: This setting can keep your vector layer fixed, even if you are rotating the camera within 3D space. The following screenshot shows the other general options for layers:

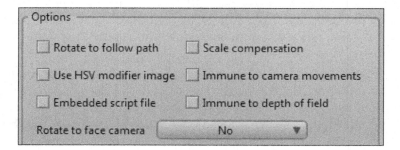

We won't be dealing with these options in this book as we start creating our animated cartoon. However, that doesn't mean you can't check them out for yourself. Different artists have different needs, and these options may be of use to you down the road.

Applying shadows and shades to the layer

Under the **Shadows** tab are three options that allow you to create different shading and shadowing effects for your layers. This can be great if you want to add a quick drop shadow or create the effect that your layer is being shaded due to different lighting.

You may keep your `LayerSettings.anme` project file open for this part of the exercise. With your **Layer Settings** panel still open, be sure to click on the **Shadows** tab to the right-hand side of the **General** tab. The following steps will help you understand how to apply shadows to your layer:

1. Check the **Shadow on** checkbox.

2. Set the **Offset** field to `50`. This value determines how detached the shadow appears from the layer.

3. Set the **Blur** value to `18`. Increasing this value will make the shadow appear more out of focus. A lower number will give the shadow a sharper look.

4. Set the **Expansion** value to `13`. Expansion determines how far your shadow reaches out from the origin point.

5. Changing the **Shadow direction** value will determine where your shadow falls on the layer. For this example, let's set the direction to a value of `230`. You can either enter this number yourself or use the directional wheel and set it using your mouse.

6. The **Shadow color** option is a colorpicker that allows you to set the color of the shadow. You can also set the transparency of the color in this box. This is indicated by the vertical slider with the white color fading into a checkered pattern. For this example, let's leave the shadow color as is. The **Shadows** tab is shown in the following screenshot:

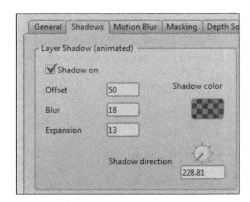

7. Click on the **Apply** button.

8. Go to **File | Preview** and view the result. You can see a shadow has been applied to the character, as shown in the following screenshot:

9. Once you are done viewing the preview, close the window and return to your **Layer Settings** window.

10. Uncheck the **Shadow on** checkbox.

A 3D shadow works in a similar fashion. The exception is that it is meant to mimic a 3D perspective. This means that the shadow can appear to be going into the horizon or towards the camera. Let's check it out in the following steps:

1. The 3D shadow is also dependent on your layer's origin point. Select the Set Origin tool and position the anchor between the two feet of the character. This will let the shadow grow naturally from the body.

2. Click on the **Perspective shadow on** checkbox in the **Layer Settings** panel.

3. As you know, adjusting the **Blur** value will alter the focus of the shadow. Let's set this to 20.

4. **Scale** will determine the size of the shadow. Enter 1 in this field.

5. **Shear** will alter the angle of how the shadow is drawn. Also enter 1 in this field for this exercise.

6. Click on **Apply** and preview the frame (*Ctrl + R* on Windows and *command + R* on Mac). You will see a shadow applied to your image, as shown in the following screenshot:

7. If the shadow doesn't look the way you want, tweak with the shear and scale settings. Creating the ideal shadow for your situation will often come down to trial and error.

8. Close the preview window and return to your **Layer Settings** panel.

9. Uncheck the **Perspective shadow on** checkbox.

The **Shading on** button allows us to automatically apply a shading effect to the layer. This usually occurs inside the layer, as opposed to outside like the shadows. The following steps will help you understand how to apply shading to your layer:

1. Check the **Shading on** checkbox.

2. **Offset** will shift the shade further from the outside of the layer if this number increases. For this exercise, let's enter 20.

3. **Blur** sets the focus of the shade. Let's enter 50 for this field.

4. **Contraction** determines how far the shade effect reaches. The bigger this number, the more of a shaded look you will have. Enter 30.

5. Click on **Apply** and preview the frame. Check out the shaded effect in the following screenshot:

Shadows and shading can add an extra dimension to your assets. While it may be more effective to create these effects yourself, don't be afraid to try out these settings first. After tweaking the settings, you may be surprised by the results!

Checking the **Inverted** checkbox under the **Shade on** section will create the effect that light is shining on your layer as opposed to a shadow being cast. Give it a try and see how it can affect your artwork.

Creating a motion blur

A motion blur can help if you want to create the illusion of an object moving incredibly fast. You may want to apply this during a quick camera pan to further sell the fast motion. Another example could be a fast-moving object, such as a car speeding across the highway or an asteroid plummeting towards the earth. Where you decide to use it is up to you!

Open the work file `LayerSettingsMotionBlur.anme`. You will see a small animation of our green character running from left to right. This will work as a basic example of creating a motion blur. The following steps will help you understand how to create a motion blur:

1. Double-click on the **Character** layer to bring up the **Layer Settings** panel.

2. Click on the **Motion Blur** tab at the top. The **Motion Blur** tab is shown in the following screenshot:

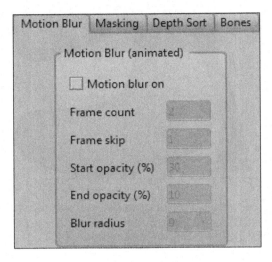

3. Check the **Motion blur on** checkbox.

4. You can adjust how the motion blur looks from here. You can choose how many frames at a time the motion blur will affect, how many frames it'll skip (if any), opacity for the trail, and the blurriness. We can leave all these options at their defaults for this exercise.

5. Click on **Apply**.

6. Page forward on your timeline to frame 24.

7. Go to **File** | **Preview** to see frame 24 rendered. This will allow us to see the motion blur as it would appear in the middle of the animation. You can see the motion blur effect applied to the character in the following screenshot:

The ability to add a motion blur is just one more feature in your vast Anime Studio toolset. The effect won't always be needed, but you may find moments where it will add an extra pop to your animations.

Masking the layer

There may come a time when you want to hide a layer in a certain way or reveal bits through the shape of another layer. Or maybe you have some pupils moving in your eyes and want them to be hidden when they intersect with the boundaries of the eyes, just as an example.

Masking can only be achieved with a Group or Bone layer with sublayers. To pull up an example file like this, open up `LayerSettingsMasking.anme` from the book's work files and perform the following steps:

1. Double-click on the Group layer labeled **Masking Group** to bring up the **Layer Settings** panel.

2. Click on the **Masking** tab. The following screenshot shows the **Masking** tab:

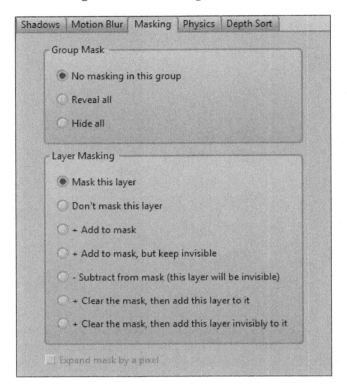

3. In order to begin masking, we first need to indicate the main layer (in this case, the Group layer) that is going to contain masking. To do this, let's click on the **Hide all** option, which is listed in the **Group Mask** section.

4. We can leave the **Layer Masking** section with **Mask this layer** selected.

5. Click on the **Apply** button.

6. With the **Masking Group** layer expanded in the **Layers** panel, click on the first sublayer named **Oval**. Your **Layer** settings will now focus on this sublayer.

7. For the **Oval** sublayer, select **Mask this layer** from the list.

8. Click on the **Apply** button.

9. Click on the **Rectangle** sublayer from the **Layers** panel.

10. Similar to what we did for the **Oval** sublayer, select **Mask this layer** from the list.

11. Click on the **Apply** button.

12. Click on the **Character** sublayer contained in the group.

13. For **Character**, we are going to select **+Add to mask**.

14. Click on the **Apply** button one more time.

What we have done here is told Anime Studio to hide the **Rectangle** and **Oval** sublayers, but to keep the **Character** layer on screen. However, since we are masking this Group layer, you will notice that the rectangle and oval are visible through the **Character** layer. This can provide some interesting results, as I'm sure you could imagine. The following screenshot is just one example of what masks can do:

Masking can be a bit difficult to understand. Because you need to work with a Group or Bone layer to get it to work, plus the many masking options to choose from, trial and error will be the key when working with this technique. Amazing things can be done with masks. We will take a look at one example in *Chapter 8, Animating Your Characters*.

Since Anime Studio 9.5, the layers on the **Layers** panel now indicate what kind of mask they are currently using. For instance, the **Character** layer has a + sign next to it to indicate it is working with the **+Add to mask** function. Additionally, if you right-click on any of these masked layers, you can choose a different mask setting from the list without having to go into the **Layer Settings** panel. This makes experimenting with masks a lot less tedious.

Designing with the Style palette

Up to this point, we have referred to the **Style** palette to change our stroke and fill colors as well as adjust line thickness. The **Style** palette is capable of much more though; it gives us many options for stylizing our assets. Through the **Style** palette, you can apply color effects, change your brush, and create universal styles that can be easily accessed at any time. The **Style** palette is shown in the following screenshot:

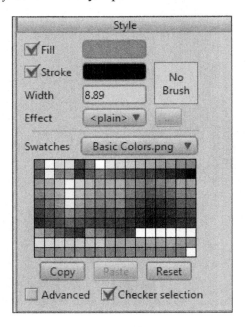

For this part of the chapter, please open the work file `StylePalette.anme`. You will see a familiar face. Our green friend will make good practice for playing with the different **Style** palette features.

The Brush types

Like your fill-and-stroke colors, brushes can be set either before or after you draw out a vector shape. This makes swapping brushes easy and experimenting a very approachable task. Learn how to change your brush type in the following steps:

1. Select the Select Shape tool from the left-hand side toolbar.
2. Click on the **Body** layer of the character.
3. Click on the body of the character with your cursor.
4. On the **Style** palette is a box currently labeled **No Brush**. Click on this box.
5. A list of several brushes will appear. As you can see, you have many options to choose from when it comes to creating stylized drawings.
6. Click through the brushes to see how each looks on the character.
7. There are options you can adjust for each brush, such as **Brush jitter angle** and **Brush spacing**. This can also alter the look of your vector. Having a higher jitter angle can create a more chaotic look, while a higher spacing number can widen the area between each part of the brush stroke.
8. The **Minimize frame-to-frame randomness** option can help control your lines if they appear wobbly or distorted during export. The **Brush Settings** panel is shown in the following screenshot:

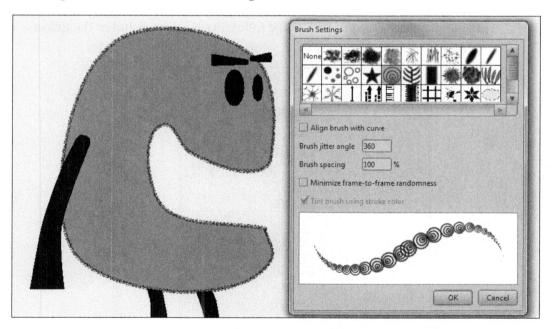

You can also create your own brushes by adding PNG files to the brushes folder, which is located in the Anime Studio Pro folder in your file browser. With Version 10, you can now make multibrushes, which allow you to add multiple images to a brush that can be randomized when drawn out. This can add an entirely new level of customization. Be sure to give it a try if you're looking for something more than the built-in brush sets.

Playing around with these brush types is the key. If you have a type of style in mind for your cartoon, this can really help solidify your look. For instance, you may want everything to look like it was drawn with chalk or crayon. Adjusting your brush type can help achieve this.

The Fill color effects

There are a few color effects you can apply to your vector graphics. These range from shading to softening effects. It is usual to apply these effects after the object has been drawn out; that way you can experiment and adjust the desired effect. We will try a few of these effects in the following steps:

1. Select the Select Shape tool and click on the shape in the **Body** layer, like you did with the brush exercise.

2. Click on the **Effect** drop-down menu to see all the effects you can apply to your vector. Each setting gives you different options that will alter the final appearance of your object. The following is a screenshot of the **Effect** drop-down menu:

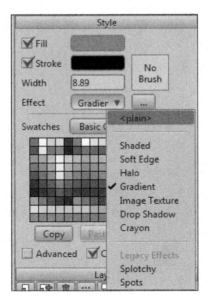

3. The following are the options listed in the **Effect** drop-down menu:

   ° **Shaded**: This effect will apply a shade to your vector, similar to how the shading effects work in our **Layer Settings**. Shading a vector has the advantage of letting you focus on one shape at a time. This may be useful if you have multiple shapes making up a layer and don't want them all affected by the shade (or if you want to apply multiple different-looking shades).

   ° **Soft Edge**: This effect will make the vector look blurry, assuming it doesn't have a stroke. The advantage of applying a color effect instead of making the layer itself blurry, like the shade effect, comes down to being able to control specific shapes of your choosing.

   ° **Halo**: This effect will create a color that surrounds the inside of your shape. This color difference will be in the shape of an oval or halo. You can adjust the size of this coloring as well as the blurriness and color.

   ° **Gradient**: Creating this color effect will allow you to choose at least two colors and have them fade from one to another. This is great for going from a dark to light color, as an example. You can choose the colors, where they appear, as well as if the gradient is linear, radial, reflected, or angled. To add more colors to your gradient, simply click anywhere below the horizontal preview to add more swatches. When you apply a gradient, a red line with two circles will appear over your object. Use the Select Shape tool to move this line or ovals to adjust the angle and spread of your gradient, as shown in the following screenshot:

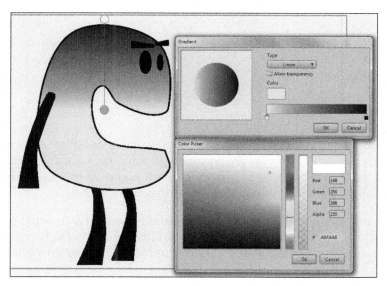

- ° **Image Texture**: With this effect, you can select an image from your hard drive and apply it as a skin of sorts to the selected object. You can choose to either tile the image (repeat it) or have the image wrap around the object as best as it can.

- ° **Drop Shadow**: This option creates a drop shadow for the selected object. This is similar to how the drop shadow in the **Layer Settings** panel works. Which one you use will come down to preference and how much control you need.

- ° **Crayon**: This effect creates the illusion that your object was colored in by a kid with a crayon. It certainly isn't an effect for everyone, but could very easily have its uses. You can adjust the intensity of the strokes as well as the density.

- ° **Splotchy**: This effect will give your object a textured or splotchy look. You can adjust the size of the splotches, as well as the intensity, to hone in on the look you are trying to achieve. This is considered a legacy effect, which means it's older and has some issues when it comes to rendering and wrapping around bones. Keep this in mind if you decide to use it.

- ° **Spots**: This effect will give your object, you guessed it, spots! You can change the color as well as how frequently the spots appear on your vector shape. This is also considered a legacy effect.

 If you're having a hard time viewing the different color effects, try unchecking the **Checkered selection** option located at the bottom of the **Style** palette.

We will be using a few of these effects as we start creating our animated cartoon. Don't be afraid to play with some of these effects yourself as you start to discover your own style.

Swatches

There may come a point where you will want to use colors only from a select spectrum. This has its uses if you are trying to go with a certain color theme for your animation, or maybe there are various colors you plan to reuse often. The **Style** palette allows you to swap and create different swatches.

With the release of Anime Studio 9.5, we now have the ability to copy, paste, or reset our stroke and fill colors in the swatch section. This can be useful for transferring colors and saves a step as it removes the need for using the Eyedropper tool.

Let's check out how swatches work using the following steps:

1. Click on the **Swatches** drop-down menu to reveal several preset swatches.

2. Explore the different color presets.

3. Click on the **Custom Image...** option on the bottom of the drop-down list. This prompts you to locate an image on your computer.

4. If you don't have an image, you can use the one included in this chapter's files, which is labeled AgnesSanta.jpg.

5. After selecting this image, you can use it as a color swatch for your project. Simply click anywhere on the image to get a sampling of the color in that area. The following screenshot shows the red color being applied from the custom swatch:

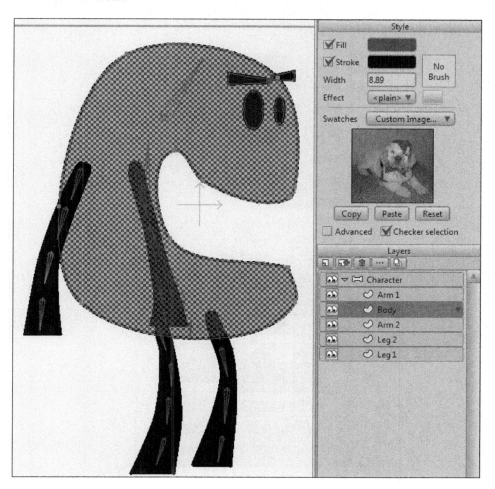

Be sure to take advantage of this, especially if you are picky about what colors go into your projects.

The Advanced style properties

At the bottom of the **Style** palette is a checkbox labeled **Advanced**. Clicking on this will expand the window to give you more options to play with. Many of these build on some of the preceding lessons. The following screenshot shows how the **Style** palette will look with advanced properties open:

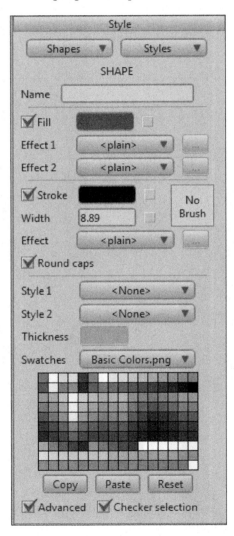

The explanation of these advanced properties is as follows:

- The **Style 1** and **Style 2** buttons allow you to create preset colors and designs for your assets. You can create a style using the **Styles** drop-down menu at the top. You can then apply that style using either the **Style 1** or **Style 2** drop-down menus near the bottom of the palette. As an example, let's say you create a skin tone in the **Styles** drop-down menu at the top and apply it to a character (by using the **Select Shape** character and applying the style through the **Style 1** or **Style 2** menus). Later, you decide to change the skin tone. You could pull that style up from the top drop-down menu and change it. The alteration will affect all assets that are currently using that style in your document. This is shown in the following screenshot:

- When in **Advanced** mode, you can place two color effects onto an object at the same time. As an example, you could use a gradient and create a drop shadow for an asset.

- Your stroke can also have effects applied to it. Not only can you use the color effects we overviewed previously, but there's also **Sketchy** and **Angled Pen**, which alters the look of your lines.

- **Round Caps** will give your strokes rounded edges.

If you're still getting used to all the options the **Style** palette provides, you may want to leave the **Advanced** checkbox unchecked until you get familiar with everything. However, once you're ready to tap into more of Anime Studio's features, the advanced **Style** palette settings can really push your work further.

Summary

Understanding what advantages the **Layer Settings** and **Style** windows bring to the table will help polish up your projects and streamline several tasks. As you follow along and start creating an animation, keep these panels in mind. Feel free to explore and apply what you see fit to solidify your own animation and drawing style, even if it's not suggested in later chapters.

In the next chapter, we will start drawing the cartoon character we plan to use for the animation. Now that we have the fundamentals, it's time to get creative and have some fun!

5

Bringing a Cartoon Character to Life

The time has come for us to start designing and rigging the cartoon character we will be using for this project. There are many elements to consider, especially when it comes to creating a skeletal structure for your character. Don't worry, this chapter will guide you through the entire process and before you know it, you will have the star of your production ready to go!

In this chapter, we will cover the following topics:

- Thinking about design
- Learning the basics of bone animation
- Animating bones
- Creating your first character
- Rigging your character

Thinking about design

At this point, you probably have a basic idea of what you want your character(s) to look like. Every cartoonist has his/her own style that gives the overall cartoon a unique look. Think about your favorite cartoons for a moment and analyze how everything is constructed. John Kricfalusi's *Ren & Stimpy* combined exaggerated character movements with retro-painted backdrops. By adding in the realistic close-up shots, they showed that when something disturbing or gross is introduced, you will have a very interesting mix of elements coming into play.

Looking at more modern works, such as Seth MacFarlane's *Family Guy* and *American Dad*, you will notice that all of the characters have a distinct style that definitely carves its own identity. The characters seen in these shows typically have large round eyes, are viewed at a three-fourths angle, and contain exaggerated facial features (such as chins or foreheads). While Kricfalusi and MacFarlane's styles are miles apart, one thing is the same—their consistency to their own styles.

Being consistent with consistency

No matter how you decide to draw your characters, whether they appear realistic or more cartoony and exaggerated, it's important to keep your character designs consistent throughout. It would be quite jarring to the audience if you had a character that looks like one from *South Park* and a character that looks like one from *Futurama* interacting with one another. Could this be done? Of course, and a creative cartoonist could think of a clever plot device to carry it out. However, as a general rule, it's best to find a style, practice it, perfect it, and then evolve with it. When in doubt, examine one of your favorite cartoons and pay attention to the character designs.

Like with the Draw tools, frame 0 (as shown in the following screenshot) is your home base when it comes to creating and editing your bones. You can also experiment with bone movements while in frame 0, without affecting the animation of your project. Be sure to keep this in mind as you start to learn the Bone tools.

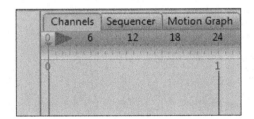

Understanding the basics of bone animation

Since Anime Studio's main focus is on bone animation, this book will be following suit and providing steps for creating rigged characters. When creating your characters, you will want to think ahead of how you'll want to draw up and eventually rig the character to a system of bones. There are three ways you can use bones in Anime Studio: **Region binding**, **Layer binding**, and **Point binding**. They all have their strengths and different uses (and cartoonists usually end up using all three in some capacity). Hopefully, the next sections will give you a better understanding of all three systems.

Using Region binding

By default, when you place bones down in Anime Studio, they will end up affecting whatever sublayers they happen to be touching or have influence over. This provides a springy, cartoony look to the movements that occur on our characters and objects. In the past, Region binding proved to be more difficult because the bones would sometimes affect other parts that you did not intend to be affected. This is no longer an issue with a new feature introduced in Anime Studio 9.5, which we will be getting to shortly.

Launch Anime Studio and open up the example file `BoneExample.anme` from your list of work files for the book. On the screen are four vector layers, each making up a part of the arm. We're going to need to put these vectors into a bone layer. Perform the following steps to do so:

1. Click on the **Add Layer** button on the **Layers** panel and select **Bone** from the list.

2. Name the bone as `Arm`.

3. Move all of the vector layers into the bone layer by clicking on the bottom vector layer (**Arm Piece 2**), holding the *Shift* key and clicking on the **Hand** layer. They all should now be highlighted, as shown in the following screenshot:

4. Hold down your left mouse button and drag the vectors into the bone layer.

 You can always create the bone layer first and place the vector layers inside it as you draw out the different pieces or objects. The order you choose is completely optional.

Now we need to draw the bones for the bone layer. These will ultimately control the sublayers inside the bone layer. Perform the following steps to do so:

1. Make sure the **Arm** bone layer is selected on your **Layers** panel.

2. Click on the Add Bone tool on the toolbar to the left. This should look like a bone with a **+** icon underneath it. You can also use the *A* key on your keyboard to select it.

3. Starting with the top of the sleeve, you are going to hold down your mouse button and drag down to where the elbow starts and then release it. A triangular red shape is now present on your **Arm** bone layer. This is what a bone looks like in Anime Studio, as shown in the following screenshot:

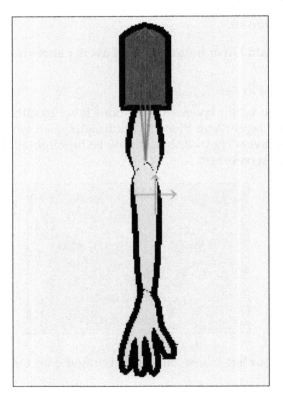

4. Repeat the same steps for the bottom portion of the arm. Draw the bone from the elbow until it meets the wrist.

5. The final bone will be for the hand. Draw a bone from the wrist to the fingers. If you desire, you can draw a bone for each finger, but for now, we'll keep things simple.

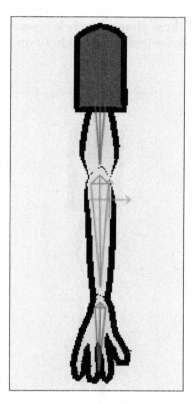

6. If you ever misplace a bone or incorrectly size it, click on the Transform Bone tool (it looks like a bone with a crosshair underneath it). This allows you to move bones by clicking and holding on the thick end of the bone and dragging it. You can also resize bones by holding down on the tapered end and dragging in or out.

If you're on frame 0 when working with the Transform Bone tool, you will simply be altering the bones before animation. However, if you alter bones with this tool while past frame 0, your bones will animate out just like any other channel. Your layers will also be affected if attached or influenced by the bones. Animating with the Transform Bone tool is useful if you want to alter just one bone at a time, unlike the Manipulate Bones tool that affects all children you are moving from the parent bone. This is also referred to as **Inverse Kinematics**.

7. If you click on the Bone Strength tool, which looks like a bone with an oval going around it, you will see some colored clouds or highlights appear over each bone. These are the areas of influence each of your bone has. The bigger the influence, the more objects will be affected in the surrounding area. You can adjust these clouds by clicking-and-dragging from left to right or adjusting the number for each cloud on the top bar, as shown in the following screenshot:

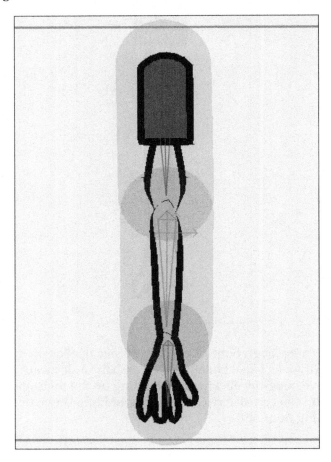

There, that wasn't so hard! Drawing the bones is only the first step. From here, we will see how these can apply to animation.

 Can't see your bone tools? Make sure you have the bone layer selected in the **Layers** panel. Only then will the tools appear for you to use.

Let's test out the movement of this arm to see what Region binding looks like by performing the following steps:

1. Click on the Manipulate Bones tool from the toolbar to the left. This looks like a horizontal bone with two black arrows pointing up and down.

2. Move your cursor over to the hand bone.

3. Hold down your mouse button and drag around. You should notice how the bones affect each other and consequently move the sublayers, as shown in the following screenshot:

If the movement doesn't look quite right, certain things can be corrected using the Bone Strength tool, such as restraining bone movements and creating **Smart Bone actions**.

Since we are in frame 0, no animation is being recorded. If you want to revert your bone layer back to its default state, simply click on the Select Bone tool. Additionally, you can page-forward to frame 1, and then come back to 0 to reset the layer.

Region binding can be a powerful animation type, especially when coupled with Smart Bone actions and other techniques. We will be exploring these additional features in a little bit.

Using Layer binding

Layer binding allows us to anchor vector layers to bones of our choosing. This not only gives you more control over some aspects of the animation but also provides limitations of its own.

Keeping the `BoneExample.anme` file open, we will build off of the bone structure we have already established by performing the following steps:

1. Click on the **Hand** vector layer in the **Layers** panel.

2. On the toolbar to the left is the Bind Layer tool. It looks like a piece of paper with a bone on it, as shown in the following screenshot. Click on it.

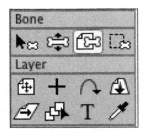

3. With the Hand vector still selected, click on the hand bone. The bone will turn red, indicating it has been selected.

4. For the sleeve and top portion of the arm, we will want to bind these to the bone that is drawn over both of them.

5. Click on the **Sleeve** layer; then click on the bone going through it.

6. Click on the **Arm Piece 2** layer, and then click on the same bone that the sleeve is attached to.

7. Click on the **Arm Piece 3** layer; then click on the bone that is drawn over it.

8. Click on the bone layer and take your Manipulate Bones tool.

9. Click-and-drag on the hand bone to move the arm. You should notice that there is a change in how the arm moves. There's much more conformity to the movement. The Bone Strength clouds have no relevance if you have everything bound to bones. In fact, you may want to disable them completely to remove some clutter from the workspace, as shown in the following screenshot:

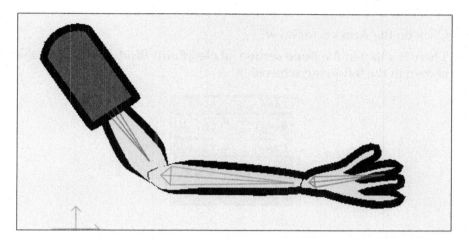

Layer binding is a much more organized way of creating movements with your assets. This is the preferred way of most longtime users, since Region binding takes a lot of effort to master. However, things have slowly evolved over the course of new versions of Anime Studio.

If you're having issues with the parts of your arm tearing or popping out of place when moving, try resizing or repositioning your bones with the Transform Bone tool. Sometimes, even a small change in size or position can help correct significant issues with layer bound bones.

Using Point binding

Point binding is sort of the middle ground between the two mentioned techniques. Here, instead of binding layers to bones, you bind individual points. This can be useful if Layer binding is too restrictive and Region binding is causing glitches or other issues. This is also the best way to bind bones if you only have one layer containing your objects.

For this example, we will open a new file titled `PointBinding.anme`. Keep the layer bound file in another tab as we will be using it as reference in the next exercise. While it looks like the same arm we used earlier, you will now notice there is only one vector layer making up the entire arm. **Bone Strengths** are off, so using the Manipulate Bones tool does nothing. Let's bind some points by performing the following steps:

1.   Click on the **Arm** vector layer.

2.   There is a tool in the **Bone** section labeled **Point Binding**. Click on that, as shown in the following screenshot:

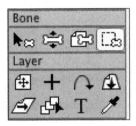

3.   This allows you to select points. You can select **Lasso Mode** from the top if you need more control.

4.   Hold down the *Alt* key and left-click on the hand bone. You could also use the Select Bone tool, but this is a nice shortcut.

5.   Select all of the points on the arm by clicking-and-dragging a box or using *Ctrl + A* (*command + A* on Mac).

6.   Click on the **Bind Points** button on the top, as shown in the following screenshot. This will ensure that all of our points are now accounted for.

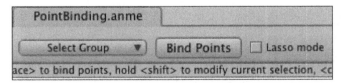

7.   Hit the *Enter* key to deselect all points.

8.   Take the Bind Points tool again, and this time only highlight the points that make up the hand (with the hand bone still selected).

9.   Click on the **Bind Points** button on the top bar.

10.   *Alt* + left-click on the forearm bone.

11. Take the Bind Points tool and select the points that make up the forearm, as shown in the following screenshot. Try to get as close as you can with the accuracy of your selection.

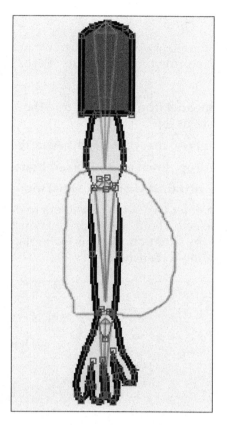

12. Hit the **Bind Points** button on the top bar.

13. Repeat these steps with the top arm bone. Making sure that the bone is selected, take the Bind Points tool, select the points that have yet to be accounted for, and click on **Bind Points**.

14. Now take the Manipulate Bones tool and move the arm around by its hand. You should notice a result similar to that of Layer binding; except, things are a bit more flexible. Pretty cool, huh?

Binding points is great if you have many assets on a layer and want to assign them to different bones. It can also be great for a more flexible look without the headaches that Region binding can bring.

Restricting bone movements

It can be helpful to restrict just how far a bone can move to avoid awkwardness with movements and positions. You can restrict the movement of any bone you wish and in varying degrees.

Let's use the layer bound (`BoneExample.anme`) arm we just set up as an example for this lesson. Click on its tab to bring the file back up. Perform the following steps to restrict bone movements:

1. Select the Select Bone tool from the toolbar to the left. It looks like a bone with a black arrow to its left.

2. Click on the middle bone that controls the **Arm Piece 3** layer.

3. On the top bar is a drop-down menu labeled **Bone Constraints**. Click on it.

4. Select the **Angle Constraints** checkbox at the top.

5. From here, you can enter two sets of numbers to determine the angle constraint for the selected bone. How far you constrain the bone will depend on your needs and the situation. For this example, let's enter -70 and 70, as shown in the following screenshot:

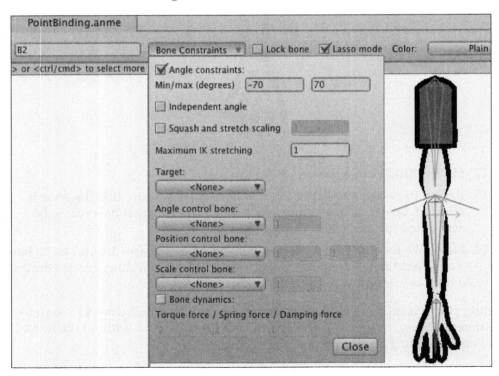

6. Two angled lines should now appear on the top of the bone. This is a visualization of the bone constraints. This helps when experimenting with different values.

7. Once you are finished, select the Manipulate Bones tool and move the arm around. Notice how the bend of the arm is restricted, yet we still have some issue with the hand moving unnaturally. Let's add some restrictions to this as well.

8. Select the hand bone with your Select Bone tool and bring up the **Angle Constraints** panel again.

9. Check the **Angle Constraints** checkbox and enter -5 and 5 for the restriction values. This will give us a little wiggle room; yet, keep the hand almost stationary during movement.

10. Now try moving the arm with the Manipulate Bones tool to see the results.

Restricting bone movements has the benefit of maintaining a certain consistency as well as hiding defects that could pop up during animation. Be sure to keep this in mind, especially as we start to design a full-fledged character.

 Anime Studio Pro 10 has introduced some great new bone constraint features that can really streamline our workflow and increase the visual flare of an animation. We will be looking at some of these options in *Chapter 8, Animating Your Characters*.

Advanced Region binding techniques

While Region binding can provide a nice "springy" cartoony look to your rigged objects, there are some issues when it comes to your bone strength spheres intersecting with other objects. Anime Studio 9.5 introduced a new feature called **Flexi-Binding**, which really helps with containing the sometimes-problematic Bone Strength spheres.

To work with this technique, let's open up the example file FlexiBindingExample. anme from the book's work files. You will see a familiar green face.

As you can see, we already have a bone structure set up for the character. We will be focusing solely on how the bones work in this exercise. Perform the following steps to work with Flexi-Binding:

1. While on the **Character Bone** layer and frame 0, select the Manipulate Bones tool.

2. Click on the bottom bone of the front arm and move it around. Notice how the Region binding is causing other parts of our character to react. Even if we were to reduce the strength of our bones as low as they can go, this will still be an issue to some extent.

3. In order to fix this, we will need to target each section of bones that we want to link to certain body parts.

4. Take the Select Bone tool and drag a selection area around the front arm. You could also select all of the arm bones by clicking on one, holding the *Shift* key, and clicking on the others. Once all of the arm bones are highlighted in red, you are set.

5. Click on the layer labeled **F.Arm** on the **Layers** panel. We are doing this because this is the layer we want to bind the bones to.

6. Now, go up to your top menu bar and navigate to **Bone | Use Selected Bones For Flexi-Binding** (*Ctrl + Shift + F* or *command + Shift + F* if on a Mac), as shown in the following screenshot:

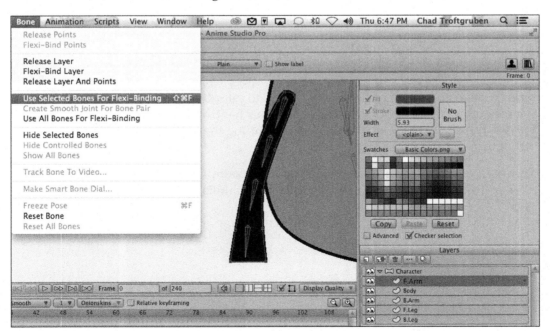

7. Repeat the preceding steps for the other arm, two legs, and body. You may need to hide the body layer to accurately identify the bones for the second arm.

After applying Flexi-Binding to all the vector layers for your bones, all your body parts should be independent and not conflict with other parts of the character.

> On frame 0, you can split up your bones and vectors using the Offset Bone tool to ensure the regions don't intersect with one another. After that, you can put everything back together on frame 1. This was the old method and is still viable. However, since Anime Studio 9.5's introduction of Flexi-Binding, offsetting bones is no longer needed.

If you decide to use Region binding for your bone structures, be sure to take advantage of the new Flexi-Binding option. It will save you a lot of headaches down the road.

Labeling, coloring, and hiding bones

If you have a lot of bones on screen, it may be a good idea to color code or display the labels of the bones on your canvas. In the file we currently have open (FlexiBindingExample.anme), the character's back arm is hidden from view due to the body. Not to mention, the body's bones intersect with this arm's bones, which can make navigating the bone structure confusing.

Let's color code the bones that make up each section of the body by performing the following steps:

1. Click on the **Select** bone tool from the toolbar to the left.
2. Click on the top bone on the front arm.
3. Keeping the *Shift* key pressed, left-click on the remaining three bones that make up that arm.

4. On the top bar is a **Color** button. It's currently set to **Plain**. Click on this button and select **Purple** from the list, as shown in the following screenshot. Notice how the bones of the arm are now purple, allowing them to stand out from all the other bones.

5. You can repeat this process if you wish by selecting other bone segments of the body and giving them different colors.

6. You don't have to color code whole limbs if you don't want to. Pick a coloring system that works best for you when it comes to organization.

7. You can also choose to switch on labels with selected bones (located next to the **Color** button). This is useful, especially if you plan to use Smart Bones, which you will be witnessing in a moment.

8. Now, with Anime Studio Pro 10, if you select a bone and navigate to **Bone | Hide Selected Bones**, the bone will vanish from your workspace. This allows you to easily interact with other bones that may be clashing with it. You can bring all bones back into view by navigating to **Bone | Show All Bones**.

Organizing bones is just as important as laying over your layers. Keep these features in mind, especially when characters start to become more complicated.

Animating bones

Like anything in Anime Studio, creating a keyframe for a bone movement is a simple matter of moving the bone when further in on the **Channels** timeline. For this, you will use the Manipulate Bones or Transform Bone tools to create the movements.

With the `FlexiBindingExample.anme` file still open, perform the following steps:

1. Select the Manipulate Bones tool.

2. Click on frame 48 on your timeline.

3. Using the Manipulate Bones tool, click on the bottom bone of the front arm and move it in any direction.

4. You will see three different channels appear for keyframes. A white bone that indicates movement is present for the bone layer, a red bone that indicates the selected bone/bones (in this case, the bottom bone of the arm), and a purple bone that shows all the purple colored bones which are currently keyed (in this case, the arm from our previous exercise).

5. If we move any other color-coded bone, we will see separate channels appearing for these as well, as shown in the following screenshot. This is of great help when wanting to identify the keyframes of certain bones.

Creating movements with your bones tends to be the easy part. Rigging the character and preparing it for animation is where most of your time will be spent.

Creating dynamic bones

A cool feature that can be applied to both Layer and Region bound bones is **Bone Dynamics**. This is where we can apply physics to certain bones so they react to movement. Good examples of this would be creating feathers that react to the movement of a wing, physics-based hair, springy objects, and so forth.

Open the example file labeled `BoneDynamics.anme`. You will see our green friend again. This time, it looks like he's sprout some antennas! We will be applying Bone Dynamics to these two layers by performing the following steps:

1. Hit the **Play** button on your timeline to see what the animation looks like. Notice how the antennas remain stationary as the character runs.

2. Go back to frame 0, take the Select Bone tool, and highlight all the bones that make up the antennas. There should be a total of six bones.

3. Click on the **Bone Constraints** drop-down menu on the top bar and notice how there is an object to enable **Bone Dynamics** at the bottom of the panel. Check the box.

4. For the **Torque**, **Spring**, and **Damping** settings, leave them as their defaults.

5. Close the panel and click on the **Play** button again. Now notice how the antennas react to the movement of the character. This is done without us having to manually animate anything out, as shown in the following screenshot:

You can change the **Torque**, **Spring**, and **Damping** settings to adjust how these bones will react to movement. Try changing the numbers to see what results you come up with. Subtle movements with Dynamic Bones can really add extra depth to your work. Try using it in different situations to see what benefits it brings.

Understanding basic Smart Bone actions

Smart Bones are actions used to correct defects that may occur during the animation process. Let's say you bend an arm using Region binding and the inside of the arm happens to cave in. You could correct this movement with a couple of actions through Smart Bones. There are more advanced uses with this feature, but we'll focus on something simple first.

Smart Bone actions are controlled through the **Actions** panel, which is located in the **Window** menu.

Open the example file `BasicSmartBones.anme` for this exercise. We will, once again, see the arm we were working with earlier in the chapter. When we bend the arm to the right, you will notice that the inside portion of the arm caves inward, as pictured in the following screenshot:

We will be using a Smart Bone action to correct this. Perform the following steps to do so:

1. Navigate to **Window | Actions**. A new panel will appear.

2. There are regular actions that can be set for animation. However, in order to determine the difference between a Smart Bone and regular action, we will need to name the Smart Bone action the same as the offending bone.

3. In this case, the middle bone is what is causing our issues. By using the Select Bone tool, we can determine that the name of this bone is **B2** on the top bar. You can rename this bone if you wish. But for this exercise, we will keep the name. Alternatively, with the bone selected, you can check **Show label** on the top bar to reveal the name of the bone on the canvas.

4. On the **Actions** panel, click on the **New Action** button and enter B2 as the name of the action, as shown in the following screenshot. Make sure you have the bone layer selected when you do this. This step is very important.

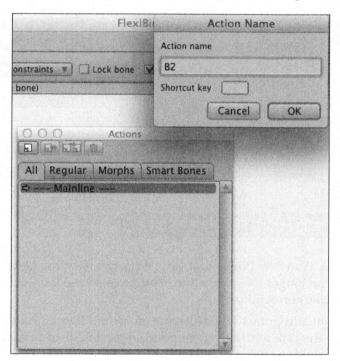

5. Click on **OK**. You will now be in the **B2** action which is signified by a red arrow pointing to the name in the list on the **Actions** panel.

6. You will be on frame 1 on the **Channels** timeline. You may also notice that the background color of your **Channels** timeline has changed to blue. All this indicates is that you are currently within the Smart Bone action. This is where we need to be.

7. Click on the **Bone** layer on your **Layers** panel and take the Transform Bone tool. It is very important to have a **Bone** layer selected before attempting to make a Smart Bone action.

8. Left-click and hold on the arm bone and bend the arm to the right as far as you can go. Notice the distortion.

9. Click on the **Arm** vector layer that is underneath the **Bone** layer on the **Layers** panel, as shown in the following screenshot. Notice how you have remained in the Smart Bone action.

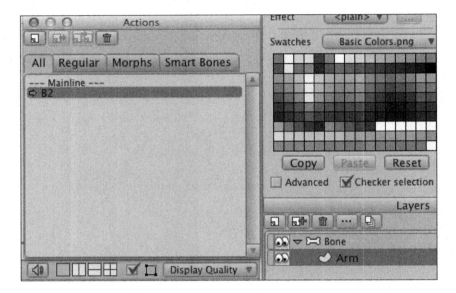

10. With your Translate Points tool, adjust the points at the bend of the arm so it no longer looks caved in. You can also use the Curvature tool to make corrections.

11. You cannot add points while altering an action. If you find you can't complete the task with the given points, you will need to back out of the action by double-clicking on **Mainline** on the **Actions** panel and then use the Add Point tool to distribute your new points. If you have to do this, you can re-enter the **B2** action by double-clicking on it to resume your work once the points are added.

12. Once you have fixed the bend, double-click on **Mainline** on your **Actions** panel.

13. While on frame 0, take the Manipulate Bones tool and bend the arm towards the right. The issue should now be corrected. If not, you can always re-enter the **B2** action to tweak the vector and bone positions some more, as shown in the following screenshot:

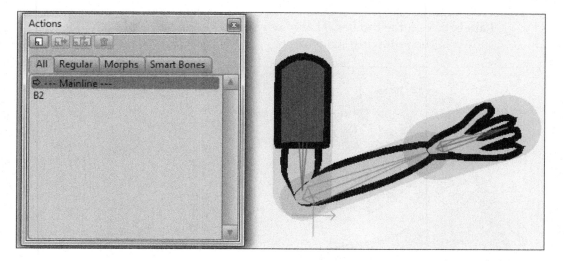

If you need to fix the arm's bend in the opposite direction, you will need to create a new action. The name of the action should be B2, space, followed by a 2 (B2 2).

Mastering Smart Bones will really help out with the animation process. In the past, Anime Studio users had to rely on manual correction whenever a bone was moved. This is no longer the case and really helps expedite the process.

Working with Smart Bone dials

Not only can Smart Bones be used to correct actions, they can also be programmed to act as dials for all sorts of different events. You can control switch layers, point animation, gradients, and more with a simple set up of bones and objects. For more advanced dials, you may need to check on **Allow nested layer control**, which is located in the main bone's **Layer Settings**. However, you more than likely will not have to bother with this as it is checked on by default.

To get an idea of how these complex actions work, open up the work file `SmartBoneDials.anme`. Here you will see our familiar green friend. He's rigged up and ready for animation. You will notice that there are additional bones sitting on the outside of the character. These have been made up ahead of time for you to play around with. They will act as dials that will set off different actions. Next, perform the following steps:

1. First, highlight all the bones outside of the character and check on the **Show Labels** box on the top bar. That way we can see the labels of each dial, as shown in the following screenshot:

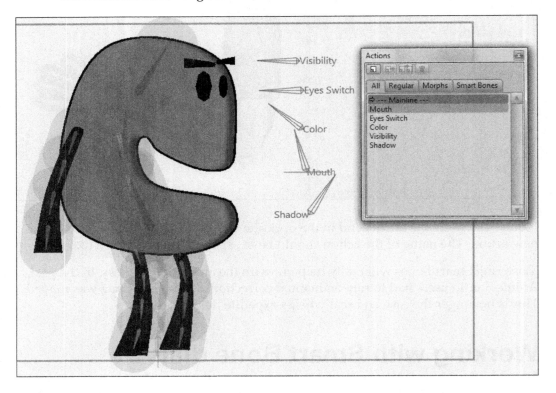

2. With the first dial (labeled **Visibility**), we can turn the layer on or off. You will need to page-forward to frame 1 to see this occur.

3. Once on frame 1, move the **Visibility** dial up. The dial's movement has been restricted greatly, but the slight adjustment will cause your layer to disappear.

4. Bring the dial back to the starting position to get the **Character** layer back into view.

5. The second dial, labeled **Eyes Switch**, controls the eyes that are currently housed in a **Switch** layer. The **Switch** layer contains two sublayers: opened eyes and closed eyes. You can see this on the **Layers** panel to get a better idea of the construction of this character.

6. Make sure you're on frame 1 again as this action can only be viewed outside of frame 0. Flicking the dial up will activate the closed position of the eye. Flicking it back down will open the eyes back up.

7. You could map out numerous switches and have them switch for different positions with the bone.

8. Try moving the **Color** dial all the way to the right. You will notice that this will gradually change the character's color from green to red. This can, of course, be used to create transitional effects for colors, even gradients. While you can do this with traditional keyframes, the dial arguably gives the user more control.

9. Moving the **Mouth** dial will result in the movement of the points that make up the mouth, as shown in the following screenshot. This can be useful for advanced lip-syncing or other animations that require precise point movements. This is similar to when we fixed the arm bend in the previous exercise.

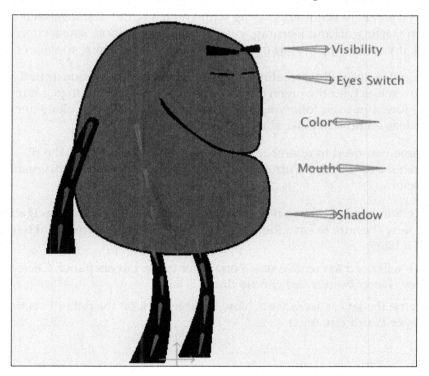

10. The **Shadow** dial is an example of how you can apply and animate color effects on your objects. Moving the dial to the right will create shading on the body. The more you move the dial to the right, the bigger the shading gets.

 Remember, any of these effects can be animated out. All you have to do is move forward on your **Channels** timeline and adjust the dials to place keyframes down. Using Smart Bones is all about streamlining the animation process.

It can take some time to get used to working with Smart Bones. As we start drawing and rigging our character, the process should become easier to understand. The great thing about creating dials is that you can custom fit them to any job you are working on.

Creating your first character

Now that you have an idea of how you want to design your characters and the importance of bone animation, let's focus on the basics of construction. In the following steps, think about your own style of design and this book's character as a template. While there is nothing wrong with you using the character style from this book when starting off and learning, you will gain much more satisfaction out of your work if you can apply your own aesthetics and personality to your creations.

For this exercise, we will be creating a human character. As demonstrated in the previous exercises with the green character, you are not limited to just humans when drawing. However, even following along with creating a human character should give you ideas on how to make different creations later on.

If at any time you need to reference the completed character, open the file CharacterComplete.anme. Perform the following steps to start with creating your first character:

1. We will need to open a new document in Anime Studio by navigating to **File | New** (be sure to save the recent example file in case you want to come back to it later).

2. We will need to create a new bone layer in the **Layers** panel. Click on the **New Layer** button and choose **Bone**.

3. Name the layer Character. Now, double-click on the default vector layer, **Layer 1**, and rename it Face.

4. Once you've done that and clicked on **OK**, grab the **Face** layer and drag it into the **Character** bone layer, as shown in the following screenshot:

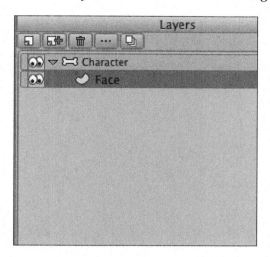

Now we can begin focusing on our drawing!

Drawing the head

The first step we will take is drawing a head for the character. This will act as a foundation for additional features we can add and adjust later on. Perform the following steps to do so:

1. Select the Add Point tool from the toolbar to the left (you can use the Freehand tool as well, if you wish).

2. On the **Styles** palette, pick a fill and stroke color along with your desired line width. Pick a line width of 4 with a black stroke color. You can alter this later if you don't like it.

3. Now, start by drawing an oval-like shape in which the top is wider than the bottom. Since this is going to be a 3/4 view of the character, you may want to scoot the thinner portion of the face forward a bit to make up a chin.

View the following example image to get an idea of what I mean. Don't worry if your drawing looks a bit different. It's all a part of the creative process.

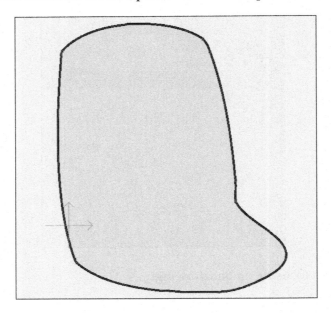

Don't be afraid to use your Transform Points and Curvature tools after tightening everything up.

Constructing the eyes

The eyes we are creating will be simple. You can certainly get very detailed with this portion of the face if you want. Don't be afraid to add or experiment with what we are doing here. Perform the following steps to construct an eye:

1. Make a new vector sublayer for the **Character** bone layer and name it Eyes.

2. Make sure to drag it above the face, otherwise our eyes will be hidden behind the head.

3. In the **Styles** palette, choose a white fill color. For your stroke, if you are not using the black color to outline your objects, you may want to select a color to compliment the fill (perhaps a light grey). You could also reduce the width size of details inside the character (such as the eyes, nose, and mouth). But this will mostly come down to personal preference and something you can explore as you advance in Anime Studio.

4. Taking the Draw Shape tool, draw out two ovals that cover the middle-right part of the face, as shown in the following screenshot. You may want to reduce the size of the second oval slightly in order to give the illusion that it's further away from the camera.

Creating small colored ovals to form irises may also be an appealing design choice for you. Remember to be creative and adapt this to your style.

5. Now let's create those pupils. Make a new vector sublayer under your bone layer and name it `Pupils`.

6. Select black as your fill and stroke color from the **Style** palette.

7. Using the Draw Shape tool again, draw two small ovals within the whites of your eyes. Make sure they're positioned evenly apart so that the character isn't cross-eyed (unless that's your intention).

8. Create a new vector sublayer for your eyebrows underneath the **Character** bone layer.

9. Select a color from the **Style** palette for your eyebrows.

10. Starting at the top of the left eye, drag out a wide rectangle that covers the length of the eye. From here, you can take the Transform Points tool and taper off the right-hand side edge of the eyebrow by moving the top and bottom points closer together.

11. Repeat this step for the right eyebrow, except taper off the left-hand side this time, as shown in the following screenshot. You can also create different-looking eyebrows by using the Add Point or Freehand tools.

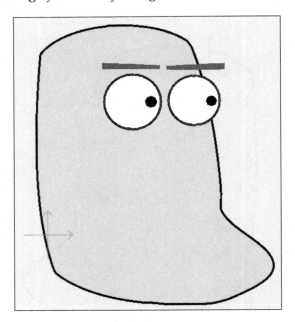

Remember, you can always copy and paste objects by selecting them with one of your selection tools and navigating to **Edit** | **Copy** (*Ctrl + C* on Windows, *command + C* on Mac) and then navigating to **Edit** | **Paste** (*Ctrl + V* on Windows, *command + V* on Mac). You could do this, for instance, with your eyes or eyebrows so that they appear symmetrical. You can also flip your objects easily, either horizontally or vertically, by using the corresponding icons on the top bar.

Making the ears

For this particular example, since we are drawing a character at an angle, we are only going to see one ear. However, you may draw two ears if you're doing things a little bit differently than instructed in the following steps:

1. Create a new vector sublayer under the **Character** bone layer and name it Ear. Make sure it is positioned above the **Face** layer in the list.

2. Take the Draw Shape tool and position the cursor near the edge of the left-hand side of the face so that it somewhat lines up with your eyes.

3. Click-and-drag out an oval that is close to the size of your eyes. Obviously, different designs will warrant different ear sizes, so in most cases it comes down to eyeballing it.

4. From here, we will want to get rid of the curve that is on the right-hand side of the oval. Select the Add Point tool and place two points above and below the point to the right.

5. Take the Hide Edge tool and click on the lines in between these two new points to hide the curves. The ear should now look something like the one shown in the following screenshot:

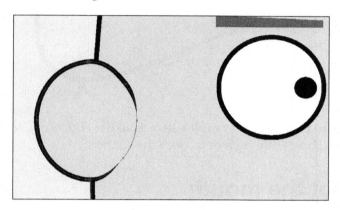

From here, you are free to alter the ear further by adding more points, details, earrings, or whatever you want!

Drawing the nose

The nose can bring a lot of personality to our character. Noses come in many shapes and sizes, so what you do with it may very well decide the fate of your character's personality and dating life. Perform the following steps to draw a nose:

1. After considering the shape of your nose, create a new vector sublayer under the **Character** bone layer and name it Nose.

2. Up to this point, if you've been using a tablet, you'll probably want to sketch the nose like anything else. If not, take the Add Point tool and position your cursor under the two eyes.

3. For this example, we'll be drawing a rather long, cartoonish nose. At the position under the eyes, create a point.

4. Now drag down and to the right a bit, and set a second point.

5. Go further right and add another. Basically, what we're doing here is creating a shape of a peanut. Keep adding points until you get a desired shape for your nose. Look at the following example picture to get an idea:

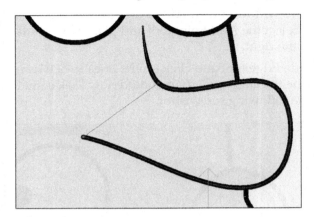

Now you can close the object in completely or take the Hide Edge tool to hide the line that is intersecting with the face to close the shape.

Laying out the mouth

With the mouth, you may want to create a switch layer and draw multiple instances of movement. This is especially true if you want to have the character talk in your movie. Or perhaps you would like to use some Smart Bone actions to create mouth movement? Either method will work. For this book, we will be showing you how to create mouth movements with switch layers. Perform the following steps to draw a mouth:

1. Create a new switch layer for the **Character** bone layer and label it Mouth.

2. Double-click on the switch layer and click on the **Switch** tab. Select the **Interpolate sublayers** option. Click on the **OK** button on the bottom of the **Layer Settings** panel.

3. Create a new vector sublayer for the **Mouth** switch layer. Label this Open.

4. Select a black stroke and fill color from the **Style** palette.

5. Taking the Add Point tool, move your cursor below the nose, but not so that it overlaps the chin.

6. For this, we will be creating a fairly simple mouth. You can get very detailed with your mouths; the design will be dependent on how your character looks. If you utilize masking, you could create teeth and a tongue and have them exposed through the mouth.

7. Create an oval shape with at least eight points making up the object. We want enough points to be present so that we can move them around to create different shapes for our mouth poses. This is the open position for the mouth.

8. Once you have the mouth drawn out and placed in the proper position, navigate to your **Layers** panel and click on the **Duplicate** layer button.

9. Name the new layer Closed.

10. Select the Transform Points tool.

11. Within the **Closed** layer, we are going to take the points and move them all together to create a closed mouth. We want it to look like a line. Right now, we are creating a neutral expression. We will use the same technique to create a grin or frown in a bit.

12. Now from here, you can repeat the steps to create different poses, including phonemes for F, Th, and S.

13. You can also create variations of these poses for happy, sad, and/or angry.

The following screenshot shows the output of the mentioned steps:

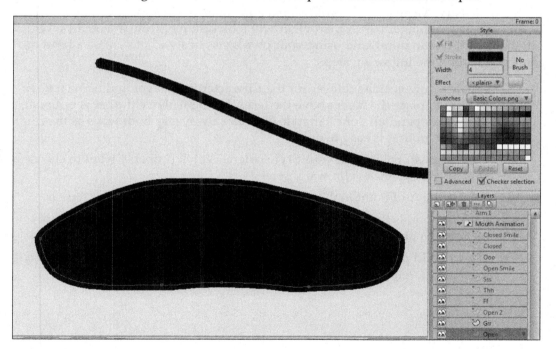

Just note that if you want to interpolate the keyframes, that is, have Anime Studio automatically animate between switches, you will need to keep the same points. This may be impossible to do when it's required to draw in teeth or other elements, unless you are using a mask.

As an example, you may want to create an S phoneme that has two poses: one with a wider mouth and one that is more closed. If you then go from an open mouth without teeth to an S phoneme, you can hide the fact that no interpolating is taking place between those two particular switches by making the mouth sizes near identical.

When in doubt, you can always open up the finished character for this lesson entitled `CharacterComplete.anme` to examine the mouth poses.

Designing the hair

You can get really creative with the hair, from the color to the flow. Hair can tell a lot about a character. Think about Fry's hair from *Futurama*. The messiness matches him perfectly as he has traits of laziness, foolishness, and so on. Messy hair could also be a sign of artistry. Meanwhile, a professional and smart businessperson may be seen with properly groomed hair. A man's hair will look different from a woman's. With all these variables in mind, and using your own sense of style, let's create a head of hair performing the following steps:

1. Create a new vector sublayer for the **Character** bone layer and name it `Hair`. Be sure to place the layer above the face. Placing it above the ear is optional; this will depend on your hairstyle (you can always try both ways as moving the layer around is easy to do).

2. Choose a hair color from your **Style** palette. You'll probably want to choose a similar color to the eyebrows.

3. Taking the Add Point tool, I will start from the right-hand side of the ear.

4. Creating points that go downward and eventually back up to form a thin rectangular shape, we will draw out the sideburn for this male character.

5. We will add points that will bring the hair up and to the right-hand side so it meets the forehead.

6. Wrapping up and around the head, we will bring our points to come back behind the ear. Finally, we will close the shape by meeting back up with the sideburn, as shown in the following screenshot:

This is a very basic example of creating a head of hair. We could, of course, add many details to create something more elaborate. This again depends on your design sensibilities.

Drawing the neck

The neck is probably the simplest thing we will draw for the character. However, there are many variables to consider. With this book's character, you will notice the neck is pretty skinny. This is matched with the disproportionate head. However, when you look at the human body, the neck really isn't that skinny as it matches the width of the bottom portion of the head. It's meant to support the head after all, so it needs to be built to do so. With this book's design, you'd think the character's head would snap off his neck. If this is something you don't like, you can always create a different-looking neck. Perform the following steps to draw a neck:

1. Create a new vector sublayer under the **Character** bone layer and name it Neck. Place the new layer under the **Head** layer.

2. Grab the rectangle from the Draw Shape tool and draw a small rectangle under the left-hand side portion of the face, as shown in the following screenshot. You may need to alter some of the points later on, but that can be determined after drawing the body.

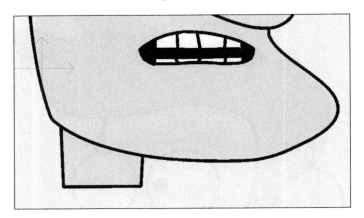

See, pretty simple! And again, this will vary with different designs.

Building the body

The shape of the body also says a lot about your character. Is your character skinny? Maybe she is elderly and has a slight hump in the back? Maybe he's an obsessed body builder? These are elements you should think about before proceeding. Perform the following steps to draw a body for your character:

1. To begin, create a new vector sublayer under the **Character** bone layer and name it Body. Place the layer below the neck on the list.

2. Next, select a color for your shirt in the **Style** palette and select the Add Point tool.

3. Starting from the bottom-left part of the neck, we will place points to drop a fairly straight line going past the neck towards the right.

4. Direct the points downward till you are satisfied with the height of the character, then loop on the bottom to create the pelvis.

5. Keep adding lines and moving up, finally connecting with the first point you started with, as shown in the following screenshot:

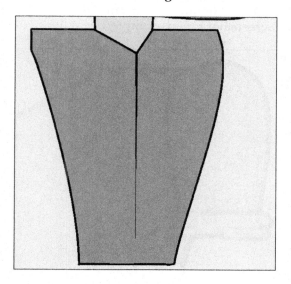

Feel free to add details such as buttons, creases, and so on.

Drawing the arms

Long sleeves or short? That will probably be your first decision. Next, you will need to tailor the arms to your body type. If you drew someone muscular, you will probably need to create some definition for the arms. Also, you have to decide on the length of your arms. A cartoony style can be more liberal with this trait. Also, keep in mind, depending on the effect you want to produce through bone rigging, that you can draw your entire arm on one layer similar to the green character example files we played with before. However, for this example, I will be creating different layers for different parts of the arm using the following steps:

1. Create a new vector sublayer in the **Character** bone layer and label it F.Arm Sleeve. The F will stand for front. Position the sleeve so that it is above the body layer. Select the same color you drew out for your body. To do so, you can select the Eyedropper tool to copy all the properties from the body object.

2. Next, take the Add Point tool and start near the front shoulder.

3. Create some points that go downward, expand near the bottom, and then close the object up by connecting to your first point. You can also create some details near the bottom if you want the sleeve to be rolled up. View the following screenshot for an example:

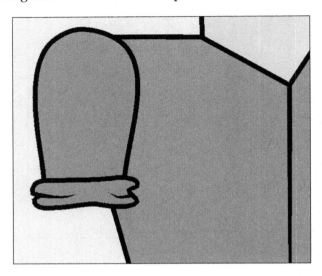

Next, let's create the top portion of the actual arm by performing the following steps:

1. Create a new vector sublayer under the **Character** bone layer and name it F.Arm Top. Position the layer so that it is under the sleeve.

2. Selecting your skin color from the face with the Eyedropper tool, take the Add Point tool and position the cursor so that it is partly under the sleeve.

3. Creating a few points going downward, we eventually want to go inward to set up the elbow and arm bend.

4. From that taper point, we will bring our points up the other side into the sleeve and connect it with the first arm point.

5. After that, we will make a new vector sublayer under the **Character** bone layer and name it F.Arm Bottom.

6. With the same colors and Add Point tool selected, place your cursor near the left-hand side of the taper point of the top part of the arm.

7. Create some points leading down that will eventually taper in again for the wrist

8. Wrap your points up and connect with the first point so that the object matches the width and length of the top part of your arm, as shown in the following screenshot:

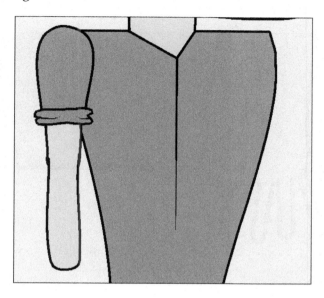

Like the mouth, you may want to create a switch layer for the hand. This will allow you to create different positions such as an open hand, closed hand, or pointed finger. Smart Bones also work here and you can create a number of preset poses using point animation and dial positions. For this exercise, we will stick with a static hand. Different hand poses can always be implemented later as well (this goes for any body part that could use a switch layer).

Drawing a convincing hand can be tough. Practice makes perfect, but it can sometimes take a few times to get it right. Just make sure you don't give up! Perform the following steps to create a switch layer for the hand:

1. Like our other arm segments, create a new vector sublayer under the **Character** bone layer and name it Hand.

2. Move the **Hand** layer above your bottom arm layer and select the Add Point tool from the **Tool** panel.

3. Placing your cursor on the right-hand side of the bottom taper point on the arm, start adding points that go down and to the right-hand side.

4. Create a small loop and bring the points back to form the thumb.

5. From here, draw the fingers by placing points to form four distinct shapes, each evenly spaced apart (with the bottom parts of the fingers being closer to each other than the top parts). The end result should look similar to the following screenshot:

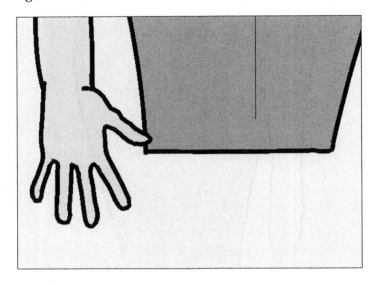

If you face difficulties drawing the hand this way, go online and find examples of hands, cartoon or real, which appeal to you. There is nothing wrong with referencing something as long as it's not blatantly copied. Finally, you don't have to draw an open hand. Sometimes, drawing a closed fist is easier to achieve, especially if you're just starting out with drawing. From here, your next task is to draw the second arm using the same steps as shown previously.

6. You will need to place the layer so that they are behind the body and match the position of the right-hand side shoulder.

7. Depending on how much variation you are shooting for, you can also duplicate your layers from the first arm and reposition them in the desired locations.

8. Just remember, when it comes to the hand, you will need to do some tweaks as we are now seeing the inside of the hand as opposed to the outside that we were seeing with the other arm.

9. By the time you're done, depending on how you are drawing your character, the second arm may be completely hidden from view by the body. When we get into character movements, the arm will make itself visible again, so don't worry about that. The outcome of these steps is as follows:

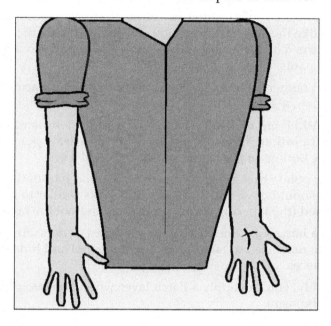

The upper body is now done! Time to move downwards.

Designing the legs

Like the arms, the legs follow a pretty basic process for construction. If your character is wearing shorts, you can create an extra layer for that and treat it like the sleeves on the character's arms. Along with the type of pants, you will need to figure out what your character will be putting on his/her feet. All of these details will form a representation of your character even without the aid of dialogue. Perform the following steps to draw legs for your character:

1. Create a new vector sublayer in the **Character** bone layer and label it F.Leg Top. Move this layer below the body on the **Layers** panel.

2. Selecting a color for our character's pants from the **Styles** palette, take the Add Point tool with **Sharp Corners** turned on (located on the top bar) and place the cursor on the bottom-left position of the body (some intersecting can occur).

3. Start by creating some points that taper downward a bit, similar to what you did with the top portion of your arm.

4. Then circle back to the top portion of the leg and connect your points to form what may appear to be a tapered-off rectangle. Don't be afraid to use your Transform Points tool to adjust any of the design attributes of the object. If you don't like the jagged design, you can always create the pants with **Sharp Corners** turned off. This will allow you to add curves, giving off an illusion of baggier pants.

5. Now, add another vector sublayer underneath the **Character** bone layer and label it `F.Leg Bottom`.

6. With the Add Point tool still selected, start on the left-hand side of the tapered-off portion of the top part of the leg and draw points downward, leaving the bottom of the leg expanded outward a bit.

7. Loop your points back up to connect with the top part of the leg. What you should have now is a piece that looks similar to your top portion, just reversed (the tapering occurs on the top and not the bottom).

8. If there is a horizontal line that intersects the two connecting leg pieces, you may need to take your Hide Edge tool and hide the line on one or both leg pieces.

9. Alternatively, you can apply a **Patch** layer where the two pieces intersect to cover up the seam.

   The following screenshot shows the outcome of the previous steps:

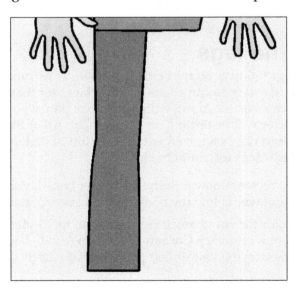

Now it's time to create the foot. Of course, you have decisions to make here as well. Barefoot? Boots? Flip-flops? Sneakers? The choices may be overwhelming, but just remember, you have complete control over this character's destiny (and shoe shopping is serious business). Perform the following steps to create the foot part of your character:

1.   Create a new vector sublayer underneath the **Character** bone layer and label it F.Foot.

2.   Choose a color for your shoe and grab the trusty Add Point tool with the **Sharp Corners** feature turned off.

3.   Position your cursor so it's under the bottom-left portion of your leg (some intersecting will probably occur).

4.   Construct some points moving downwards a bit, then move to the left and create a bulge (this will be our heel).

5.   Moving right (and creating the bottom portion of the foot), we will create a horizontal line going across for as long as you want (the longer the line, the bigger the foot).

6.   We will create a slight curve moving up, then a wider curve that moves inward. Points should start to come up to match the y axis of the first point, and from here we will need to reconnect to complete the shape. The following screenshot shows our completed character:

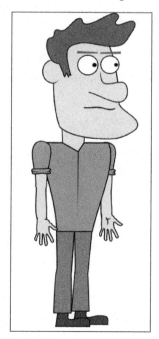

This is a very basic example of a boot-like shoe and your methods will vary depending on the design you choose. For the second leg, repeat the previous steps. Or, if you wish, you can duplicate the existing layers to build the limb.

Rigging your character

The final step of constructing our character is setting up the bones for the **Character** bone layer. After all, what good is a bone layer without bones? There is certainly a method to this when it comes to bone order, position, and so forth. Luckily, bones can be easily reshaped or positioned if things don't work correctly the first time.

Drawing the bones

Drawing bones is easy. The important thing to remember is that there is a hierarchy to your bones. This should make more sense as we start rigging. Keep in mind that you can always check out the completed character for this exercise to break down how everything works. Perform the following steps to draw the bones:

1. Make sure you have the **Character** bone layer selected.
2. On your tool bar, grab the Add Bone tool and place the cursor near the pelvic area of your character.
3. Starting with the top of the bone, hold down your left mouse button and drag downwards a little to create a small pelvis bone.
4. Upon releasing, the top part of the bone should be thick and the bottom part tapered off. This bone will be used for tilting our character at the waist.
5. Next, place your cursor above the pelvis bone so there is a small space between the two.
6. Starting from the bottom going up, hold down the left mouse button and draw a bone that reaches from the bottom portion of the body to the middle, as shown in the following screenshot:

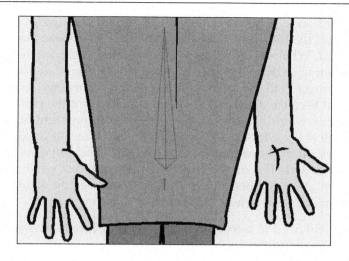

7. Add another bone that goes from the middle to the top of the body (near the neck).

8. Place two more bones that cover both the neck and the head.

9. Draw at least two bones that branch off from the head and intersect with the hair. Make sure that when you draw the second hair bone, you select the head bone first so that both hair bones link to the head, as shown in the following screenshot:

For these first few bones, what we have done is created a simple hierarchy. To see this in action, select the Reparent Bone tool. Arrows will appear that show where each bone is linked. What you should see are arrows leading down from each bone, eventually connecting to the pelvis. So, in other words, the head is connected to the neck, which is connected to the torso, which is in turn connected to the pelvis. This order is important because if we had the head connected to the pelvis, for instance, the structure simply wouldn't work. If you ever need to reparent or reconnect a bone, simply use the Select Bone tool to select the offending bone, take your Reparent Bone tool, and then click on the bone you want to link it to. You can also, as a shortcut, hold the *Alt* key and left-click on the bone you want to select while using the Reparent Bone tool. You are then free to click on the bone you want to connect it to. Perform the following steps to add the bones for the arms:

1. First, we will need to select the top torso bone. It only makes sense to have our arms linked to the torso.

2. Select the Add Bone tool, and starting with the top of the arm, draw down until you meet the bend of the arm.

3. Move the cursor down slightly and draw down, creating a second bone that ends near the wrist of the hand.

4. Finally, draw down from the wrist, covering the hand with a small bone.

5. You will want to repeat the preceding steps for your second arm. Just remember to select the top torso bone before drawing out your bones.

6. With our legs, we will need to select the pelvis bone as the parent bone.

7. With your Add Bone tool, start with the top-left part of the leg and draw down until you meet the top of the bend or knee.

8. From the bottom of the bend or knee, draw down until you meet the ankle.

9. With the foot, you're going to want to start at the heel and draw a horizontal line that meets the tip or toes.

10. Repeat the steps for the second leg. Be sure to select the pelvis bone before proceeding.

11. By clicking on the Reparent Bone tool, you will see how every bone is connected to ensure you did things correctly, as shown in the following screenshot:

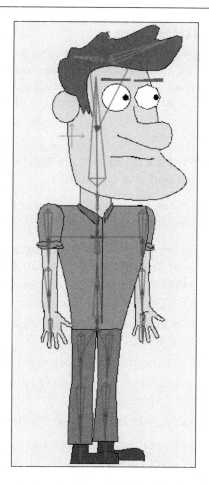

It looks like our bones are good to go! Now we just have to bind everything.

 Additional bones can always be added to the character. Examples of this may include shoulder bones or additional torso bones. If the rig in this chapter is too limited for you, don't be afraid to branch out and explore.

Binding the bones

As of now, if you try to move your bones around with the Manipulate Bones tool, you'll probably get some weird things occurring, far from the desired effect you're looking for. As discussed before, by default, Anime Studio uses Region Binding to control bones. Using the new Flexi-Binding features to bind our layers to bones can control these distortions.

There is no harm in mixing the techniques. Some objects may be better bound to layers while others work great for Region or Point Binding. Smart Bone actions can really help clean up any defect that you encounter.

We will be implementing all three binding techniques for the final portion of this exercise, by perform the following steps:

1. Let's start with the first bone and work our way up. Our pelvis bone, at least for this character design, has no layer to bind to. So we can leave it alone and move on to the torso bones.

2. With the Select Bone tool, select the bottom bone for the torso.

3. Click on the **Body** layer and select the Bind Points tool. Highlight the entire body and click on **Bind Points** at the top.

4. Now, highlight the lower points of the torso and click on **Bind Points**.

5. Deselect the bottom bone by clicking on the *Enter* key. Press *Alt* + left-click on the top torso bone to select it.

6. Highlight the top torso points and click on the **Bind Points** button.

7. If you have other layers relating to the torso (ties, collars, and so on), be sure to select those layers and include them with your binding.

8. Moving up, we will use the Layer Binding method. Take your Bind Layer tool; bind your neck layer to the neck bone and bind all face layers (eyes, nose, mouth, and so on) to the head bone. Remember, you will need to select the vector layer you want to bind to do this; then click on the desired bone with the Bind Layer tool.

9. For the hair, we will be using Region Binding. Take the Bone Strength tool and enlarge both hair clouds so that they cover the entire area of the hair.

10. Highlight both hair bones with your Select Bone tool and click on the **Bone Constraints** drop-down menu. Select **Bone Dynamics**. Set the values for **Torque**, **Spring**, and **Damping** to 1. This will give our character's hair some extra bounce when moving.

11. With the arms, we will use the Bind Layer tool again. We will bind the top portion of the arm and sleeve to the top bone, bottom part of the arm to the middle bone, and hand to the hand bone.

12. The legs will follow a similar method, with the top portions being bound to the top part of the legs, the middle bones being bound to the bottom part of the legs, and the feet being bound to the horizontal bones.

The following screenshot shows the outcome of the previous steps:

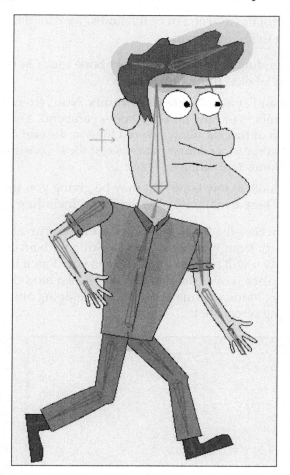

Look at that! Our character is alive!

Polishing things up

Even with all the precautions we've taken up to this point, very rarely does a rigged character work right the first time. Try taking your Manipulate Bones tool and moving some limbs around. One of the following things will probably occur: limbs will move unrealistically, layers will have visible lines or seams intersecting with limbs, or layers will move outside of the intended bounds. The first issue is, fortunately, easy to fix. The other two will require some trial and error on your part.

First, in order to control the movement of the limbs, we can place restrictions or constraints, using the following steps:

1. Select the offending bone with the Select Bone tool. On your top bar, you will have a button labeled **Bone Constraints**.

2. Click on that and enable **Angle Constraints**. Now, from here, you can adjust the numbers of how far your bones can bend. You have a visual representation of this showing two red lines at the end of the bone on the canvas. And you can, of course, always test these constraints by using the Manipulate Bones tool while on frame 0.

3. Apply constraints to any bone that may be giving you undesired movements. These usually involve the limbs, including hands and feet.

For the seams, that's where the **Patch** layer comes in. You can also go in and manually hide the seam from view if you are working with an earlier version of Anime Studio. What you will need to do is create a new **Patch** layer, link it to the offending layer, and place it over the seam. You can also bind the patch to the closest bone so the seam stays hidden no matter what you're doing animation wise, as shown in the following screenshot:

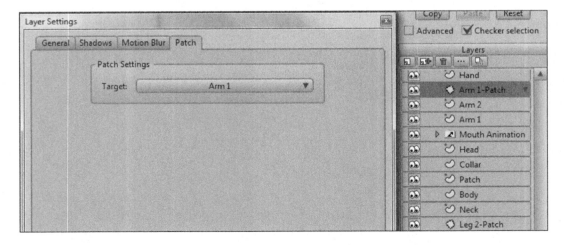

The last problem, layers poking out and breaking, will require some tweaking with the bones and vectors. You may need to reposition your bones slightly, adjust the size, or alter the shape or size of your vectors. This process will take the maximum amount of time and it requires a lot of patience. Sometimes, even seemingly minor things can cause an ugly-looking body movement, so be sure to consider all options when working. Smart Bones can also be used to help correct these issues.

Feel free to add shading, shadows, and other effects to enhance the character's visual properties.

If you'd like to compare your character, remember to open the file `CharacterComplete.anme`. This should also allow you to troubleshoot any problem you may be facing.

Summary

Rigging a character for bone animation is the heart and soul of Anime Studio. While there are many elements to consider, mastering bone placement, learning the three binding types, and experimenting with Smart Bone actions will take you a long way when animating characters. Finally, keep practicing your design skills. As you get better acquainted with the drawing tools, your characters and assets will start finding a life of their own.

In the next chapter, we will focus on designing the scenery for our cartoon. We will look into creating props and other elements as well.

6
Developing Your Cartoon's Scenery

Now that you have your cartoon character drawn and rigged up, it's time to focus on creating an environment for it to interact with. A lot of what you will be doing here will be similar to designing your cartoon character. We will continue to use the draw, fill, and layer tools to create a sense of depth.

In this chapter, we will cover the following topics:

- Being consistent
- Discussing scene design
- Drawing your scenery
- Creating scene depth
- Polishing up your scene

Being consistent

As discussed in earlier chapters, when planning and designing your characters, having a consistent design is essential in order to create a visually pleasing production. Unsurprisingly, the same goes for scenery. As you start with the initial stages of your production, you will want to make sure your backgrounds compliment the main attraction, which will more than likely be your characters. There is really no direct route to achieve this. You can browse the mass catalog of online animations and discover everything from painted scenery to more minimalistic backgrounds. The key is that once you discover your look, you strive to maintain it throughout your work.

Discussing scene design

While there are several routes you can take when designing scenery, or characters for that matter, the following are a couple of tips that may help you when planning out your scenes:

- Keep the outlines of your backgrounds lighter or thinner than those of your characters. At the very least, don't make your background outlines thicker than that of your foreground objects. Of course, this doesn't apply if you decide not to use strokes at all for your designs. However, this technique will allow your foreground objects, such as characters, to stand out more while animating your cartoons. If you're using black outlines for your characters, you could probably try changing the color of your outlines for the background to see if it provides more of a *pop*. The following screenshot demonstrates how lines and colors can clash with background objects if not careful:

- The same concept applies for fill colors. If you have bright, vibrant colors making up the background, they could wash out the appearance of your foreground objects. The same applies if you have a man wearing a green shirt against a green hill as an example. Depending on the variations of green you use, it could make the character hard to see.

- To give your cartoon a more cinematic quality, you can apply a depth of field effect, or in other words, blur out certain elements of your scene to showcase your main characters or objects. You will see this technique done all the time in films and television shows. As discussed in the previous chapters, you can apply this effect automatically or manually in Anime Studio. To have the software take care of it for you, go to **File** | **Project Settings** and check on the **Depth of Field** option. Here, you can adjust the variables for the distance and focal depth to dictate when things go out of focus and just how blurry they look. For more control, it's usually best to manually blur the layers as opposed to relying on Anime Studio to do it for you. The following screenshot shows an example of applying the mentioned suggestions. With these corrections, you can see that the character now stands out more from the background.

Setting up shots effectively

While working with your characters and scenes, displaying the elements on screen in a particular way is just as important as any of the steps outlined in the point we are going to discuss. Composing shots well can really make the difference between an animation that looks amateurish and one that looks professional. When starting out, you may be more concerned about the story or learning the tools to pay too much attention to these details. However, it's something you will want to pick up quickly for the sake of your work.

Composing shots, like anything in animation, is something that will improve with practice and research. The following are a couple of tips for you when you set up your assets and camera positions:

- First, watch your head room. One of the biggest offences seen in animated works (especially if the animator is new) is one that displays a close-up shot of a character, yet leaving ample head room that displays nothing of importance, as shown in the following screenshot:

- There is nothing wrong with slightly cutting off the top or bottom of the head in cases like this. At least, in a scenario like this, you will have a primary focus on the screen.
- Try to eliminate any dead space the scene may have. Having room above the head is a good example of this, but a good rule of thumb is that if the element you are showing isn't important, don't show it. The following screenshot shows a shot that is more properly composed than the previous attempt:

If you have two characters situated on the right-hand side of the screen holding a conversation, and nothing but a solid blank wall on the left, try to spruce things up a bit. Add some props to the left, or even some commotion (people, or cars moving by, and so on). This doesn't mean you should add elements that have no relevance to your work. Just think about what looks interesting and breathe some life into the universe you are creating. This will not only help in composing shots but also make the cartoon more engaging.

Drawing your scenery

While designing the scenery, there are many ways in which you could approach your scene depending on what your script calls for. Does your story lead to a spooky cave? Maybe it all takes place in a house. Perhaps you have many different scenes that take place in a variety of exotic locations. Whatever the case, you will need to plan your background according to where your story is taking the viewer.

For this piece of scenery, you can browse for the project file named `OutsideScenery.anme`, which you downloaded with this book in the `Chapter 06` folder. Use this if you face issues with parts of this section or if you just want to see the finished result.

To get started, let's create a new document in Anime Studio so that we have a blank slate to work with. After going to **File | New**, we will be ready to draw up a simple, yet effective backdrop. For this example, we will be creating an outside shot, something you may find in the countryside. This simple exercise should hopefully kick your creative juices in gear and allow you to build more complex and diverse scenes in the future.

Overlaying the sky

The sky is probably the simplest thing we will end up producing with this backdrop. Perform the following steps to overlay the sky:

1. In your new document, rename Layer 1 to Sky. This will help with organization.

2. Select the Draw Shape tool from the left-hand side toolbar and select the Rectangle option on the top.

3. Depending on your style, we could just draw the sky using a solid color. In this case though, we will be taking advantage of the gradient fill option to create the effect of different colors in the sky. This may be especially effective if you want to depict a sky in the morning or at dusk.

4. From the **Style** palette, click on the **Effect** drop-down menu and select **Gradient**, as shown in the following screenshot:

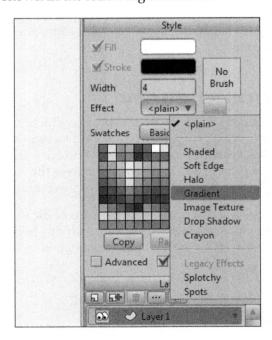

5. From here, a new panel will appear where you can alter the colors.

6. To change the color of the left side of the gradient, double-click on the left-most box underneath the color spectrum. A color swatch will appear, and you can choose any color you wish.

7. In this case, let's select a light blue color. Click on **OK** to close the panel.

8. Now, follow the same steps with the right-hand side box. This time, choose a dark blue color. Once you click on **OK**, you should see how this color will look with the oval example in the panel.

9. You can make any adjustments to the color (for instance, if you don't like how the different blues merge), even add another color swatch if you wish, by simply clicking anywhere underneath the color spectrum, as shown in the following screenshot. If you wish, you can also move the boxes around by clicking-and-dragging. This can alter the intensity of the gradient where the selected color is.

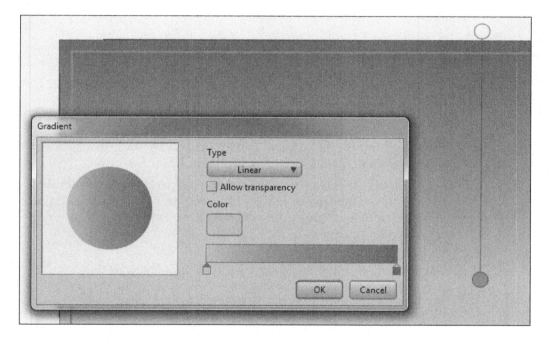

10. Once the gradient color appears to your liking, simply click on **OK** in the panel.

11. Now, let's draw out the sky. With the Rectangle tile selected, click-and-drag to create a rectangle that covers the entire document area. If you go outside the document's boundaries, that's fine. It's better to have too much than have a part of the document not covered, as shown in the following screenshot:

12. Finally, to make sure the sky doesn't pan around on us while using the Camera tools, we will need to select an option in Layer Settings.

13. Double-click on the Sky layer in your **Layers** panel, and on the **General** tab at the bottom, click on **Immune to camera movements**. Now, we don't have to worry about the rectangle area going off the canvas when we perform pans and other camera movements.

Remember, if your gradient isn't displaying how you want it to, choose the **Select Shape** tool and adjust the gradient with the red line and ovals that appear. You can change the spread and direction of the gradient to change the intensity. Play with this to get an effect you are happy with.

Creating the first piece of land

Let's draw up a chunk of land on which our main action will take place. There are several ways to approach this, but we will choose to use the **Add Point** tool to lay out the land, and perform the following steps:

1. We will need to create a new layer to keep the land separated from the sky. In the **Layers** panel, click on the **New Layer** button, choose **Vector**, and name it Land Piece 1.

2. Along with this, you may want to choose a new color from your **Style** palette. Since our goal here is to create some grass, we will be using a variant of green (color code **#5CB44E** to be exact). You can continue to use gradients if you wish or go for a solid color. Make sure you turn **Gradient** off in the **Effect** drop-down menu if you wish to go the solid color route.

3. Also, for this example, we will be using a dark green stroke color to offset the background elements from any characters.

4. Select the Add Point tool, as shown in the following screenshot:

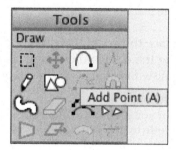

5. Placing your cursor past the left side of the document, yet nearly centered vertically, move the cursor to the right while you place some points down.

6. In the case of an outside environment, we want the ground to be slightly uneven in order to give it a more natural look. So, while adding points, move down slightly and then back up to create this look.

7. Once you have set down points across your document, you will need to circle back to the first point and close off the shape to fill everything in. To effectively do this, make sure you create your ground to extend outside of the left and right boundaries of your document, as shown in the following screenshot:

When circling back around, place those points below the bottom boundary of your document. As far as connecting the dots and creating a solid shape is concerned, that should be something you are now familiar with due to our character-creation exercise.

> Remember, when you are in the color selector, you have the ability to enter a color code to get an exact tone (located at the bottom right of the panel). This is why numbers for scenery pieces in this chapter are provided, in the event you want to copy the color verbatim.

Compare your drawing to the preceding screenshot to ensure you have come up with something similar.

Laying down the second piece of land

To add some depth to this backdrop, we will create a second piece of ground that will be placed behind the first. Most of the steps will remain the same with just a couple of adjustments, which are as follows:

1. We will need to create a new layer for this piece of land. In the **Layers** panel, create a Vector layer and name it Land Piece 2. Drag the layer downward so that it is placed below **Land Piece 1**.

2. Select a solid or gradient color that is slightly darker than that of the first piece of land. In this case, I will continue to use a solid color with a fill green variant of **#509745**, as shown in the following screenshot:

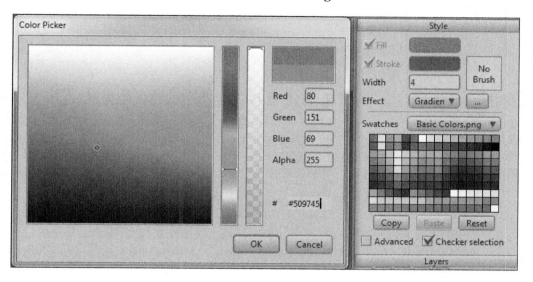

3. With the Add Point tool, move the cursor up so that it is a couple of inches above the first piece of land. Lay out some points.

4. You can follow a similar process to that of **Land Piece 1**; just make sure you vary the points so that the shape isn't identical to the first.

5. Once you've created your outline from left to right, loop back around and close the shape off just like you did before.

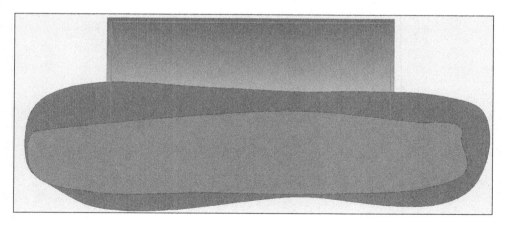

The previous screenshot shows two land pieces down! Pretty easy, right?

Would you like to use an image as a reference while drawing? That's easy! Simply go to **File | Import | Tracing Image**. Select the image you want from your computer, and it will be brought onto your workspace. The best part? It's transparent and fixed, allowing you to easily see everything while you trace. The image will go away once the document is closed.

Drawing hills with the Draw Shape tool

To finish off with our grassy land pieces, we are going to place some hills in the background. This should give the illusion that we are in a wide open space. To spice things up, we could add a forest of trees, snowy mountains, or any other type of landmark. Draw hills using the following steps:

1. Create a new Vector layer and label it `Hills`. Make sure it is placed below **Land Piece 2**.

2. Take the Create Shape tool from the left-hand side toolbar and select a darker green color from the **Style** palette (the exact color we will be using is color code #304F29). Your outline should blend more with the hills' fill color, as we don't want the hills to be seemingly popping out for us. You could even make the stroke the same color as the fill; it depends on your own style and preferences.

3. We will start by creating a simple oval, hiding the bottom portion of it with the second land piece. For a good point of reference, hide the middle of the hill with the second land layer.

4. Repeat this step from left to right until your backdrop horizon is covered with hills, as shown in the following screenshot:

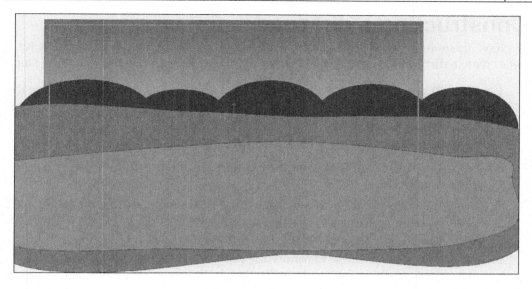

As we are creating a grassy area, our hills are simple, green, and round. However, if you were designing a desert or snow-covered area, you would want to change things up, perhaps change the shape of the hills and apply a different color.

You may notice that as you draw the hills, the one that was last drawn appears to overlap with the previous one (if you chose to make your outline darker than the fill). If you want to mix this up, you can click on the shape that you want to bring to the front with the Select Shape tool, hold down *Shift* on the keyboard, and hit the up arrow key. Additionally, you can use the down arrow key to shift objects behind others that are on the same layer.

Constructing a dirt road

We have the main piece of land, but it could probably do with a little more character. Let's create a dirt road to add to this countryside's backdrop, using the following steps:

1. We will need a new Vector layer for this. Label it Road and place it above the **Land Piece 1** layer.

2. Select a brown solid or gradient color from the **Style** palette and set your stroke color to compliment the fill. The fill color we will be using is #C6C0AC.

3. Select the Add Point tool from the left-hand side tool bar if it isn't already selected.

4. In a similar fashion to how we created the land pieces, from left to right, position a few points on your new layer. You will probably want to position these so that they're near the top of the first land mass.

5. Also, it may make sense to follow the path of the line of this land mass as closely as possible, since technically they both take up the same plane.

6. Once you've added your points, loop back around and connect to fill in the object, as shown in the following screenshot:

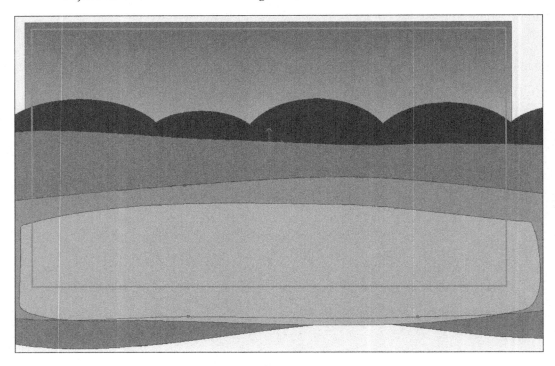

There we go. It looks like our scene is coming along!

Building a fence Group layer

Our scene would look good with a fence added to it. Since this is taking place out in the country, it's not hard to imagine what an old wooden fence could look like placed in this shot. To build the fence, perform the following steps:

1. Create a new Group layer (remember, this is on the one that acts like a folder and houses sublayers), name it `Fence`, and place it below the **Road** layer.

2. In this Group layer, we will create two Vector layers. The first will be named `Horizontal Pieces`, which will be placed on the top in this Group layer. The second will be labeled `Vertical Pieces`, which will be at the bottom position of the two sublayers.

3. Starting first with the **Vertical Pieces** layer, take the Add Point tool, select a brown fill color (and a complimentary stroke color), and position the cursor a little bit above the first land piece. The color we will be using for the fence is #A7937D. Make the fill color darker than that of the road to make the two set pieces stand apart from one another.

4. If you wish to make sharp or pointy pieces of wood, be sure to turn on the **Sharp Corners** option that is located on the top.

5. Now, draw some points down towards the top of the road. Add a point or two going to the right and then bring the outline back up.

6. Close off the piece of wood to create a rectangle-looking shape. You could add some details while doing this, such as dips and points.

7. Using the same methods just described, create three or four more vertical fence pieces going over to the right. Be sure to add variation to each piece by positioning points in different spots. Make some posts taller than others, add divots, and be creative! Take a look at the following screenshot for your reference:

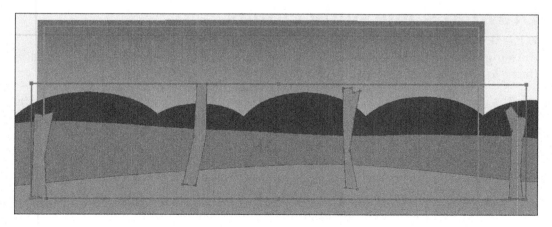

8. Now, for the horizontal pieces, first make sure you are on the **Horizontal Pieces** layer.

9. Starting from the left, you are going to create one long post that connects to all of the vertical pieces. The pole can bend and twist a bit, depending on the size variation of your vertical posts.

10. Like the vertical posts, feel free to create divots and such things.

11. Add two or three of these, positioning them vertically offset from one another. Your fence should look similar to what is displayed in the following screenshot:

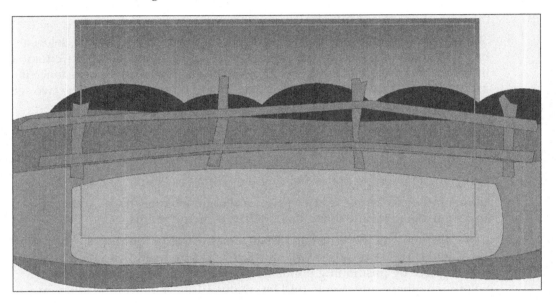

Drawing some puffy clouds

What sky would be complete without some clouds? You can really approach drawing clouds in numerous ways. For our work, we will be creating some pleasant, fluffy-looking clouds, using the following steps:

1. First, create a new Vector layer and label it Clouds. Place this layer above the sky but underneath all other layers in your **Layers** panel.

2. Select a white fill color with no stroke from the **Style** palette.

3. Taking the Add Point tool (and make sure **Sharp Corners** is turned off if you are using this option for the fence), position your cursor on the sky.

4. Start by creating some points that form a dipping line. Follow this pattern in a circular motion until your points meet back at the beginning.

5. Connect your first and last point to fill in the object.

6. From here, you can take the Transform Points tool and move the individual points to create varying degrees in your dips and curves for the cloud.

[

If you are looking to soften up the edges of your clouds, try using the Soft Edge fill effect in your **Style** palette. Reducing the transparency can help too.
]

7. You could copy the first cloud, paste it, move the copy to another location, and manipulate the points to form a different-looking asset. You could also create another cloud from scratch using the steps just provided. However you approach it, try creating three or four puffs that fill the sky, as shown in the following screenshot:

Adding details to the road with different brush types

Now that we have all the major elements in place, it's time to go back and add some details and touch up some things. Let's concentrate on the road first. As it stands now, this will work on a basic level, but it would be nice to give the road a bit of texture. Perform the following steps to use the brush types to add details to the road:

1. We can do this easily with the Freehand tool and a different brush type. Be sure to select this tool for this exercise.

2. Let's create a new layer for these details. You could place these new brush strokes on the same layer the road is on. However, if you like to keep things separated, like me, create a new Vector layer and name it `Road Details`.

3. Now, you could create a Group layer and stick the **Road** and **Road Details** Vector layers inside of it for even more organization. This is optional but recommended.

4. While on the **Road Details** layer, take the Freehand tool and go over to your **Style** palette and select the rectangle that is labeled No Brush.

5. We have looked at this panel before, so you should be aware of the different brush types at this point. For our purposes, let's select the seventh or eighth variation. Also, be sure to turn the **check Minimize frame-to-frame randomness** option on in order to keep things from moving about, as shown in the following screenshot:

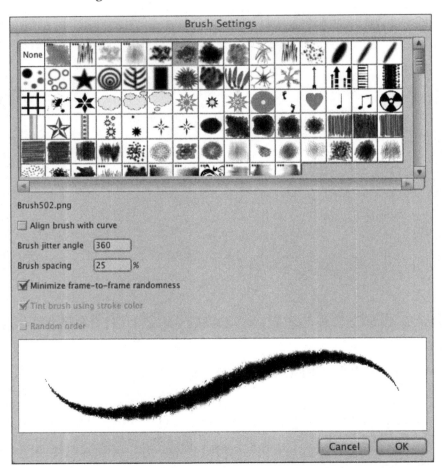

Chapter 6

6. For the stroke color, choose something that is a little bit darker than your road fill.

7. Finally, place your cursor on the road and start drawing some arched lines. They should vary in size, but try to keep a fairly consistent look to them. When complete, this will hopefully add some more character to your scene. The result is shown in the following screenshot:

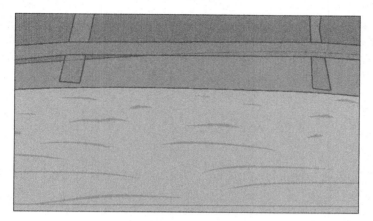

Using the Scatter brush for our grass blades

Like our road, it will be beneficial to include some details for at least the first land piece that we have placed at the front. This will also help with the look of the fence as we can use grass blades to cover up the bottom portions of the posts. This will make things look like they're not *floating* as much. Perform the following steps to detail the grass:

1. You will need a new Vector layer for the grass details. So, create a new Vector layer, name it Grass Details, and place it above **Fence**. The following screenshot shows the proper layer order:

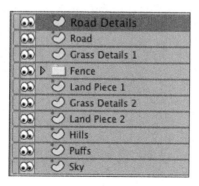

2. Take the Add Point tool and go to your **Styles** palette to reapply your normal brush.

3. Select a green fill and stroke color that is slightly darker than your land piece.

4. Place your cursor on the land piece and add a couple of points going up, coming to a point, and then coming back down towards the base.

5. Close the grass blade off at the bottom.

6. To get rid of that line at the bottom, take the Hide Edge tool and click in between the bottom points. This will make the grass blade appear to be closed off everywhere except for the bottom, as shown in the following screenshot:

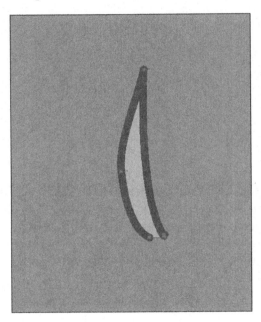

7. So, we have a blade of grass, but how do we easily populate the area with this asset? We could copy and paste, or draw every single blade manually. There is an easier way though. You will remember that we took a look at the Scatter Brush tool back in *Chapter 2, Drawing in Anime Studio*. Now, it's time to put it to use.

8. Take the Select Points tool and highlight the entire blade so that all points are selected.

9. Go to **Edit | Copy**.

10. Now, go to your toolbar and select the Scatter Brush tool.

11. On the top bar, there should be a drop-down menu with **Bubbles** as the default choice. Click on this and go all the way to the bottom of the list and choose **Use Clipboard**.

12. On the top-left of the options bar, there is a **Scatter Brush Options** button. Click on it.

13. Adjust **Angle Jitter** to a value of 20 and **Color Jitter** to 100, and select **Flip X**.

14. You can close this window. Now, what we are doing here is not only copying the grass blade, but applying some variations to it to easily populate our first land piece with grass.

15. Place your cursor over the first land piece and click to apply some grass blades. Keep your mouse button held down and move around to keep applying the assets.

16. If you feel you need to adjust how the blades vary in look, go back to your **Scatter Brush Options** button and play around with the values.

17. You can also adjust the size of the grass using the **min width** and **max width** value boxes. You can also adjust these values to apply a range of sizes (for example, 20 for minimum and 40 for maximum). Try to apply a good amount of grass to the layer, as shown in the following screenshot:

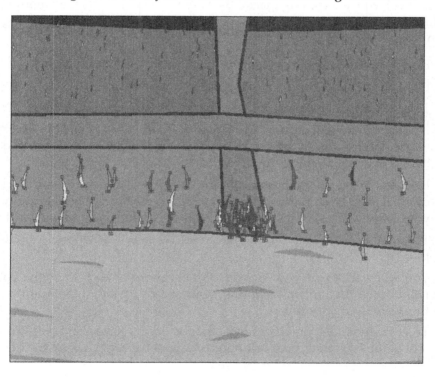

Finally, try applying the same method to the second land piece, except that this time, use smaller blades. Be sure to create a new layer for this second set of grass blades. If there is too much detail, try blurring the grass blades by going into your Layer Settings and adjusting the blur value or using single-line strokes to create the grass.

Creating scene depth

This section deals with how the camera will react to our assets when it tracks them across the screen. Right now, everything is on one plane, indicating that all assets will react to a camera movement in the same way. This is optional as some people like to keep everything on one plane (this is also the reason why we didn't create layer depth while we were creating the assets). To create this effect, we will need to go through each layer and decide just how far back we need to push them into our document.

Depth shifting your layers

Since Anime Studio 9.5, it's now easy to adjust the distance of objects from the camera without having to do a bunch of resizing after the fact, because if you push something away from the camera, the layer will appear smaller, which can be annoying if we have everything placed the way we want it. This new method, which streamlines the process, is called **depth shifting**, and can be performed using the following steps:

1. First, take the Transform Layer tool and select the **Clouds** layer.

2. Hold down the *Alt* and *Shift* keys on your keyboard.

3. Take the cursor and place it on the clouds in the workspace.

4. Hold down the left mouse button and drag upwards a little bit. You will notice that the clouds appear to be shrinking. However, what we're doing here is actually pushing the clouds further away from the camera.

5. Release the left mouse button and the clouds will appear to snap back to their original size. What has happened here is Anime Studio automatically resized your layer while keeping the new distance you have just applied as the same.

6. To verify this, look at your top bar to see the new Z position. It should be less than 0.

7. You will want to get your clouds to sit between -10 and -13 on the Z value. Hold down *Alt* and *Shift* and drag your clouds up and down until you reach the desired target number.

8. To get a good look at what this method is doing, select the Orbit Workspace tool at the bottom of your left-hand-side tool bar and click on the document.

9. You should notice that the clouds are pushed further back than any of the other assets, as shown in the following screenshot:

10. Click on the **Reset View** button on your top bar and go back to the Transform Layer tool to resume our work.

11. We are going to apply the same method to most of our other assets. Click on the **Hills** layer and set the Z properties to -7 using the depth shifting method.

12. For **Land Piece 2** and **Grass Details 2**, place the Z property at -4.

13. For **Land Piece 1**, **Grass Details 1**, and the **Fence** Group layer, place the Z value at -1.

14. We will leave all the other layers as they are (resting at a value of 0).

15. You can test the depth by using the Orbit tool again or selecting the Track Camera tool, and moving the document around. You should notice that there is a definite illusion of depth going on with the layers, as shown in the following screenshot:

Polishing up your scene

You may have noticed that when we test the Track Camera tool with our scene, certain elements such as the land pieces come up short, so to speak. In other words, we can see the edges of these pieces while panning, which may not work to our advantage if we want to have a long pan of the scenery. This is where you will want to go back and lengthen your elements if needed. You can do this by using the Transform Layer or the Transform Points tools. It may be necessary to build on manually, especially with assets such as the fence where you may need to add more posts. You may be able to copy and paste and mirror some elements to create a seamless effect as well. This is all part of the process, so plan accordingly!

Again, if you would like a reference file for this exercise, refer to the Anime Studio project file OutsideScenery.anme in the Chapter 06 folder.

The methods we applied here can be used for many types of scenery. Be sure to keep an open mind and play around with the tools!

Summary

Building a scene is similar to drawing out your cartoon character. As you can see, we end up using many of the same tools, and everything works together. Your characters and the backdrop must complement each other stylistically. As you practice and continue to build scenes for your own production, all of this will come together.

In the next chapter, we will look at how to create a library of assets and actions that we can reuse throughout one or multiple productions.

7
Creating a Library of Actions and Assets

As you start animating your project, you will discover that assets will accumulate quickly. Characters, props, sounds, scenery, and even animation tend to get repeated often, especially if you are creating a multi-episode series. One thing you can do to cut down on time is create a centralized library and organize it with folders to store your files. That way the assets can be brought in whenever you need them, no matter which file you have open. If you animate an asset out, the library will retain the keyframes as well. The Actions panel works in a similar fashion.

In this chapter, we will cover the following topics:

- Setting up a content folder
- Saving assets to the library
- Importing assets from the library
- Creating reusable animations with the Actions panel
- Working with scripts

Setting up a content folder

In order to take advantage of saving and reusing assets, you will first need to set up a content folder. Back in *Chapter 1, Stepping into the World of Animation*, we set this folder up after Anime Studio prompted us at startup. Assuming that you followed those directions, your content folder should already be set. However, if you decide at some point that you'd like to reassign the content folder, follow these steps:

1. Go to **Help | Set Custom Content Folder**.

2. The prompt gives you three options: **Never**, **Not Now**, and **Choose**, as shown in the following screenshot:

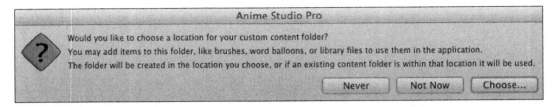

3. Select **Choose** and your file browser will appear.

4. You will now choose where you will be storing your custom Anime Studio assets on your computer, as shown in the following screenshot:

5. Pick a location that is easy to remember. If you've already made a folder for the files we have saved for our character and scene, you may want to pick that as your folder and store future files in there. Once selected, you should be set.

Saving assets to the library

Let's try saving an asset to the library. First, you will need to open an existing project file that has an asset you would like to save. For this case, let's use the character we created back in *Chapter 5, Bringing a Cartoon Character to Life*. If you don't have the file you made yourself during that chapter, you can open the `CharacterComplete.anme` file and then perform the following steps:

1. There are three ways to open the library. You could go to **Window | Library**. There is also a handy icon on the top-right of the screen that looks like a set of books, as shown in the following screenshot. Also, *Ctrl + Shift + L* (*command + Shift + L* on Mac) is the shortcut.

2. You will see buttons that represent different categories (**Characters**, **Props**, **Images**, **Scenes**, and so on).

3. Since we are saving a character, it makes the most sense to select the first button that houses characters.

4. You should now see two folders, `My Characters` and `Characters`. It'll be best to save your characters in the `My Characters` folder to keep things separated from the other built-in assets, so open it now.

5. Within this folder, you can create a new folder if you wish to organize things even further (indicated by the folder with the **+** sign on the bottom of the panel). Maybe you want to create one folder for human characters and another for animals, or perhaps you want to separate your character folders by project or cartoon episode. For practice, let's click on the **Add a Folder** button and name the new folder `Book Characters`, as shown in the following screenshot:

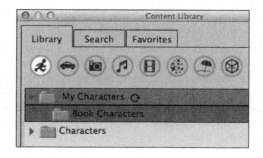

6. Click on **OK** to apply the new folder.

7. To add your character to the library, you will first need to make sure the character layer is selected. In the case of the example, to add a character in the `CharacterComplete.anme` file, click on the character's bone layer.

8. Now click on the **+** button in the center of the library panel. This is the Save to Library button.

9. You will see that the character asset has been added to the selected folder in your library, as shown in the following screenshot:

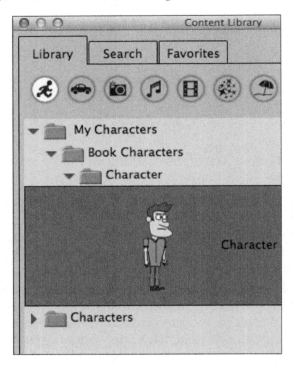

You can click on the asset to get a larger thumbnail view. This can help if you have many assets and are searching for a particular one.

 Where did the character go? Since you saved it to the library, it must be stored somewhere, right? If you ever need to manually delete or change the location of your library files, simply browse to the content folder that you set up in the previous step. This also allows you to share your library files with other Anime Studio users, should the need arise. You can also go to **Help | View Custom Content Folder** to bring up the folders for your library.

If you realize at any point that you no longer need an asset in the library, just select the asset and hit the - button that appears at the bottom of the panel. This will not only remove the asset from the library but also from your computer. So make sure you want it gone before hitting that button.

Searching for assets and adding them to the Favorites folder

As you start to accumulate a lot of assets, you may find it difficult to locate exactly what you want, in spite of organized folders and filenames. Luckily, you have the ability to single out assets that you may end up using a lot. Additionally, you can search through all library assets with a couple of clicks on the button; perform the following steps:

1. To favorite a library file, select it in the **Library** panel. In this case, let's select the character we imported.

2. On the bottom of the panel is a button that has a star on it; this is the Add to Favorites button. Click on it.

3. You will now need to choose which favorite folder you would like to put the file in. You can organize your Favorites folders just like any ordinary folder in the library. For example, you could make a folder titled Favorite Characters. In this case, we'll just put the character in the default Favorites folder and click on the **OK** button, as shown in the following screenshot:

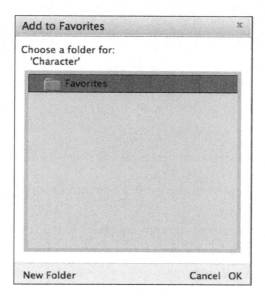

4. When you click on the **Favorites** tab in the **Library** panel, you will see the character displayed in the list.

5. If you are looking for a specific file, use the **Search** tab on the top of the **Library** panel.

6. You can filter out which categories you want to search in here. For instance, if you're looking for a character, you may just want to select the **Characters** category option to narrow your options.

7. Enter the name of the file in the search bar and click on **Search**, as shown in the following screenshot:

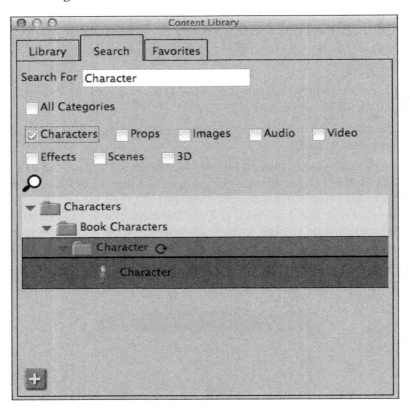

8. The file should appear in the list if it's currently stashed in the library.

Deleting an asset from your favorites list will not remove the file from the computer. You will need to find the asset's original location in the library and click on Remove if you want it removed from the computer.

Importing assets from the library

Assets in your library are of no use if you can't, somehow, bring them into your animations. Well, don't worry, because that's just as easy as importing! To demonstrate this, let's open up the scene you made in the previous chapter and perform the following steps. If you don't have that file, you can always open up the one entitled `OutsideScenery.anme`, which is included with this book.

1.   With your scenery open, make sure you have the **Library** panel open by clicking on the Library icon on the upper-right corner of the screen.

2.   Open up the `My Characters` folder in the library and locate the character that you placed in it.

3.   With your character file selected, click on the button that looks like a double checkmark on the bottom of the **Library** panel to add the character to your scene, as shown in the following screenshot. In addition, you can double-click on the file to add it to the scene, if you prefer.

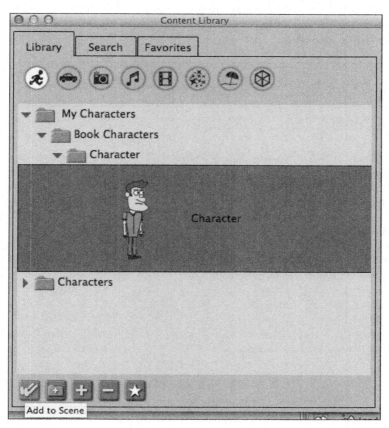

Editing your library assets

Just because you saved an asset to the library, doesn't mean you can't alter it. Once your asset is on screen, you can go into any of its layers and make the necessary alterations. Changing the properties of the asset once it's on screen will not affect the original library file it is referencing.

Now, if you want to edit the original library asset, it will require a little more work. Just remember that once you alter the original library asset, it will be changed for any future project you apply that asset to.

The first thing you need to do is locate the file you want to edit, and then perform the following steps. Remember, all your library files are stored in the content folder you had set up.

1. If you want a shortcut to access these files, simply go up to **Help | View Custom Content Folder**.

2. In the case of the character we just imported, you will want to browse to the folder in your file browser labeled Library, as shown in the following screenshot:

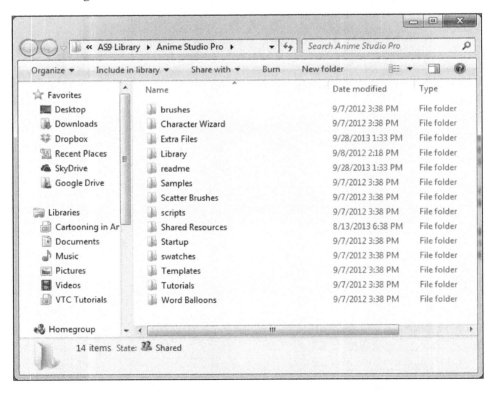

3. Enter the `Character Wizard` folder.

4. You will find a folder for your character here; enter that folder.

5. You should now see two files; a thumbnail image and an Anime Studio project file, as shown in the following screenshot. The thumbnail is automatically generated for the library's use; the Anime Studio project file is the one we are interested in.

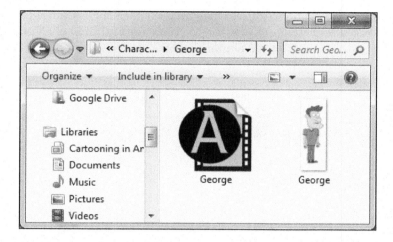

6. Double-click on this file to open your character's Anime Studio project file.

7. With the Anime Studio project file open, you are free to make any changes you see fit. Perhaps, you decided at some point that the character should wear a red shirt instead of a green shirt, as an example.

8. Once the alterations are made, go to **File | Save**.

9. The next time you import the character from your library, these changes will be reflected.

Creating variations of your library assets

Let's say, from our previous example, you would like to alter your character's library asset so that he is wearing a red shirt. Well, that was a simple matter of altering the original library object. But what if you want him to have a green as well as a red shirt? A character needs style choices, right? Or maybe you have built your assets to have animations in them and you want to create a library of different actions (walking, sitting, waving, and so on). You can do this pretty easily through Anime Studio.

Now, you could enter your file browser, make some duplicates of the original `Library` file, enter each file, make the alterations, and then save them all under different names. However, the following steps show an easier way to approach this:

1. Create a new document in Anime Studio by going to **File** | **New**.

2. Open the **Library** panel if it's not already open.

3. Browse to your character and bring him/her onto the document. Remember, to do this, double-click on the character, as shown in the following screenshot, or click on the character and then click on the button with the double checkmark icon:

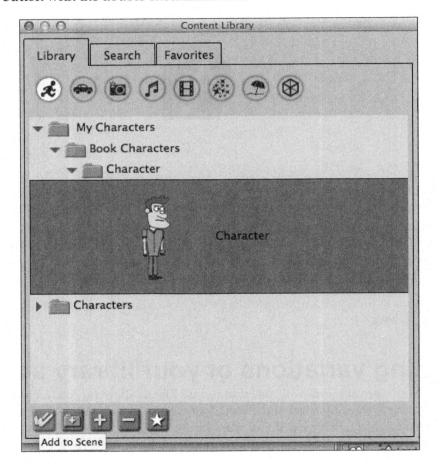

4. Now make your alterations. In this case, let's give the character a different colored shirt, as we discussed before. Let's try red!

5. Once you have colored his shirt, double-click on your character's bone layer on the **Layers** panel.

6. Rename the layer. In this case, let's choose `Character - Red Shirt`. Then click on **OK**, as shown in the following screenshot:

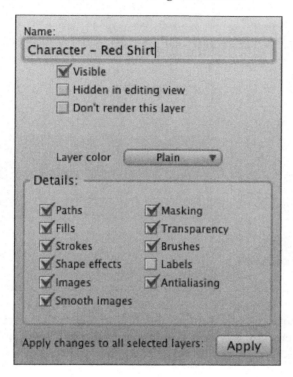

7. With that layer still selected, click on the **My Characters** button on your **Library** panel.

8. Click on the Save to Library button. Your new altered asset has been saved alongside the original. Now all you have to do is reference your library when it's time to give your character a change of clothes, as shown in the following screenshot:

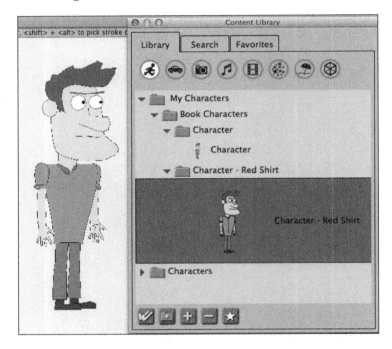

For further organization, you could move all your assets that pertain to one character into their own folder; that way you don't have multiple folders and files spread throughout the My Characters folder.

 If you ever run into an issue where changes you are making to the library aren't showing up, try clicking on the refresh button that appears at the right-hand side of your folders and files (the circular icon).

Importing a project file's assets directly

You don't have to bring assets into the library in order to use them in other project files. In fact, if you plan to use an asset only once, it may be easier to just use the direct import option.

1. As an example, let's open the CharacterComplete.anme file again.

2. Go to **File | Import | Anime Studio Object**.

3. Your file browser will appear. Browse for your scenery file. Remember, you can always use the file included with the book, if needed (OutsideScenery.anme).

4. A box will appear asking which assets you want to import.

5. You can check off all the assets that you need. This is useful if you need to bring in multiple references from another file.

6. Once you're done, click on **OK**, as shown in the following screenshot, and the assets will be applied to the file:

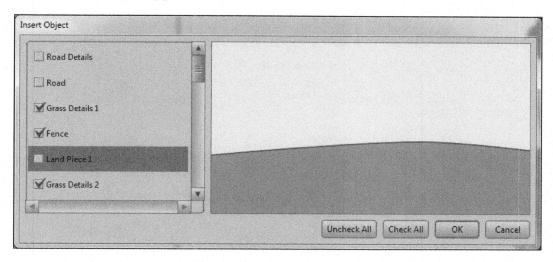

The files should all position themselves as they appear in the project file you are pulling them from. This is nice for when you bring in whole sets and don't want to worry about moving things around after the fact.

Bringing in third-party library files

While surfing the Internet, you may discover a generous artist willing to share his/her artwork for you to use in your own projects. To do this, you can follow one of the two methods mentioned earlier; that is, move the desired asset in a folder inside your content folder or import the file using the **File | Import | Anime Studio Object** method.

If you're looking for a good collection of files, check out www.ContentParadise.com. This is Smith Micro's own file and service exchange powered by community members; they bring many assets to the table for you to utilize. Keep in mind that some members may charge for their files.

Importing other file types

With Anime Studio, you're not just limited to importing objects made within the software. You can also import images, videos, audio, vector graphics, Photoshop files, and more. As you know, some of these can be imported by creating a layer (such as the image or audio files).

To import different file types, go to **File | Import**. All the items listed below **Anime Studio Object** are options for importing outside files, as shown in the following screenshot. You can even import 3D objects, which can make use of Anime Studio's 3D workspace.

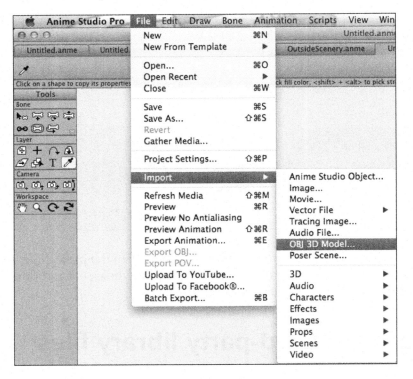

As we discussed earlier in the book, if an external file is altered, this change will be reflected in Anime Studio, which includes file location. Keep this in mind as it can save you from a lot of headaches later on.

Using built-in library assets

Anime Studio comes preinstalled with several different library assets that you can use in your own productions. These assets include characters, props, vehicles, scenery, special effects, and more. You may recall the character we played with in *Chapter 1*, *Stepping into the World of Animation*, which appeared in a new document by default. This is an example of one of those built-in library files.

You can access these files in the following two different ways:

- First, with the **Library** panel open, you can browse the different categories and click on the corresponding folders to view the assets. As an example, under the Character button, click on the Characters folder and you will get to see all the character assets accessible in Anime Studio. To bring the asset into the project file, simply double-click or click on the double checkmark button, as shown in the following screenshot:

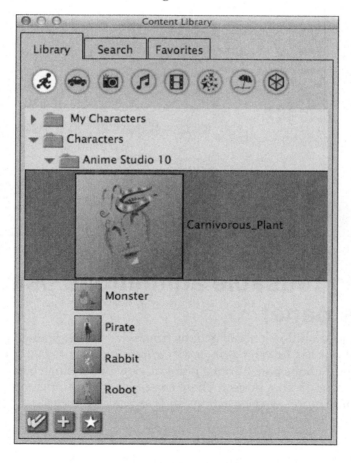

- Another way you can access the built-in assets is through the **File** menu. If you go to **File | Import**, the items in the upper section are the built-in library content items for Anime Studio, as shown in the following screenshot. The folder structure will appear similar to that of the **Library** panel, allowing you to pick and choose any item. This may be a bit harder to navigate as you don't have thumbnails to distinguish what each file looks like. However, if you know what you're looking for, this may not be such an issue.

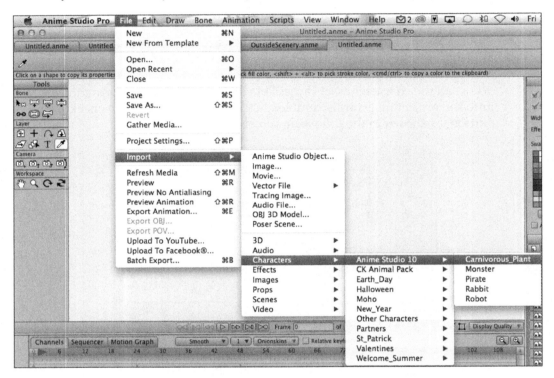

Creating reusable animations using the Actions panel

You already know a little bit about actions from what was explained about the Smart Bone actions in *Chapter 5*, *Bringing a Cartoon Character to Life*. We will now be approaching the Actions panel from a point of view of creating character actions that can be reused throughout a project. These can range from simple motions such as moving an arm to more complex actions such as walking cycles.

For this demonstration, let's open our character file CharacterActionsStart. anme. If at any time you want to see the end result of this exercise, open the file CharacterActionsEnd.anme. Of course, if you have your own file, feel free to use it. However, be sure to make a copy of this file before you start (by going to **File | Save As**) in the event something doesn't go right and it alters your original file. We don't want to lose anything important. All said, let's try creating a simple walking motion that we can reuse using the Actions panel, using the following steps:

1. Open the **Actions** panel by going to **Window | Actions**.

2. Create a new action by clicking on the **New Action** button on the top of the panel.

3. Let's name the action Walk, as shown in the following screenshot, and click on **OK**:

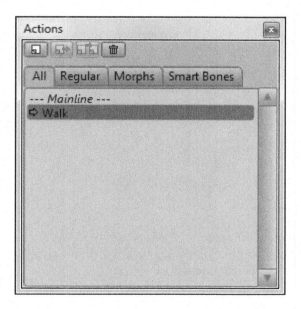

4. When creating a regular action, refrain from naming your action the same as any of your bones. Naming an action the same as one of your bones will create a Smart Bone action.

5. We are now inside the action. A big red arrow on the **Walk** action indicates this, plus the timeline is now red. This is different from the Smart Bone blue timeline color, indicating you are creating a regular action.

6. Within the action, our Channels timeline will be set to frame 1 by default, thus ready for animation.

7. Using the Manipulate Bones tool, move the character's left leg forward and left arm backward. Do the opposite for the right leg and right arm. Try to bend the knees a bit to give the action a more grounded look, as shown in the following screenshot:

8. Now page forward to frame 12. Move the limbs in the opposite direction of their starting points. So, left leg backward, left arm forward, right leg forward, and right arm backward.

9. We are going to want to create a looping animation for this. So on frame 24, copy the bone keyframes from frame 1 (*Ctrl + C* on Windows, *command + C* on the Mac) and then paste them on frame 24 (*Ctrl + V* on Windows, *command + V* on Mac).

10. Go back to frame 1 and hit the Play button on the timeline. You should see one cycle of movement take place for the character walking, as shown in the following screenshot:

11. Double-click on **Mainline** in the **Actions** panel to return to the main timeline.

12. Make sure you're still on the character's bone layer, advanced to frame 1 on your main timeline.

13. Click once on the **Walk** action.

14. On the top of the **Actions** panel, click on the Insert Reference button. It's the second one from the left with the icon of a sheet of paper and a red arrow, as shown in the following screenshot:

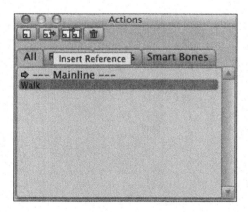

15. On your timeline, you will see a red area appear that takes up the duration of your walk. If you page forward, you will see the character is now performing the walking action.

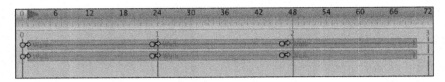

16. To create a looping effect, page forward to the end of the action on frame 24 and insert another reference. The walk should continue seamlessly, allowing you to create the animation as long as you want without having to move any keyframes.

17. If you want, you can use the Transform Layer tool and move the character across the screen to correspond with the walking movement. You can use your tools in conjunction with the actions to create more diverse animations.

18. If you need to delete an action at any time, simply highlight the action on the timeline and hit the *Delete* key on your keyboard. Now, if you delete an action from the **Actions** panel (by clicking on the action and using the trash can button), you will delete any reference of it that you inserted on the timeline. Be sure you really want that action gone from your project before you do it.

Remember, if you're having trouble or need to reference what we have done here, open the CharacterActionsEnd.anme file to see what everything should look like.

Multiple actions can be mixed together. However, if you insert an action that animates limbs which are already playing out from another action, you can end up with some broken results. Feel free to play around, but make sure to keep a copy of your original file as a backup in the event something goes wrong and you need to recover.

Actions are optional and some artists opt out of using them. It does make sense to utilize the panel if you are creating a cartoon that uses repeated movements. Keep this lesson in mind as you advance forward with your own work.

Inserting references versus inserting copies

Whenever you insert a reference of an action, just like we did in the previous exercise, you are actually bringing the action into the animation. This means that should you decide to alter the actions in the Actions panel later on, the changes will be reflected with all references you place down on the timeline. So, if we decided to alter the walking action we just made, the reference on the main timeline would instantly reflect that.

Now, this could be an issue, especially if you want to use an action as a starting point to create a different action. Luckily, you can still do such a thing by inserting a copy as opposed to a reference.

You will notice that on the top of your **Actions** panel, there is a button next to the Insert Reference button (it looks like two documents with a red arrow between them), as shown in the following screenshot. Clicking on this will simply transfer keyframes from the action onto the main timeline. This means you are free to alter these keyframes without fear of it affecting the action in the **Actions** panel or any of its references that may appear in the project.

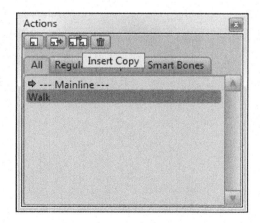

The same holds true for deleting actions. If you delete an action from the Actions panel, any reference of it will be removed from your project file. Copies will not be held to this same rule.

In the end, just stay alert when altering or deleting your actions. The last thing you want is your project coming to a screeching halt because of a simple mistake. As always, save often, so that you can revert if needed. Plus, navigating to **Edit | Undo** can really be your friend in sticky situations like this.

Working with scripts

Scripts in Anime Studio serve many purposes. They can add new tools to your toolset, make certain aspects of animation easier, or add special effect options to your cartoons. While there are a few scripts built into Anime Studio, the real power of this feature comes from community members who program their own scripts and share them online.

Using built-in scripts

Let's open the OutsideScenery.anme file again for this demonstration and perform the following steps. You can make a copy if you wish in the event you don't want to override the original file with script effects. You can use the scene you created previously for this exercise as well.

1. Go up to the file menu bar. You should see an option called **Scripts**. Clicking on this will reveal an assortment of options.

2. Let's go to **Camera** and choose **Handheld Camera**, as shown in the following screenshot:

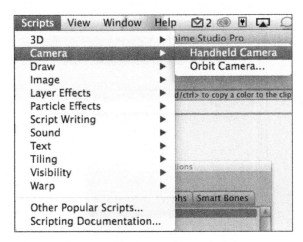

3. Immediately, you should notice that this effect has been applied if you page through your timeline. It creates random movements for your camera tools to simulate the effect that someone is holding the camera.

Try applying some of the other scripts to see what other effects you can come up with. You may be surprised by the results.

Downloading third-party scripts

As stated before, the biggest benefit of scripts comes from members of the community who create additional tools and features that can enhance the workflow or visual appeal of your project.

Go to **Scripts** and choose **Other Popular Scripts** at the bottom. Your web browser will launch and `www.AnimeStudioScripts.com` should load. This website is the best place to acquire new scripts created by members of the Anime Studio community.

Installing scripts is just as easy as putting files into your library. The exception is, instead of putting the files into your `Library` folder, you will put them into the `Scripts` folder. The website has a short installation video on its homepage that you can watch if needed.

Anyone can code scripts for Anime Studio; that's one of the program's most powerful features. You will need to learn the Lua programming language if you're interested in pursuing this. Unfortunately, this section is as far as we will be discussing scripts in this book. If you are interested in the programming language, you can check out `www.lua.org` to learn more!

Summary

When you start to build a collection of assets, it may be best to look towards creating a library so you can easily access your files at any time. Remember that you can use built-in assets and scripts as well as import external files to enhance your project. Finally, creating and reusing actions may be helpful, especially if you plan to recycle a lot of content.

In the next chapter, we will focus on animating a scene in Anime Studio. That idea for your cartoon is closer to becoming a reality!

8

Animating Your Characters

Building off everything you have learned to this point, we can now begin to implement animation techniques and start work on our very own project. This chapter aims at getting you going on the animation process. It will be up to you where you ultimately want the animation to take you through your script, creativity, and lessons learned in this book.

In this chapter, we will cover the following topics:

- Following your blueprint
- Animating characters non-linearly
- Finding a workflow
- Putting it all together
- Experimenting with character animation

Following your blueprint

The building blocks are set. It's now time to mold these elements into an animated masterpiece. This can be the most overwhelming part of the process, but just remember to keep your script and storyboard handy for the duration of this process. These two items make up the blueprint or map of your animation and things will move a lot smoother with them close by. Also, remember that a blueprint can change. Don't be afraid to make edits to your script, even this far into the process, when certain obstacles come up during animation.

Animating characters nonlinearly

If you have ever worked on films or read up on the process of filmmaking, you will discover that scenes, more often than not, are shot out of sequence and edited together later on. This can be due to location restrictions, weather, scheduling conflicts, and a multitude of other issues. It stands to reason that linear work is more feasible with animation due to having a more controlled environment. You don't have to worry about scheduling locations or weather as all work is done on a computer and actors don't have to get together for recordings (although the latter arguably helps in creating more authentic emotions). All said, you may have to prepare for the event that non-linear animation will happen. If you need to meet a deadline, for instance, you may need to move forward with scenes you have voices for while other actors finish up their portion of the script. The same can be said if you're collaborating with a team and you're waiting for assets needed for certain scenes. Maybe you need to rewrite portions of the script but are good to go on others. The bottom line is: be flexible and keep an open mind.

Finding a workflow

Sometimes, while animating, if a scene or environment appears multiple times throughout an animation, it may be best to animate all shots for this scene first, no matter where they appear in the script. That way, you can finish one scene project file and move on to the next, as opposed to jumping back and forth throughout the animation process. This, of course, goes with non-linear animation, but it's also a workflow choice. It could drive some people nuts. There are those out there who like to create characters and scenes as they animate. Another method is to have everything designed before beginning the animation process. Should you render each shot out as you do it? Or should you wait until everything is animated and then export everything out at once? These are just a few small examples of what will define your workflow.

For this book, a basic workflow was set up for you to follow. First, we designed a character. Then we created a scene. And now, we will combine the two to create an animation. As you dig deeper, you will find a rhythm that best suits you.

Finally, a common question is how do you create separate scenes or shots for your animation? Some people choose to lay everything out on one project file. This can be confusing. Many prefer to create a separate project file for every scene that's animated. This allows for keeping things more organized and is easier to access while editing later.

Putting it all together

Taking all the elements we have assembled to this point, we are going to create a short animation. This is mostly an introduction to what will undoubtedly become a more complex process. But it should hopefully give you an idea of what is required to assemble an animated project. We will be taking everything we have learned so far and combining it to create this animated scene. Advice will be offered on several aspects. However, ultimately, you will choose where you want to take this character and scene once you have a handle on the basics of animation. If you're ever in doubt, refer to the previous chapters as they contain all the basics you will need to get going.

Opening the scene file

First, we will need to open a scene or backdrop for our character to interact in. As we created a scene for the book, let's go ahead and use it. Remember, this file is called `OutsideScenery.anme` and is located in the `Chapter 6` work folder. The following are some tips for bringing your scenes and characters together:

- You can open the scene file or import it to your library so that it can be accessed any time.

- If you open the file outright, be sure to go to **File | Save As** and save the file so that you can keep your original scene untouched. You may want to name this new project file `Scene 1` or something that indicates what the scene or shot entails.

- For more complex animations, you may want to consider organizing scenes and shots into separate folders on your computer. This can make things more accessible when working on animations with multiple scenes later.

Bringing in your characters and props

The next step is to import our characters and props into the scene. If you still have your character saved in the library that we worked on, you can bring him/her into the document through that panel. If you don't have the character in the **Library** panel, you can always go to **File | Import | Anime Studio Object** and browse for the file you saved when you created your character. Once the character and props are on the screen, be sure that a layer is placed above the backdrop on the **Layers** panel.

If you want, you can organize your scene assets into a **Group** layer, which is something you can certainly do. Sometimes, having a lot of layers on the **Layer** panel at once can get confusing.

Experimenting with character animation

What do you want your character to do in this environment? Is she taking a nice leisurely stroll through the countryside? Perhaps, a monster is chasing our protagonist? Maybe he's hauling a huge seed, which he will bury to grow a large plant that leads to a new and exciting world? It may not seem like it, but your possibilities, even with just one character and a scene, are virtually endless. What's important is that you now have the know-how to create what you want. We learned about bone animation, actions, keyframes, and all the tools. You just need to learn how to execute what you want or what your script calls for.

This section will outline some basic animations you could use in your own works. The goal here is to take these small elements and apply them to a larger project. In other words, we won't be creating any linear narrative here. Treat these as separate exercises to strengthen your soon-to-be-made cartoon.

Running, waving, jumping, and more; animation contains the art of motion, and it stands to reason you will have some character movements occurring in your projects. We already covered a basic walking animation in the previous chapter. Now, we will look at some other actions. The book will provide some advice in regards to these motions.

To follow along, you can open a file containing the character we made in the character creation chapter. But if you like, you can open the file `CharacterJumpStart.anme` to follow along with.

Jumping

Maybe your script calls for your hero to leap over a lava pit? Or maybe you just need him to leap for joy? The following are some tips on creating a jumping action:

- You will want to start with the character bending forward slightly; this includes the knees bending outward. This should be an easy task with a character rigged up for bone animation.

- However, when you bend the knees, your feet are going to move upward. This will create an undesirable effect when creating the animation.

- One way to correct this would be to take the Transform Layer tool and move the character as you go from standing to bent position. This may require some fine-tuning to make it look like the feet aren't shifting as the animation takes place.

- If you need additional help with positioning, turn on **Onionskins**. This is located on the top of the timeline. Now, if you click on the number of a frame on your timeline, an outline will appear for that frame, giving you a reference for future or past frames you're working on. This is great if you want to set down a similar position for an asset or need to do some fine-tuning with animations. You can have onionskins on as many frames as you want. Simply click on the frame again to remove the onionskin. The following screenshot shows the options for the **Onionskin** menu:

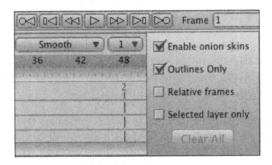

- After the bend, your character's legs will need to straighten. The torso should tilt up along with the arms coming up.

- Depending on if the jump is straight up or to the side, your legs will animate differently.

- You may want to pause for a few frames before the jump animation occurs. How long your character waits may depend on the length of outside circumstances occurring within the scene.

- You will need to move the character bone layer with the Transform Layer tool once the limbs have been set for the height of the animation. How far your character leaps will of course depend on your needs.

- As the character descends, you will want to start bringing the limbs back to the bent position. Also, use the Transform Layer tool to guide the character back to the ground.

- After the character lands, you will more than likely need to do some correcting with the feet by using the Transform Layer tool as he/she stands up from the bend. Again, onionskins are your friend here.

- For extra detail, feel free to add a shadow to the bottom of the character that enlarges a little when he/she launches into the air and then returns to normal size, along with following the character's path, when contact with the ground is made.

- Dust clouds could also help with detail. Be sure to take advantage of using a fade effect with the opacity layer setting. Remember that? As you can see, our character is now in the air.

If you need to see the completed exercise, please open the file
`CharacterJumpComplete.anme`. Again, this could be used in a number of different
ways. All it takes is a little patience and some tweaking with the Transform Layer tool.

Cycling keyframes

From looping backgrounds to spinning wheels, sometimes it's necessary to be able to
create a looping animation that can be applied to a scene. In this case, we will be using
our character and scene to create a looping animation and background. It will give
the illusion that the camera is following our character as he walks from left to right.
Open the file `CharacterLoopingAnimationStart.anme` from your chapter work files.
What is set up here is a basic walking animation for the character that cycles once. You
will also notice that the scenery assets are extended out to the left and right. These
assets were copied and pasted to create the illusion of a more real estate. This is so
that we can create a seamless looping animation. All the assets have been pulled to **0**
on the *z* axis position. This part isn't necessary, but it'll make moving our assets a little
easier. We will still be creating a parallax effect. However, we will have to control this
manually with each piece of scenery and not through any of the camera tools.

Looping the walking animation

To get started, let's make the character's walking animation a loop. We could
continually copy-and-paste the keyframes for as long as we need to keep this
animation going. But there's an easier way that automates the process for us:

1. With the **Character** bone layer selected, go to frame 24 on the timeline.

2. Right-click on the top bone channel's keyframe and choose **Cycle** from
    the list.

3. A box will appear, asking you if you want to do a **Relative** or **Absolute** cycle.
    We will leave the **Absolute** option checked and put 2 as the value in the box.
    This means that once the animation reaches frame 24 on this layer, it will
    jump back to frame 2 and repeat the process. As we set this up so that frames
    1 and 24 are identical, we want to avoid going back to frame 1 so that the
    cycle appears to loop seamlessly. Otherwise, we will essentially see the first
    frame repeat twice.

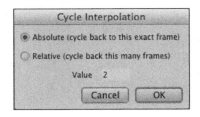

4. Once you click on **OK**, a red arrow will appear on frame 24 for both bone channels, pointing back all the way to frame 1. Let's do the same thing for the Transform Layer tool's frame 24 keyframe.

5. Once your cycles are applied, try clicking on the timeline's **Play** button. You should see the walking animation continuing to cycle even as the scrubber moves past the keyframes for the action.

As it appears right now, our character is walking in place. He's not getting anywhere fast, but don't worry, we'll be changing that soon.

Looping the scene assets

The next step is to allow the scene pieces to loop. This will require use of the Transform Layer tool and lining things up just right so that no break appears in the cycle.

On the **Layers** panel are two group layers, **Road** and **Road 2**. Each of these contains the original road asset plus the road details overlaid on top. We grouped these two things together from the previous work file to make looping the background easier.

While on frame 1, we'll want to highlight both Road **Group** layers from the panel (remember, you can do this by clicking on one layer, holding down *Shift* and then selecting the second layer).

Advance forward to frame 120. What you would to do here is move the road pieces so that the one on the right matches the position of the piece on the left on frame 1. Onionskins are also useful for this. The following are the steps we'll take to create a looping background:

1. To make things easier, hold down *Shift* when moving the pieces with the Transform Layer tool. This will disable the ability to move the assets vertically.

2. Pay attention to the road lines when doing this. This will be the easiest way for you to match things up. Zoom in on the workspace to get a better view.

3. Once you get it where you want it, right-click on frame 1 for both the layers and choose **Linear** from the list:

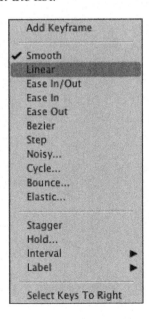

Linear is the animation option that creates consistent movement with no slowing down or speeding up. By default, Anime Studio animates on the **Smooth** option, which creates a slight bounce to movement in the form of slower speeds at the beginning and end of the interpolation.

> There are other animation types you can play with as well. **Ease In/Out** will create a more exaggerated speed up and slow down effect for your keyframes, **Hold...** will hold onto a keyframe for a specified duration of time, and **Noisy...** can create a randomized effect to your animation based on an amplitude number you input. **Stagger, Bounce...,** and **Elastic...** are three new options introduced in Anime Studio Pro 10, all giving your animations unique results. Try out different combinations to fit your needs!

4. Right-click on frame 120 for both layers and choose **Cycle**. Enter 1 into the field and click on **OK**.

5. Try to get it to match as closely as possible. If it's slightly off, you may be able to tell. You can always play back the animation to check and then tweak it until you get it just right. Remember to turn on onionskins!

6. You will want to apply the same method to all the other scenery assets. If you are looking to create the parallax effect we originally had when we created the scene, you will need to increase the frame durations as assets appear further in the distance.

7. For your reference, the project file for this book cycled at frame 120 for the road, 144 for the fence, 192 for the first land piece, 216 for the second land piece, and 336 for the hills. The clouds were left alone, but you can choose to move them as well.

Playing the animation back on the timeline, you should see a seamless looping animation occur for our character. If anything looks to pop or jump when looping, just go back to that frame and correct the position. It will take some patience and practice. But if you keep at it, you will be able to create your looping animation in no time. If you need to see the completed file for this exercise, please refer to the CharacterLoopingAnimationComplete.anme file in your Chapter 8 work files.

The following is a screenshot of our character running on the looping background:

Cycling keyframes isn't only useful for scrolling backgrounds; try using it on spinning wheels and other repeatable animations too.

Creating keyframe intervals

One interesting setting for keyframes is the ability to create intervals. In essence, this allows you to choose which frames get animated between two keyframes. While it may make sense to just adjust the overall frame rate of a project to suit a certain movement, it may sometimes be desirable to have one layer skip every other frame while your camera pans are shot at the project's original frame rate. Basically, this can provide a cool low-tech or pseudo frame-by-frame effect. Perform the following steps to create keyframe intervals:

1. With the walking cycle project file still open, select your **Character** bone layer.

2. Highlight all keyframes for every channel, with the exception of frame 24; right-click and choose **Interval** and then **2** from the list, as shown in the following screenshot:

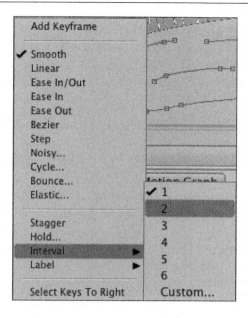

3. By selecting **2**, we are telling Anime Studio to animate this character at every other frame. Since we are on a project file that is animated 24 frames per second, the character will essentially be animating at 12 frames per second while everything else around him is running at 24 frames per second.

4. Play the animation back on the timeline to see the result. The character should be running at a choppier rate compared to everything else.

Keyframe intervals aren't for everything, but you may find occasions where it does come in handy. If you want to see the final result of this, open the file CharacterLoopingAnimationIntervals.anme.

Incorporating facial expressions

Before we start creating a basic conversation, it's best to explore how to create different emotions by manipulating facial details. You can create your own character to do this; or, you can use the work file entitled CharacterFacialExpressionStart.anme if you'd prefer to use the book's character.

An anxious expression

There are a few ways we could create the illusion that a character is anxious. This will mostly come down to the way the eyes move, along with the eyebrows. Your character probably won't be smiling as well in this case. The following are some tips for creating an anxious expression:

- **Shifting eyes back and forth**: This can be effective with dialog. This is one reason it was suggested that it may be best to create your pupils in a separate layer than that of the whites of the eyes. That way, it's easier to grab the pupils, create keyframes, and shift them.

- **Tilt the eyebrows outward**: This can be used when creating sad expressions, but it can also be applied to a case like this.

- **Biting the bottom lip**: This can help sell the expression. A slightly open mouth works too. Again, smiling probably won't sell the expression unless they're devious or trying to laugh the situation off, as shown in the following screenshot:

To see an example of an anxious expression, open the file `CharacterFacialExpressionAnxious.anme`. Creating movement with the body, which we're not focusing on here, will help sell this expression.

An angry expression

You could create an angry expression with the same template as the anxious one. All that's required is to adjust the eyebrows and change the mouth. The following are some things you can do to create an angry expression:

- **Tilt the eyebrows inward**: The lower the eyebrows are, the more they cover the whites of the eyes, and the angrier your character will look.

- **Create a frowning mouth**: This could even progress with animation, from a neutral-positioned mouth to one showing teeth.

- **Shifting the eyes**: This makes the anger appear more chaotic while static pupils make the character appear more focused. This will have to be a judgment call that you make.

If you'd like to see an example of an angry expression, please refer to the file `CharacterFacialExpressionAngry.anme`.

A happy expression

Depending on how you position your eyebrows, you could create something that is a bit cocky or more genuine for a happy expression. The following is how you can create a happy expression

- **Tilt the eyebrows inward**: This will create a more determined or cocky look for the character; the outward position will have an opposite effect.

- **A smiling mouth position**: The mouth is really what will sell this expression.

- **A simple closed-mouth smile**: This is to show that teeth can really determine the degree of happiness. If your character is talking while happy, be sure to create the appropriate mouth poses for such an action.

To see an example of a happy expression, open the file `CharacterFacialExpressionHappy.anme`.

Creating a conversation

There's a good chance that your cartoon will contain characters talking to one another. This is how a plot progresses in films and the same goes for cartoons as well. To approach creating such a sequence may be a bit overwhelming. How do you keep things interesting? Should you do any animation other than the mouth movements? This lesson should help with that.

First, let's open the file `ConversationStart.anme`. This file contains two characters we can use to create a conversation.

Situating mouth poses and audio files

To begin with, you will need to decide how you want to approach animating mouths. You will remember that we discussed techniques such as use of Smart Bones and the **Switch** layers. Pick one that you are comfortable with.

In the case of this exercise, we will use the **Switch** layers and draw out a series of mouth poses. We will refer to these as phonemes. Phonemes are the poses our mouths make when we make different sounds. This includes "S", "Th", "O", and "F".

When creating mouth poses, you may want to consider reusing them for multiple characters. This can save on time and make things easier when it comes to creating a workflow.

Let's position the audio files properly using the **Sequencer** timeline:

1. You will need to bring in some voices so that we can begin voice syncing. If you go to **File | Import | Audio File** and browse to your book's work files, you will find two audio files Audio1.wav and Audio2.wav. Import both of these into your project file.

2. The audio files will automatically appear on the timeline. In the current state, they will be overlapping each other, which doesn't really benefit us much, as shown in the following screenshot:

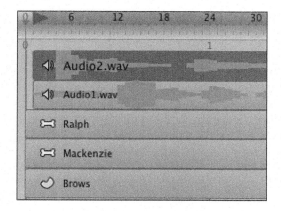

3. Go to the **Sequencer** timeline and drag **Audio2.wav** to the right so that it comes immediately after the first line. As we are creating a conversation where one character speaks after the other, we will want just a small beat (about five frames) in between each file.

4. Play the timeline just to hear how the audio files work together. If the second line appears to be delivered too quickly in relation to the first (or if it doesn't come quick enough), just use the **Sequencer** timeline again to line up everything correctly.

5. If you don't want the scene to start with a dialog right away, you may want to leave about one to two seconds of screen time before any audio starts. This will allow you to establish the scene and give the audience a breath before diving in. As we're basically doing a snapshot of a potential action that could take place in a larger project, this establishing rule will vary depending on what has come before this shot.

If you're having trouble visualizing any of this, take a look at the following screenshot:

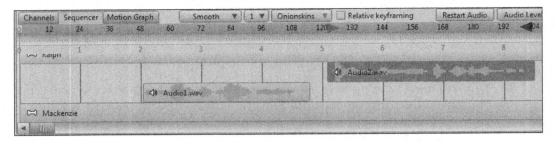

Note the space between the two audio files plus the two seconds of room left at the beginning of the timeline.

Syncing the mouths to the audio files

Now, it's time to go back to the beginning where the first audio line starts; figure out which line this character belongs to, and start animating his or her mouth. As we are using the **Switch** layers for this example, this is a matter of advancing forward frame-by-frame and listening for changes in the line. Remember to change positions with a **Switch** layer, right-click on it on the Layers Panel, and choose the phoneme you want. The following are some tips for syncing up the voices with your characters' mouths:

- When you hear the first character (Mackenzie) start to say a word starting with, for instance, an "S" sound, you will want to position your character's mouth so that it makes this pose.

- Once you are finished with the first line, hop over to the second character and do the same thing. The goal is to get all the mouths animated before proceeding to the next step.

- When you hit the **Play** button, you should have your first character talk along with the second following up. Your mouths should be in sync with the voices. If there are some places where the mouths don't quite match up, just do some adjusting with your **Switch** keyframes.

The following screenshot shows the **Switch** keyframes placed for the first character's mouth on the timeline:

If manually animating the mouth poses is too time consuming for you, there are other options. In the **Layer Settings** panel of the **Switch** tab, you can sync your sublayers to a targeted audio file. View the **Switch** tab to see this option. The **Layer Settings** panel is shown in the following screenshot:

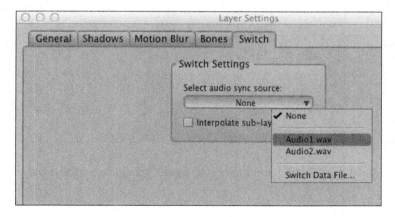

Additionally, Papagayo, an extension to Anime Studio, offers an alternative way to lip sync. For more information, visit http://anime.smithmicro.com/papagayo.html.

Animating a mouth with Smart Bone dials

As we have discovered throughout the book, Smart Bones are great for many different situations, including animating mouths. If the **Switch** layer route isn't cutting it for you, try setting up a dial or two. To see how this could be done, open the example file SmartBoneMouthMovmentsStart.anme. You can keep the conversation file we are working on open in another tab for now. Be sure to save it just in case! When opening this new file, if Anime Studio asks you where the audio file is, click on **Yes** and choose Hello.wav from your work files.

As you can see, we have a character rigged up and ready to go. He even talks! However, we could probably add a little bit more movement to the mouth to further sell the phonemes. Let's use the new dial setup system of Anime Studio Pro 10 to achieve this by performing the following steps:

1. You can see we already have one dial working with the mouth. It moves back and forth as the animation plays out.

2. To add a second dial for the mouth, click on the **Monster** bone layer in the **Layers** panel.

3. Make sure no bones are selected. To ensure this, hit *Enter*.

4. Take the Add Bone tool and draw a small bone next to the **Mouth** bone on the outside of the character. Try to make the dial about the same size as the **Mouth** dial. Start from the bottom and draw up when creating this dial.

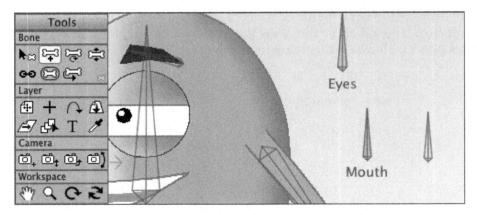

5. With your new bone selected, go to **Bone | Create Smart Dial**.

6. Here, you can enter a name along with other various parameters. Let's name the bone Mouth 2. You can keep everything else as is and click on **OK**.

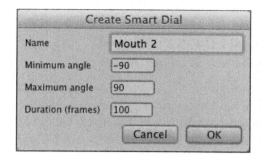

7. We are now inside the new Smart Bone action with 100 frames to play with (that was the default lifetime frames from the previous panel).

8. Starting at frame 1, go to the **Mouth** group layer on the **Layers** panel and choose the **Mouth** vector layer.

9. Take the Transform Points tool and hit *Ctrl + F* (*command + F* on Mac) to create keyframes for this position. We want this starting position so that we have something to contrast the movement with at frame 100, which we will create next.

10. Advance forward to frame 100.

11. Select all the points and then take the Transform Points tool and scale the points inward so that the mouth looks like it's creating an "O" shape. You can even move some of the points around individually, if needed.

12. Once you're done, double-click on **Mainline** on the **Actions** panel.

13. Advance to frame 1, take the Manipulate Bones tool, and try moving that new dial you made. You should be able to control the mouth in a different way now.

14. Go through the animation and try applying this new dial to the existing animation to enhance the mouth movements.

If you need additional help, refer to the work file `SmartBoneMouthMovmentsEnd.anme`. While we used the new bone dial setup feature for this exercise, you can create dials through the normal Smart Bone setup process like we did in *Chapter 5, Bringing a Cartoon Character to Life*.

Creating facial expressions

Going back to the conversation we are building, you need to decide if the lines warrant more expressions beyond the mouth movements. How about the eyes? Do they need to move? How about eyebrows? Pay attention to the dialog and your script, and create the facial expressions accordingly.

For the case here, when the first character says *You smashed my car!*, we will have him emit anger through his eyebrows. The second character, when responding innocently, will have neutral positioning of eyebrows, as shown in the following screenshot:

We will also have the second character look away when answering the first character's accusation. This could be seen as a sign of guilt or shyness.

Animating body movements

The final step is to create some movements through our character rigs to sell the dialog exchange. Like many aspects of animation, this will require trial and error. The following tips should help get you going:

- Focusing on the first character, it's obvious that his words are more heated; he's clearly angrier with the situation. We can probably make his movements a bit more exaggerated when it comes to the hand, head, and torso.

- When the character says *you*, we may want to add a finger point. This could be done through a **Switch** layer with the hand or animating the points to go from a neutral positioning of the hand to a finger point. Of course, there's always Smart Bones to control such changes as well. In the case of this lesson, we will be using a **Switch** Layer.

- Once you have that hand drawn and in place for the **Switch** layer, we can begin the animation process.

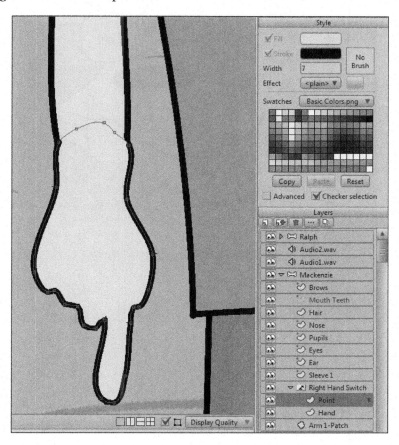

- As the character escalates his line, we can lift his arm up and switch the neutral hand position out for the point.

- We can also tilt his head slightly forward and shift the torso. As he is angry, remember that his actions will be a bit more exaggerated.

- When the line comes to an end, we can bring everything back to a more relaxed state.

- When the second character replies, we could have him shrug his shoulders or lower his head suspiciously. Or maybe he's more direct with his innocence. Be creative and try different things!

Creating camera movements

Finally, you will need to choose if this scene contains a static camera position. Maybe you will want to go with something that's a bit more dynamic? One idea would be to have a close up on whenever one character speaks his/her line. You could do this in a couple of different ways. The first option would be with no panning. Whenever one character speaks, the camera cuts to a close up of that character. The second option would be to do quick pans back and forth as each character delivers a line. This could make for a more chaotic scene. We will now explore both methods.

Before we get started, we need to consider the establishing portion of this shot we created when we delayed the delivery of the lines by two to three seconds. We should probably leave the shot as is for these seconds and then have the cut appear as the first character starts to talk. To do this, perform the following steps:

1. Advance forward on the timeline right before the first character starts to speak.

2. Select the Track Camera tool. Click once on the screen. This will create a keyframe for the tool without altering the scene. This is exactly what we want right now.

3. Now take the Zoom Camera tool and do the same thing. Click on the screen once. A second keyframe for the Zoom Camera tool track on your **Channels** timeline should now be present.

4. To do the camera cut, first advance forward one frame, and then take the Track and Zoom Camera tools and zoom in so that the first character's face takes up a good chunk of the frame. Remember that we want to compose these shots in a pleasing manner. We talked a bit about this in *Chapter 6, Developing Your Cartoon's Scenery*. See the close up of our character in the following screenshot:

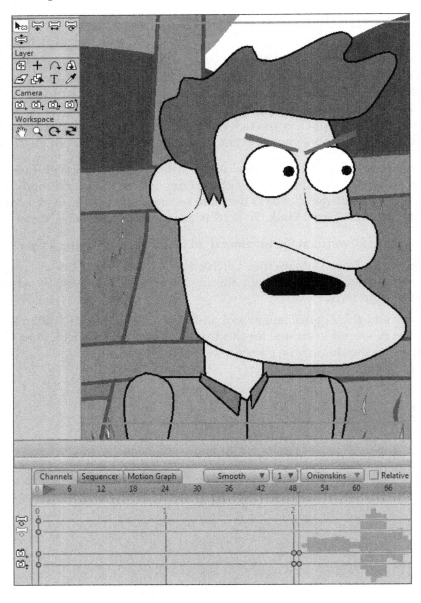

5. You will now have two sets of keyframes back-to-back for the two Camera tools. If you page back and forth, you should go from your establishing shot to a zoomed-in shot of the first character's face. Having these keyframes in such close proximity prevents a pan from occurring. This is exactly what we want in this case.

6. Now, when the time comes for the second character to talk, we will do the same thing as we did before for the Track and Zoom Camera tools; page forward right before the second audio file starts.

7. Double-click on the **Track and Zoom Camera tracks** on your **Channels** timeline to create these two keyframe copies.

8. Paging forward one frame, change the position of your camera with the Track and Zoom Camera tools so that we now have a nice close-up shot of the second character.

9. If you page backward and forward between these two keyframes, you should see that the camera just cuts from one character to the other.

10. So, how about creating camera pans? That's easy! Do you know the two keyframes we added before each zoom-in cut? Highlight both these **Track and Zoom** keyframes and shift them back. The further away they are from the zoom-in keyframes, the slower your pan will be. It will be up to you to establish just how fast you want things to pan and zoom. In this case, as the characters are arguing, it may make more sense to make everything move at a quicker pace. Different situations will warrant different approaches.

This is just one scenario in how a conversation could be animated. It will all depend on what is occurring in your script. If you'd like to see the completed version of this animated conversation, refer to the work file ConversationComplete.anme.

Animating with the new bone constraints

Anime Studio Pro 10 has introduced some new **Bone Constraint** options that can really add an extra coat of polish to an animated work. You may have to rig your character differently to take advantage of most of these enhancements, since the **Layer Binding** techniques we used in this chapter don't really apply. So, what do they do exactly? The best way to explain it is to have you open a work file titled NewBoneConstraints.anme that we made just for Bone Constraints. Anime Studio may ask you to locate a file named Arm.png. You will find this in your Chapter 8 work files folder.

The first thing you will notice is that the file is made up of multiple layers. Only one layer is visible right now. This is good because we want to view one layer at a time as they each contain different examples. Let's take a look at the Bone Constraint features:

- With the **Independent Angle** layer, we see a crane. Take the Manipulate Bones tool and move the third bone from the left. Notice anything unusual? The child of this parent bone, the small piece at the end, has a stationary angle. Normally, this bone would bend and react along with the others. In a way, this acts sort of like a camera crane. This can be useful for locking the angle of, let's say, a foot when moving a leg, so you can make manual alterations later if you wish. To turn this constraint on, simply select a bone, go to the **Bone Constraints** menu and check on **Independent angle**, as shown in the following screenshot:

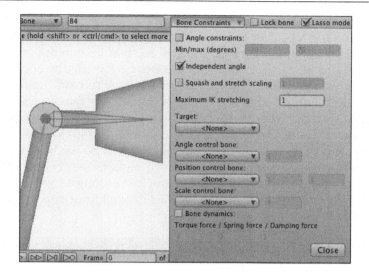

- Let's hide the **Independent angle** layer (by clicking on the eye icon next to the layer on the **Layers** panel) and make **Squash and stretch scaling** visible. With the Transform Bone tool, we can adjust the size of any bone, even during animation. But when selecting a bone and checking on **Squash and stretch scaling** in the **Bone Constraints** menu, the selected bone will now create a more cartoony squishing effect when scaling. You can also enter a number for this option. The higher the number, the more obvious the effect. Try scaling the bone in this example to see the effect take place. Feel free to adjust the number in the **Bone Constraints** menu to try out different effects. And remember, you must be on frame 1 to affect the layers attached to the bone. On frame 0, you will simply be adjusting the bone itself, and consequently, not see the squash and stretch effect.

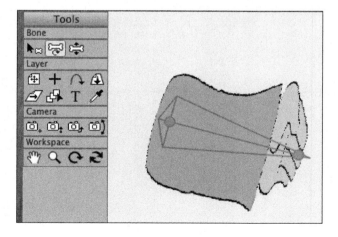

- **Smooth Joint**, which is the next layer on the list, shows an example of two bones creating a perfect bend when using the Manipulate Bones tool. Give it a try! When moving the hand, you will see that no bowing or glitching occurs at the bend of the arm. While Smart Bones can be used to correct such issues (as we looked at before), this doesn't work if we're working with images, as their points cannot be altered. So now, if you have two bones making up a bend, click on the layer in the **Layers** panel that is attached to the two bones, select the two bones with the Select Bone tool, and go to **Bone | Create Smooth Joint For Bone Pair**. Anime Studio will do the hard work for you and the two bones will now create a nice, smooth bend. This isn't limited to just limbs and can be applied anywhere, just as long as you have two bones in a straight line to apply it to. Also, this doesn't limit you to just images. Vectors will work too!

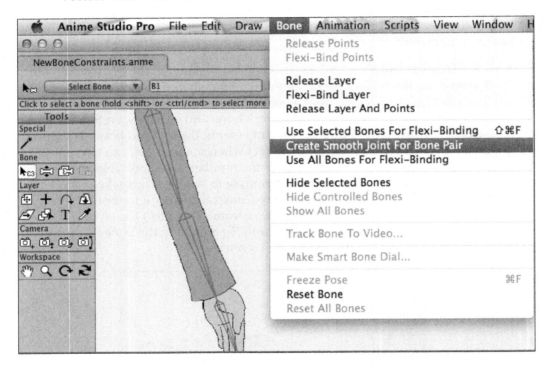

- With the **Target Bones** layer, you will notice we have two bones that seem to be touching the heels of the character. Take the Manipulate Bones tool and try moving these targets. Notice how we can control the legs. Additionally, try taking the Transform Bone tool, clicking on the pelvis bone, and moving the character around. You should notice that the Target Bones act as magnets, having influence over the legs wherever the character is moved to. Combining this with **Independent angle** attached to some bones, you could get some really cool-looking results. To create a target bone, simply draw the bone similar to how you see it here. Make sure it isn't attached to any other bone on the character (to ensure this, hit *Enter* before placing the bone). For human characters, placing the bones close to the feet and touching the heels are best. Then to target a bone, select a bone you'd like to link it to; in this case, the bottom leg bones work best. Under **Bone Constraints**, choose the name of the desired target bone from the **Target Bone** drop-down menu. In the case of this example, our bottom leg bones will be targeted. This is because of the fact that the skinny portions of these bones are touching the target bones.

- Auto-Bone Scaling works with Target Bones. Click on the **Auto-Bone Scaling** layer. Now take the **Transform Bone** tool and move the pelvis bone, like we did before. Notice now how the legs stretch as they move away from the targets. You can set a number for this in the **Bone Constraints** menu under **Maximum IK Stretching**. 1 is the default and will have no scaling effect; any number higher than this will have a scaling effect.

Our current example is set to 2. Try raising the number to see what happens!

Remember, with the **Transform Bone tool**, you have three functions: moving, scaling, and rotating. Placing your cursor on the bone allows you to rotate. Placing your cursor on the red dot near the thick part of the bone allows you to translate or move. Placing your cursor near the skinny part of the bone allows you to scale.

- The last layer, entitled **Everything,** has all of the above methods working together. Enable that layer and hit the **Play** button. As you can see, we can create some really smooth results with these new options!

Remember, the use of these **Bone Constraints** options is simply optional. The great thing about Anime Studio is you have many ways to tackle a project. Don't limit yourself; be bold. Try new things!

Summary

It would be impossible to detail every single animation situation you will run into as you begin your production. Each script carries different traits as well as the creator behind the animation. But by learning how to create basic character movements in conjunction with facial animations, you will be able to do a lot. While the conversation we made is pretty simple, your creativity will launch you to new heights once you start working on your own production.

In the final chapter, we will take a look at how to preview, compile, export, and publish your animated movie.

9
Exporting, Editing, and Publishing

Now that you have a scene animated, polished, and ready to go, you will need to export your cartoon for the world to see. Is this scene just one part of a larger cartoon that you plan on editing together? Maybe you're looking to export the file so it will be compatible with a website such as Newgrounds. Or maybe you just need to create a quick render to test how the animation plays out on video. Whatever the case, this chapter will cover all that you need to export your file out, test it, and get it ready for distribution.

In this chapter, we will cover the following topics:

- Previewing your work
- Choosing your file format
- Exporting your scenes
- Exploring different video editors
- Breaking down the editing process
- Exporting your completed project
- Finding your audience

Previewing your work

With Anime Studio Pro 10, there is a new preview option that allows you to do a quick render and view your animation as it appears on the workspace. This is ideal for complicated projects that may drop frames when viewing the project with the timeline and the **Play** button. Accessing this new feature is easy. Perform the following steps to do so:

1. Find the portion of animation you want to preview. To do this, pick a starting frame on your timeline, hold in the *Ctrl* key (*command* on Mac) and left-click. A green rectangle should appear on the timeline.

2. Find the frame you want to end on, hold in the *Ctrl* key (*command* on Mac), and right-click on it. A red rectangle will appear on the timeline, as shown in the following screenshot:

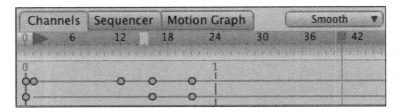

3. Navigate to **File** | **Preview Animation**. The shortcut for this is *Shift + Ctrl + R* on Windows (*Shift + command + R* on Mac).

4. The timeline will play from your start to end point.

5. Your computer will then automatically launch a default video player. You can preview the animation by hitting play.

Rendering can take a lot of time, so this is a great way to preview a scene before committing to an export. If you need a different view of the action, simply zoom in or move around on your workspace before previewing. Another trick is to use *Ctrl + J* (*command + J* on Mac) to darken everything outside your project boundaries. This can give you a better visual of what your animation looks like before exporting it.

> If you would like to save a frame preview, you can use a drop-down menu on the bottom, which is labeled **Save As**, after clicking on *Ctrl + R* (*command + R* on Mac). Here, you can choose from different image file types. Pick one, name it, and that's it!

Choosing your file format

If you are looking to share your animations on streaming websites such as YouTube or Vimeo, or if you're looking to submit your cartoon to a film festival or a similar vendor, you tend to export your files as videos. Anime Studio handles the exporting of videos better. The thing you have to decide is which format and codec you should use when exporting out your animations. The .swf files, which are not videos, can also be created. However, you have a chance of limiting your audience by taking this route because only a certain number of services use the .swf files. Not to mention, you eliminate the possibility of altering the animation further in a piece of video editing software.

Exporting QuickTime files

QuickTime is a video format that was created by Apple. However, you don't need an Apple computer in order to utilize or view videos using this format. If you are using Windows, you will need to download QuickTime Player, which is free, from Apple's website so that you have access to the format. From there, you will be able to select QuickTime from the list of file types in the **Export** panel.

There are a couple of things to point out with regards to QuickTime. First, this is the recommended format as it usually delivers the best results in terms of video quality, file size, and render speed. There are codecs or compression types you can choose after selecting QuickTime. When rendering out your scenes initially, try using the **Animation** codec, it's the best middle ground for quality and file size. If you're having some quality issues (sometimes weird trails can appear in movement), move to either **PNG** or **None**. These files tend to render out rather large (depending on duration and detail) and can cause resource issues when editing, depending on computer hardware. One option is to render this file out as **PNG** or **None**, and then convert it to a lighter weight format before editing if you're having issues with playback.

When it is time to distribute your animation online, **H.264** seems to be the best option. This is another reason why QuickTime is the best option; it's versatile and you can usually find a compression type to fit your situation. The second thing to keep in mind is that Windows users will need to open the 32-bit version of the software in order to access all QuickTime files. This is due to QuickTime not being available natively as a 64-bit application for Windows users. This isn't as big a deal as it may seem, it just requires a few extra clicks at the time of rendering.

Exporting AVI files

The **Audio Video Interleave (AVI)** format is Microsoft's video format and your only other video option next to QuickTime. While there are people who like this format, we suggest using it only if you absolutely cannot use QuickTime or if you're really opposed to switching between the 64- and 32-bit versions of Anime Studio. The .avi format also has codecs to choose from, and by default, your selection is limited. The standout is **Uncompressed**, which gives you a really nice render, but at the cost of huge amounts of hard drive space. You may also run into the issue cited with QuickTime's **PNG** or **None** codecs — choppy playback if computer resources aren't up to snuff.

Exporting SWF files

There was a time when Internet cartoons were broadcast almost exclusively as embedded .SWF files. Back when YouTube didn't exist, the next best thing was to stream cartoons through these small Flash files, thereby kick-starting the success of websites such as Newgrounds. Today, the .swf format isn't used much for cartoons and there are several reasons for this. First, most cartoonists like to edit their cartoons in programs outside of the animation software and this is best achieved through video. Next, YouTube and other streaming sites have made video the standard for broadcasting cartoons on the Internet. Finally, .swf files are being slowly phased out due to Apple's refusal to allow the file type to be viewable on iOS devices.

However, there may still be instances where an artist wants to export with this format, particularly if the goal is to import the animation into another software, such as Flash, to implement interactive elements or target a website such as Newgrounds, which still uses the format to broadcast some of its content. However, in most cases, .swf is considered outdated for cartoonists and, because of that, this chapter will focus primarily on exporting your animations as video.

Exporting your scenes

Whether you decide to export everything at once or as scenes are completed, you will need to know the proper procedure for exporting your files.

The following is what you need to do to export:

1. Once you have completed a scene, navigate to **File | Export Animation** (*Ctrl + E* on Windows, *command + E* on Mac). Here, a panel will appear giving you a wealth of options.

2. The frame range at the top is the same as you'll find on the top of your timeline. You can use this to dictate which frames you want to be included in this render. This can be useful if you want to test or re-render a certain portion of the animation. Given this is your first time rendering, you'll probably want to select the number of frames that your animation runs for on the timeline.

3. Below this is the **Output format** drop-down menu. This is where you can select one of the three file types we just discussed in addition to a few other image types. Select **QuickTime Movie** from the list of choices, as shown in the following screenshot. Remember, if you're running the 64-bit version of Anime Studio in Windows, you will need to switch to the 32-bit to access the **QuickTime Movie** file type.

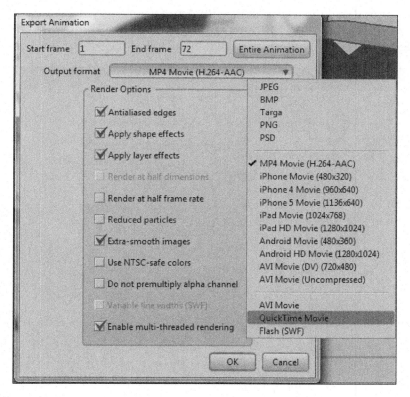

4. The checkboxes underneath allow you to alter the quality of the video, such as reducing the number of frames or cutting the dimensions in half. You would only want to do this if you are looking to quickly test a file out. Otherwise, leave everything as is and click on the **OK** button.

5. You will now be prompted to locate a folder to save your video file(s). Create a new folder within your project folder (where you have been keeping all your Anime Studio scenes) and save it there. Name the folder `Videos`. It's good to keep things organized with subfolders in a single project folder. If you have a lot of shots, you may want to organize this further by creating more subfolders within the `Videos` folder.

6. Now you can choose the compression type, also known as a codec. The options were discussed in the *Choosing Your File Format* section, so choose your codec appropriately. If in doubt, start with **Animation** and see what results you get. For best results, select **Millions of Colors+** from the **Depth** section and bump the quality meter to **Best**, as shown in the following screenshot:

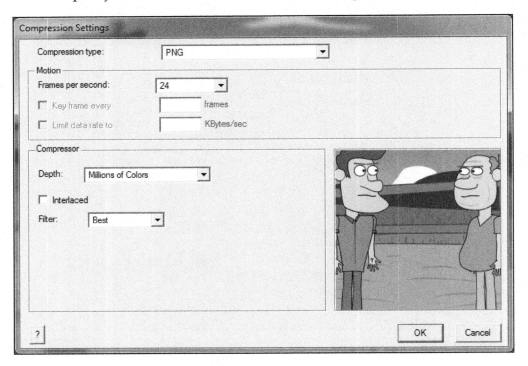

7. Once you have your settings, click on **OK** and prepare to be patient. Rendering a video can take a long time, depending on the amount of detail and the duration of the clip.

This is why it's always good to make sure you are set before attempting a render. Sometimes though, it's hard to see the details of your animation until they are rendered, so redoes are all a part of the process.

When the file is done, it should automatically open in your default media player. If you're a Windows user, you may need to open the file in the QuickTime Player in order to view it because Windows Media Player sometimes has issues with certain QuickTime codecs. And that's it! You now have a clip to either distribute or edit. If you have multiple scenes you plan to edit together, you will want to go through and export them all out.

Exploring different video editors

It's now time to put all the pieces together. We have all these separate video clips lying in folders on your computer, so how do we bring them together to form a cohesive narrative that reflects your script? First, we are going to need a video editing software. These come in many types and, depending on what you need, you could spend upwards to $1,000. Obviously, these expensive software are loaded with features, but if you're looking for something a bit lighter and basic, there are free alternatives you can choose from. In fact, without even knowing it, you probably have one of these free programs installed on your computer right now.

Using free video editors

For Windows users, **Windows Live Movie Maker** comes installed on all modern iterations of the operating system (starting with Windows XP). If you're an Apple user, **iMovie** is the Mac equivalent. Both allow you to import, trim, and rearrange clips as well as alter audio, add titles, create clip transitions, and export for distribution. You can definitely use these base programs to assemble your cartoons. However, you get what you pay for, and lacking the ability to add more than one video and audio track (in other words, not being able to stack clips on top of one another), just as an example, may turn some people towards premium solutions.

The following is an example of the iMovie editing window:

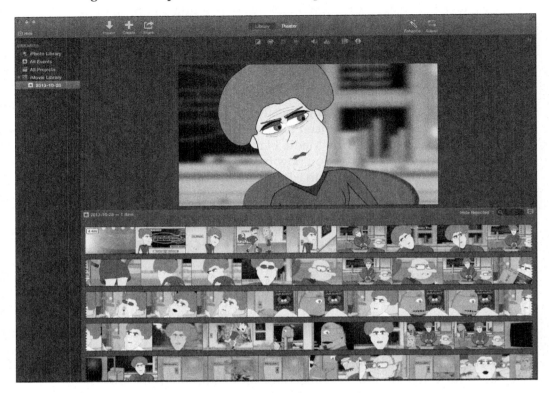

Using premium video editors

There are a few options out there if you're looking to splurge and get something that is a bit more robust in terms of features. **Adobe Premiere** and **Final Cut Pro** share many similarities and are the most popular video editors. Many cartoonists find one of these programs to more than fit their needs. Another software that has made a name for itself is **Sony Vegas**, which holds its own against Premiere and Final Cut Pro. Also, you have **Avid**, which is seen as the industry standard for many professional editors.

These advanced video editors will give you much more freedom, enabling you to do the following:

- You can overlay multiple video tracks, which is great if you want to take advantage of alpha channels or line-up sequences more accurately

- You can implement several different types of video effects, and audio is usually much easier to work with
- The interfaces tend to make complex projects easier to work with

If one of the free editors works for your current needs, definitely use it. But if you feel you need to expand your tool set, look into something more advanced.

Final Cut Pro is only available for Mac OS if that is the route you are thinking of taking. Also, Premiere is now part of the Adobe Creative Cloud suite. You will need to pay a monthly fee to use it. However, the good news is that you can gain access to every other piece of Adobe software, including **After Effects** and **Audition**, which can help with advanced editing.

The following is a sample Premiere interface. Notice how the timeline contains more information than iMovie, giving you more options when editing.

Finally, a section on video editing cannot be written without touching on Adobe After Effects. While the four programs mentioned previously are made for assembling footage, After Effects is for editors looking to add advanced special effects. The work you can do in After Effects is truly amazing and can really add a nice coat of polish to an animated project.

Breaking down the editing process

For this section, we will be using Adobe Premiere as a reference. However, most video editing software work in a similar fashion, so you should be able to apply these steps to whatever you are currently using.

To follow along, you can use your own clips or refer to some of the book's work files, export them out, and play around with the editor from there.

Creating a new document

When creating a new document with a video editor, you will have similar considerations as you did when making a new Anime Studio document for the first time. In the case of Premiere, perform the following steps:

First, create a project file. You will then be prompted to create a **Sequence**.

When saving your project file, simply give it a name and place it in the folder where you have been saving your clips and Anime Studio project files. This will help keep things organized.

You can have multiple Sequences within a project file, depending on how you want to work. As an example, you could create a Sequence for every scene you have. Once they are edited and arranged in the form you want, you can bring all the Sequences together to assemble the final animation. It just depends on how you want to work.

When creating your Sequence, you will have some templates to choose from, each pertaining to resolution and frame rate. You will, more than likely, want to create a Sequence that mirrors your animated clips. So, if your clips are rendered at 1280 x 720 at 24 frames per second, you will want to find a template that has those properties. You could create a higher resolution Sequence and put your clips inside it. However, the clips will appear smaller within the frame. If you try to enlarge them to fit in the frame, the video quality won't be as good. So, it's always best to keep your videos and sequences consistent in terms of resolution and frame rate. You can downsize later, if needed.

To create a new project and Sequence in Premiere, perform the following steps:

1. When the welcome screen appears, select **New Project...** from the right-hand side, as shown in the following screenshot:

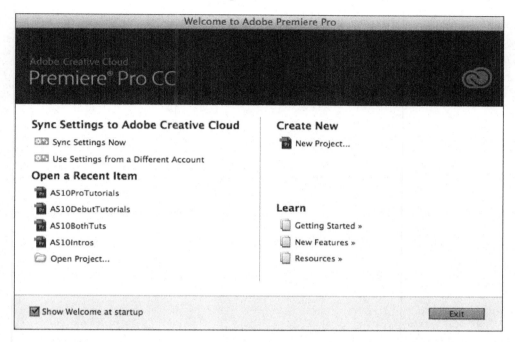

2. Enter a name for your project into the **Name** field. Something related to your cartoon would be best for organizational purposes.

3. Set the location of the file by clicking on **Browse**. We will set the file somewhere inside your main project folder. It may be best to make a new subfolder and label it Premiere Files.

4. After clicking on **OK**, your workspace should come into view.

5. Navigate to **File | New | Sequence...**, as shown in the following screenshot:

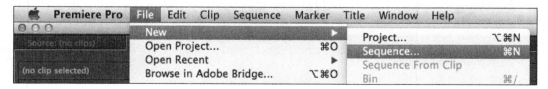

6. Here is where you will choose the dimensions for your Sequence. In the preceding example, we cited 1280 x 720 at 24 frames per second. Under HDV is a template labeled **HDV 720p24**. Select it, as shown in the following screenshot, and click on **OK**:

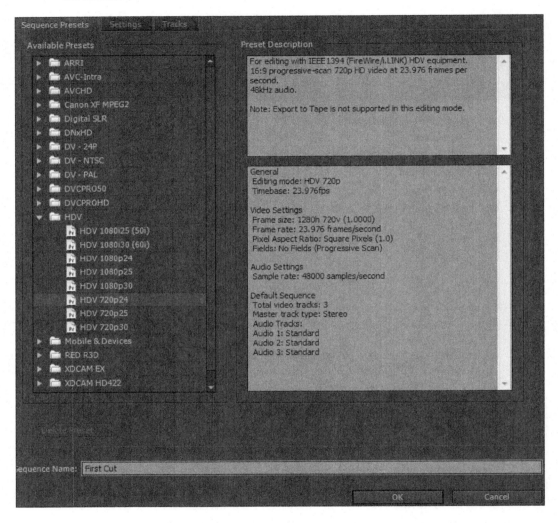

Your workspace should now have a Sequence ready to go.

Importing clips to bin

Once you have a Sequence, you will want to import your clips into what is called a bin. By default, this is located on the left-hand side of Premiere's interface. A **bin** is essentially a file browser for all your assets within the project file. Sequences can share these assets. It's advised to create sub-bins in the bin for your clips. You can even arrange these further if you want to split the clips up by scenes. Organize these bins however you see fit. Perform the following steps to import clips to bins:

1. To import the clips, you can navigate to **File | Import...** or right-click on the bin panel and choose **Import...**, as shown in the following screenshot:

2. Browse to your clips, select them, and click on the **Import...** button. It may take some time to bring everything in, depending on the complexity and duration of the clips. There will be a meter in the bottom-right corner indicating the process.

3. Using the media browser, you can drag your clip(s) into any bin you wish. It's best to do this early in order to keep things organized.

Assembling the clips

Now comes the part where you grab the imported clips and place them on your Sequence's timeline in the order they would appear in your script. Now, you will probably see why animating in a non-linear fashion really has no effect in the long run; everything comes together in the end. Assembling your clips is a simple matter of dragging-and-dropping. By default, your clips will snap together when they come into close proximity, making it easy to line-up clips so they seamlessly transition from one to the next. You can also cut or copy clips and paste them where you see fit. Adding transitions, such as fades, are really easy to do in a video editor. With Premiere, you can drag-and-drop transitions along with other video effects by using the **Effects** panel in the bottom-left corner of the software, as shown in the following screenshot:

You can also take this time to trim or edit your clips, if needed. This is arguably easier to do in a video editor than Anime Studio because the timeline permits greater flexibility. You may discover that some shots go on longer than they should, or maybe something pops up in the video that you don't like. While you can edit some errors out, if something is serious, you will need to go back into Anime Studio and take care of the problem at the source most times.

Incorporating audio

Once your clips are assembled, you may want to import some audio files to overlay on the timeline. It's advised that you redub or replace any audio that was brought over from an original Anime Studio clip. One reason for this is that the audio in Anime Studio can sometimes become distorted on export. Another reason is that if an audio layer is moved off center, you will get an audio pan effect, which can be distracting. Perform the following steps to remove the original audio from the clip:

1. Click on the lock icon next to the video track.

2. Select the audio below it and click on the **Delete** key. You are now free to reimplement the audio files.
3. Click-and-drag your audio files onto the timeline and arrange them as you see fit.

You will also find that overlaying music is much easier to do in a video editor. For instance, if you have multiple clips and want to have the same music play throughout, this is a simple task to achieve with software such as Premiere. In Anime Studio, because you are working with separate files, things become a bit more complicated. You can also adjust the volume of these clips and trim them, if needed. So, take this opportunity to spiff up the audio of your animation.

Using the audio sources correctly

When it comes to hunting for pieces of music or sound effects, it's advised you refrain from grabbing copyrighted material. In the event that your work does become a success, you don't want to go through any legal issues while trying to promote or distribute your work. The bottom line is it's bad practice. How would you feel if someone took your cartoon, or elements of it, and stuck it into their own work to pass it off as their own? Stay away from doing this, and either get permission to use someone's work that you like or seek out sources for royalty-free media. It may seem like a pain, but in the end, your work will be better off for it.

With the copyright lecture now over, if you're looking for some good places to get royalty-free sound effects and music, here are some recommendations: http://freesound.org and http://incompetech.com. They both contain a wealth of files for you to pick and choose from. Just note that most sound creators ask that you credit them somehow in your production notes. For more information on these guidelines, check out the FAQ or Help pages on these websites.

Creating titles in a video editor

While you can create titles and text with Anime Studio's text tool, you may find it's easier to create such clips within a video editor. With Premiere, you can go very simple with the text or create some more detailed designs. There are even templates that can help bolster your titles. If you're looking to create some good-looking credit sequences with 3D and other special effects, After Effects may be worth checking out.

Adding basic titles in Premiere is easy, as shown in the following steps:

1. Go to the top and navigate to **Title | New Title | Default Still...**, as shown in the following screenshot:

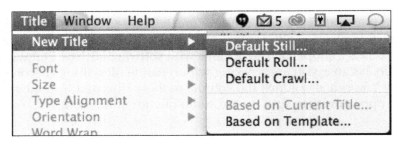

2. Choose the resolution and frame rate (which should default to your Sequence's settings) and write a name. Maybe this could be Movie Title or Credits.

3. Once you click on **OK**, you will be brought to the title editor. Here, you can choose the position of your text as well as its font, color, size, effects, and more. What options you choose is up to you!

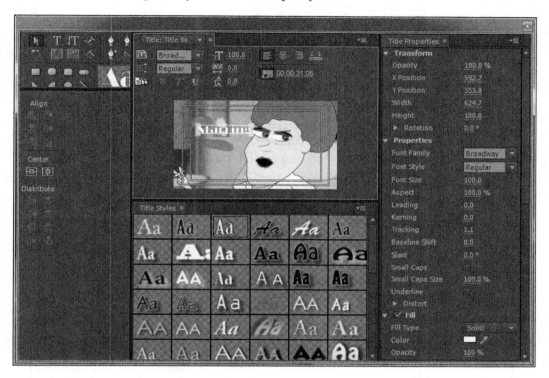

4. Once you are done, you can click on the **X** button.
5. To apply the title to your timeline, locate it in the bin and drag it out as you would any other clip.

> Just note that if you edit this title at any time, whether it's in the bin or on the timeline, any instances of it will be altered as well.

6. If you are looking to create a new title with the same properties, go to the file in the bin, right-click and select **Duplicate**. Rename this new file. You are now free to edit the new file without fear of altering the old one.

Be sure to credit others when appropriate. Okay, so maybe we're not done lecturing about copyright yet. For instance, as described with the two audio sources, you will find that there are credit guidelines to using their files. Be respectful and give credit where it's due!

Exporting your completed project

Once you have assembled your cartoon, added audio, polished, and test viewed it, the final step is to export the entire animation.

1. In Premiere, you can navigate to **File** | **Export** | **Media** (*Ctrl + M* on Windows and *command + M* on Mac) to create the file.

2. You will have similar options present for when you export your clips from Anime Studio. As before, it's recommended that you stick to QuickTime. If you're targeting the Internet, go with **H.264**.

3. This will present you with different templates, as shown in the following screenshot, some relating to YouTube, Vimeo, and so on. Going with the appropriate template (depending on the resolution of your video) should give you some pretty good results.

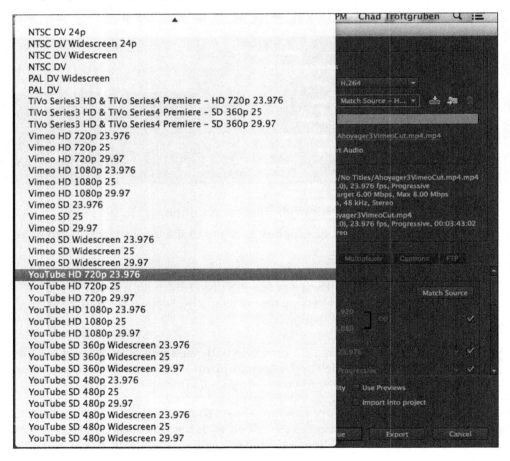

4. If you want to distribute the animation in a different, high-quality fashion, **H.264** offers high-quality HD exports. But, if you want to burn to DVD or Blu-ray, **MPEG2** may be a good option.

5. There are other options you can play with too. First, if you click on the **Output Name** field, you can name the clip as well as point to a folder to save it in, as shown in the following screenshot:

6. After picking a template, you can adjust the properties, such as resolution, frame rate, and bitrate. You should probably leave these options alone, mainly because the templates do a good job of delivering a video for whatever venue you are targeting. However, after exporting once, if things aren't looking good, feel free to play with the settings.

7. Once you have selected your template, click on **Export**. As you know by now, this process may take some time, depending on duration, effects, and complexity.

Once the process is complete, locate the video and test it out. Make sure it is exactly the way you want it. If something is wrong, you may need to go back to the timeline and make corrections. Or, you may discover a deeper problem that needs to be addressed in Anime Studio. Whatever the case, make sure it's just the way you want it. From here, it's all about distribution.

Finding an audience

It's probably safe to assume at this point that you have a pretty good idea of how you want to distribute your work. The most popular way today is through websites like YouTube and Vimeo, but traditional methods such as DVD and film festivals are still viable. And, maybe, you plan to do a combination of online and traditional distribution. Regardless of how you do it, this final section is meant to give you some insight on the process in terms of marketing and finding an audience.

Taking the traditional route

We are living in an age where online media is quickly becoming the norm. However, there is still a market out there for more traditional distribution. While you could burn your animation on DVDs and try your hand at selling or giving them out, the best course of action would be featuring your work in a film festival.

Now, not all festivals accept animated works, and there may be other rules to consider. For example, many festivals will not accept a work if it's already been distributed online. So be sure to read through all of the fine print before slapping down money for a submission. There is no guarantee that this method will gain you an audience or pique the interest of an executive, but it's probably the best shot you have in the traditional realm. The bottom line is to believe in your work and hope everything else falls into place.

Exploring the online realm

The absolute best way to get your work out there, reach the widest audience possible, and maybe even catch the eye of some higher-ups is to distribute your work online. Luckily, we live in a world where online streaming media is incredibly popular and easy to handle. With mobile devices taking up a large market, people can even access and watch your cartoons on the go. There are several options out there, but your best bet is YouTube as it has a huge user base and high retention rate. Vimeo has gained traction over the years as being the best place to distribute creative works, and it is a great service. And there is nothing stopping you from putting your work on both services. Another benefit is that these services allow you to easily embed your works onto other websites.

Obtaining views and constructive criticism

So, you've created your YouTube or Vimeo account and have uploaded the cartoon. Now what? You're not getting any views (except for perhaps the one from your mom) and your channel is pretty bare. What can you do to change this?

First, keep making cartoons! You'll have a better chance of attracting attention by keeping the content flowing. Not just any content of course, but good content. There seems to be a misconception that short, funny cartoons don't need to be up to par in terms of production values. Try to avoid this pitfall. If possible, try establishing a schedule. Maybe release a cartoon once a month so your viewers can learn when to expect fresh content. This would take considerable commitment, but it may be worth it if you're willing to put in the work.

The next step to gaining viewers is pushing your videos anywhere you think is relevant. This doesn't mean outright spamming of random forums and websites with links to your videos. Try finding websites that have communities that focus on animation; a good example is the **Lost Marble** forum (http://www.lostmarble.com/forum/). These are the official forums for Anime Studio and have a strong and supportive community interested in animated works. Try connecting with other YouTube or Vimeo channels that are based on animation or distribute other creative works. Utilize social media and spread the word by creating a Facebook page and tweeting to your followers on Twitter. The bottom line is to reach out and make connections wherever possible. The more you expose your work, the more views you will get.

With regards to having your work appear in search engines, keywords are important. You can put keywords on any YouTube video and it's always best to have a large, yet relevant, pool of relatable words. Research and discover what terms people are using to search for relating to your content. This in itself can take considerable time and dedication.

You can also pay for advertising. **Google AdWords** is the most popular form of online advertising as it aims to target keywords used by websites. For instance, if a website based on animation uses Google to fill ad space, your advertisement could pop up. Honestly, paid advertising is something that should be a last resort, or if you really have the money to spend. This type of advertising may work well for businesses, but trying to get people to click on a cartoon may be a tough sell.

Stay away from "traffic sellers". You will find many people or companies out there that claim if you use their "revolutionary" system for only so many dollars a month, you will see a huge increase in traffic. The bottom line is that most of these services are scams and their huge "lists" are nothing more than poor saps following an endless futile circle to pull in traffic.

Partnership opportunities

The biggest draw YouTube brings is probably the ability to monetize your work. In other words, you can set up your account so that ads can be placed on your videos. If people watch or click on the ad (depending on the ad type), you get compensated. Now, in order to set up your account like this, you will need to either partner with YouTube or another service. There are pretty strict guidelines with getting a partnership agreement, such as how many viewers and subscriptions you are pulling in at that time. Also, make sure the videos you are uploading contain no copyrighted material, such as images or music, as that can lead to issues down the road should you be granted the ability to monetize. But you've already been lectured on this twice. So this section will spare you the details.

If you are looking to partner directly with YouTube, you can submit an application using the link `http://www.youtube.com/yt/partners/`. Again, there are strict guidelines in place, mostly pertaining to viewership, which may prevent you from getting accepted. These guidelines seem to change from time to time, but if you feel you are holding a steady and substantial viewership, submit an application and give it a try!

Another big partnership program out there is through Fullscreen, which holds the same benefits of a YouTube partnership, but with additional perks through their own service, such as access to a large collection of royalty-free music, community forums, and additional stats.

MotionPXL, as shown in the preceding screenshot, is their animation network and you can submit an application using the link `http://apply.fullscreen.net/motionpxl`.

Summary

Editing is just as important as animating. Whether you decide to use a free or premium editor, the techniques you use will ultimately be the same. What's important is for you to find a consistent flow, just like you did with your character designs and animation techniques. Once you perfect this, it will stick with you for the rest of your life. The hardest part will be finding your audience. As long as you're persistent and maintain a high threshold for quality, there should be nothing stopping you from achieving your dreams of becoming an animator.

Although you may not want to hear this, there is a very good chance that things will start off slow when trying to push your content on the Web. YouTube is a big place with countless videos, and it takes a lot of effort to stand out. This is especially true with how fast interests or trends change. A video that is a viral sensation one day can be thrown aside the next when something new comes along. You may encounter people who give you negative feedback. Some of it will be constructive, which you can use to grow stronger, while others will be nothing more than feeble attempts to knock you down. It can be easy to get discouraged. But if this is something you want to do, and you believe in it, you must keep pushing. Don't let your content stagnate during this time either. Keep perfecting your craft, as your goal should always be to outdo yourself with each video release. There is an audience out there; you've just got to be willing to find it.

If you would ever like feedback on the cartoons you're producing, look up the *Incredible Tutorials* channel on YouTube. We are always happy to look at works created by our subscribers! Good luck and we'll be keeping an eye out for your work.

Index

mouse drawing
  versus tablet drawing 37
mouth
  animating, with Smart Bone dials 286-288
  poses, situating 282
  syncing, to audio files 284, 285
mouth, character
  laying out 196-198
Mouth dial 189
My Characters button 253

N

Name field, Layer Settings panel 139
neck, character
  drawing 199, 200
Noise tool
  about 79
  used, for creating random line
    movements 80, 81
nose, character
  drawing 195
note layers 123

O

objects
  filling in, Paint Bucket tool used 57-59
Opacity field, Layer Settings panel 141, 142
options tab
  about 28
  Consolidate timeline channels 29
  Enable drawing tools only on frame 0 29
  Startup file 29
**Outline settings, Layer Settings
    panel 143, 144**
Output Name field 319
OutsideScenery.anme 269

P

Paint Bucket tool 57, 58, 106
particle layers 120, 121
patch layers 116, 117
Perspective Points tool
  about 74
  used, for creating pseudo effects 74, 76
Play button 302

point binding
  using 173-175
Point Reduction tool
  used, for polishing 88-90
points
  altering, Transform Points tool used 50-55
preferences
  about 28
  Editor Colors tab 30
  GUI Colors tab 30
  options tab 28, 29
  Web Uploads tab 29
Premiere
  basic titles, adding 316, 317
preview option 302
project
  exporting 318, 319
project files assets
  direct import 255
project settings
  adjusting 32-34
Pro version
  and Debut version, selecting
    between 21, 22
  purchasing 21
pseudo 3D effects
  creating, Perspective Points tool used 74, 76
purchasing 21

Q

QuickTime
  about 303
  files, exporting 303

R

random line movements
  creating, Noise tool used 79-81
region binding
  techniques 177-179
  using 167-171
Render Style section 34
reusable animations
  creating, Actions panel used 258-262
road details, scenery
  adding, brush types used 233-235
Rotate Layer XY tool 101, 102

Rotate to face camera option 147
Rotate XY Layer tool 76

S

Save as Defaults button 34
Scale compensation option 147
Scatter Brush Options button 237
scatter brush, scenery
  using, for grass blades 235-237
Scatter Brush tool
  about 82
  using 83-85
scene assets
  looping 276, 277
scene file, characters animating
  opening 269, 270
scene heading 11
scenery
  depth, creating 238
  depth shifting 238, 239
  design 218, 219
  dirt road, constructing 230
  drawing 221, 222
  fence Group layer, building 231, 232
  hills drawing, Draw Shape tool
      used 228, 229
  land, creating 226
  land first piece, creating 225, 226
  land second piece, creating 226-228
  polishing up 240, 241
  puffy clouds, drawing 232, 233
  road details adding, brush types
      used 233-235
  scatter brush, using for grass
      blades 235-237
  shots, setting up 219-221
  sky, overlaying 222-224
scenes
  exporting 304-307
Screenwriting 10
scripts
  about 264
  built-in scripts, using 264, 265
  third-party scripts, downloading 265
Select Points tool
  about 55

used, for selecting vector points 55-57
Select Shape tool
  about 59
  used, for altering shape properties 59, 60
Sequencer timeline 128, 129
Set Origin tool 97, 98
shaded effect 159
shades
  applying, to layers 148-151
Shadow color option 148
Shadow dial 190
shadows
  applying, to layers 148-151
shape properties
  altering, Select Shape tool 59, 60
shapes
  drawing, Add Point tool used 41-43
  perfect shapes creating, Draw Shape tool
      used 46-48
Sharp Corners option 231
shearing
  Shear Points tool used 76, 77
Shear Layer tool 102, 103
Shear Points tool
  about 76
  using 77
Shock Wave File (SWF) 39
shots
  setting up 219-221
sky, scenery
  overlaying 222-224
Smart Bone dials
  about 187, 188
  Color dial 189
  Mouth dial 189
  Shadow dial 190
  used, for animating mouths 286-288
Smart Bones
  about 184-187
  actions 171
  dials 187-190
Smooth Joint 296
soft edge effect 159
Splotchy effect 160
Spots effect 160
Start frame field 33
Startup file 26-29

storyboard
  illustrating 13
Stroke Exposure tool 67, 68
Style palette
  Advanced style properties 162, 163
  brush types 157, 158
  designing with 156
  fill color effects 158-160
  swatches 160, 161
style properties
  removing, Delete Shape tool used 70, 71
swatches, Style palette 160, 161
SWF files
  exporting 304
switch layers 117-120

T

tablet drawing
  versus mouse drawing 37
Target Bones layer 297
text layers 122
third-party library files
  about 255
  bringing in 255
third-party scripts
  downloading 265
timelines
  about 123
  channels timeline 127
  Channels timeline 126, 128
  Motion Graph timeline 129-133
  Sequencer timeline 128, 129
titles
  creating, in video editor 316, 317
tools
  about 37
  Add Point tool 41-43
  Bend Points tool 78, 79
  Blob Brush tool 86
  Create Shape tool 63, 65
  Curvature tool 48, 49
  Curve Profile tool 81, 82
  Delete Edge tool 68, 69
  Delete Shape tool 70, 71

  Draw and Fill tools 40, 41
  Draw Shape tool 46-48
  Eraser tool 87, 88
  Freehand tool 44-46
  Hide Edge tool 65, 66
  Line Width tool 72, 73
  Magnet tool 61, 62
  Noise tool 79-81
  Paint Bucket tool 57, 58
  Perspective Points tool 74, 76
  Point Reduction tool 88-90
  Scatter Brush tool 82-85
  Select Points tool 55-57
  Select Shape tool 59, 60
  Shear Points tool 76, 77
  Stroke Exposure tool 67, 68
  Transform Points tool 50-55
top bar 40
Transform Layer tool 94-97
Transform Points tool
  about 44, 50
  used, for deleting points 50-52
  used, for moving points 50-52
  used, for rotating points 54, 55
  used, for selecting points 50-52
tweening 19

V

Variable line width option 45
varied copies
  creating, Scatter Brush tool used 82-85
vector graphics
  about 39
  example 39, 40
vector layers 111, 112
vector points
  selecting, Select Points tool used 55-57
video editors
  about 307
  advanced video editors 308
  free video editors, using 307
  premium video editors, using 308-310
  titles, creating in 316, 317
Visible checkbox, Layer Settings panel 140

W

Wacom tablets
about 38
URL 38
walking animation
looping 274, 275

Web Uploads tab 29
Windows
32-bit and 64-bit versions 24
Windows Live Movie Maker 307
workflow, characters animating
finding 268
Workspace tools 133-135

Thank you for buying
Learning Anime Studio

About Packt Publishing

Packt, pronounced 'packed', published its first book "*Mastering phpMyAdmin for Effective MySQL Management*" in April 2004 and subsequently continued to specialize in publishing highly focused books on specific technologies and solutions.

Our books and publications share the experiences of your fellow IT professionals in adapting and customizing today's systems, applications, and frameworks. Our solution based books give you the knowledge and power to customize the software and technologies you're using to get the job done. Packt books are more specific and less general than the IT books you have seen in the past. Our unique business model allows us to bring you more focused information, giving you more of what you need to know, and less of what you don't.

Packt is a modern, yet unique publishing company, which focuses on producing quality, cutting-edge books for communities of developers, administrators, and newbies alike. For more information, please visit our website: www.packtpub.com.

Writing for Packt

We welcome all inquiries from people who are interested in authoring. Book proposals should be sent to author@packtpub.com. If your book idea is still at an early stage and you would like to discuss it first before writing a formal book proposal, contact us; one of our commissioning editors will get in touch with you.

We're not just looking for published authors; if you have strong technical skills but no writing experience, our experienced editors can help you develop a writing career, or simply get some additional reward for your expertise.

jQuery 2.0 Animation Techniques: Beginner's Guide

ISBN: 978-1-78216-964-2   Paperback: 292 pages

Bring your websites to life with animations using jQuery

1. Get going with jQuery's animation methods and build a toolkit of ready-to-use animations using jQuery 2.0.

2. Over 50 detailed examples on different types of web page animations.

3. Create both simple and complex animations using clear, step-by-step instructions, accompanied with screenshots.

Mastering Manga Studio 5

ISBN: 978-1-84969-768-2   Paperback: 298 pages

An extensive, fun, and practical guide to streamlining your comic-making workflow using Manga Studio 5

1. Make Manga Studio 5 your own personalized software by creating your own workspace, tools, page layouts, and materials.

2. Explore using 3D models, actions, ruler tools, and creating projects to save you time.

3. Full of examples, illustrations, and tips with a lighthearted and fun style to make comic creation fun and easy.

Please check **www.PacktPub.com** for information on our titles

Blender 2.6 Cycles: Materials and Textures Cookbook

Over 40 recipes to help you create stunning materials and textures using the Cycles rendering engine with Blender

Enrico Valenza

Blender 2.6 Cycles: Materials and Textures Cookbook

ISBN: 978-1-78216-130-1   Paperback: 280 pages

Over 40 recipes to help you create stunning materials and textures using the Cycles rendering engine with Blender

1. Create naturalistic materials and textures—such as rock, snow, and ice—using Cycles.

2. Learn Cycle's node-based material system.

3. Get to grips with the powerful Cycles rendering engine.

Direct3D Rendering Cookbook

50 practical recipes to guide you through the advanced rendering techniques in Direct3D to help bring your 3D graphics project to life

Justin Stenning

Direct3D Rendering Cookbook

ISBN: 978-1-84969-710-1   Paperback: 430 pages

50 practical recipes to guide you through the advanced rendering techniques in Direct3D to help bring your 3D graphics project to life

1. Learn and implement the advanced rendering techniques in Direct3D 11.2 and bring your 3D graphics project to life.

2. Study the source code and digital assets with a small rendering framework and explore the features of Direct3D 11.2.

3. A practical, example-driven, technical cookbook with numerous illustrations and example images to help demonstrate the techniques described.

Please check **www.PacktPub.com** for information on our titles

CPSIA information can be obtained at www.ICGtesting.com
Printed in the USA
BVOW09s1652220215

388760BV00005B/93/P